LYCOS PERSONAL WEB PAGE GUIDE

que®

201 West 103rd Street, Indianapolis, Indiana 46290

Lycos Personal Web Page Guide

International Standard Book Number: 0-7897-1834-0

Library of Congress Catalog Card Number: 98-86993

Printed in the United States of America

First Printing: July 1999

01 00 99 4 3 2 1

Trademarks

All terms mentioned in this book that are known to be trademarks or service marks have been appropriately capitalized. Que cannot attest to the accuracy of this information. Use of a term in this book should not be regarded as affecting the validity of any trademark or service mark.

Warning and Disclaimer

Every effort has been made to make this book as complete and as accurate as possible, but no warranty or fitness is implied. The information provided is on an "as is" basis. The authors and the publisher shall have neither liability nor responsibility to any person or entity with respect to any loss or damages arising from the information contained in this book.

Publisher
John Pierce

Development Editor
John Sleeve

Managing Editor
Thomas F. Hayes

Project Editor
Tom Stevens

Copy Editor
Molly Schaller

Indexer
Chris Barrick

Proofreader
Terri Edwards

Technical Editor
Mark Hall

Copy Writer
Eric Borgert

Layout Technician
Eric S. Miller

Cover Design
Jay Corpus

Interior Design
Louisa Klucznik

Contents at a Glance

Contents

About the Author

Digitalmill is a technology project development firm based in Portland, Maine. An active developer of written content for companies in and out of the technology industry, the company has produced books, newsletters, and articles for many leading publishers and publications with a focus on emerging technologies, e-commerce, software development, technology business development, and consumer uses of technology.

Acknowledgments

Digitalmill would like to thank Mary Millhollon, Stephanie Mabee, and Justine Clegg for their contributions to this book. We would also like to commend John Sleeva, development editor, and Tom Stevens, project editor, for helping make this book better than it would have been otherwise.

Also deserving praise are Matt Goldberg and everyone at Tripod.

Tell Us What You Think!

As the reader of this book, *you* are our most important critic and commentator. We value your opinion and want to know what we're doing right, what we could do better, what areas you'd like to see us publish in, and any other words of wisdom you're willing to pass our way.

As the publisher for Que, I welcome your comments. You can fax, email, or write me directly to let me know what you did or didn't like about this book—as well as what we can do to make our books stronger.

Please note that I cannot help you with technical problems related to the topic of this book, and that due to the high volume of mail I receive, I might not be able to reply to every message.

When you write, please be sure to include this book's title and author as well as your name and phone or fax number. I will carefully review your comments and share them with the author and editors who worked on the book.

Fax: 317-581-4666

Email: que@mcp.com

Mail: John Pierce
Que
201 West 103rd Street
Indianapolis, IN 46290 USA

PART I

Know the Pod

CHAPTER 1

Tripod FAQ

What is Tripod?

Tripod is a free home page service that lets anyone who wants to publish his or her own Web site do so without cost. Tripod is also a community of Web page builders who share their knowledge and interests with each other through their own homepages, chats, and message boards. After you register with Tripod, you can build your own home page and participate in the various communities available on Tripod.

Tripod is broken into dozens of interest communities called Pods. There are Pods for dozens of different themes, topics, or interests, such as Classical Music, Extreme Sports, Mac Computing, and Travel. Although you or your site needn't be a member of a Pod, you can submit your site to be considered for its Pod Publisher's list. This way, your page is seen and visited more by members who have the same interests as you.

Tripod was purchased by Lycos in 1998 and is part of the Lycos Network of online services. The Lycos Network also includes Lycos.com, a full-service Web destination that includes search and navigation resources, personalized services, chat, and free email, and HotBot, the award-winning search engine.

How was Tripod Started?

Bo Peabody, a Williams College graduate, founded Tripod in 1992 to provide an informational site for young adults trying to deal with the real world. As originally planned, Tripod was supposed to be a Web community with a Generation X focus. However, what the company soon realized was that, aside from the community and information they were building, the interest in the free home page option was growing at an amazing rate.

Realizing that the members themselves should control the content and take Tripod to new levels, the company went full force into the free Web page business. However, by retaining its community focus, Tripod offers more than just a free home site—it offers an online community in which people can come together and learn from each other. Though its original strategy shifted a bit toward home pages, and even though people of any age can join, Tripod still retains a key focus on the needs of young adults.

Tripod, which was purchased by Lycos in 1998, is one of the most visited sites on the Internet. It is a combination of original content, a vibrant online community, and interesting subject matter. The purchase gives Tripod the strong partnership it needs to continue building its services and finding more ways to help people build their own pages on the Internet and meet other interesting people.

How Do I Become a Tripod Member?

To begin building your free home page and participating in Pods, chats, and conferences, you need to become a Tripod member. This is a simple sign-up process in which you fill out a form with your name, mailing address, and email address and choose the pods in which you want to participate.

NOTE

For more information on becoming a Tripod member, see Chapter 2, "Getting Started with Tripod."

Why Would I Want a Free Home Page?

There are dozens of reasons to have your own home page. A home page can be a place to share your thoughts with the world—or with just your family and friends. Because the Web is so open to all sorts of possibilities, your page is capable of doing almost anything—from being a site dedicated to your favorite movie or sports star to offering a tutorial on your favorite subject. Because you're reading this book, you might already have a page or an idea of what you want to put on a home page. If you don't, this book contains dozens of examples of the types of pages you can build.

In the end, the most important reason to have a free home page is sharing. The Web has unleashed all sorts of great information, but it has done very little in the way of sharing it. Publishing a free page isn't about keeping information to yourself, it is about giving that information to people with similar interests. The ultimate form of this notion is Tripod. Tripod not only takes the financial cost out of Web publishing, but also gives you the means to directly find and interact with other people from around the world who share your interests.

Do I Need to Build a Home Page to Be a Member?

Although it defeats the purpose of this book, and you deny yourself one of Tripod's main offerings, you don't have to build a home page to be a member of Tripod. If you just want to chat or participate in conferences, you can do that.

Your home page also doesn't have to be a stellar creation. Although certain types of content are not allowed on Tripod, your pages don't have to be the work of a master page builder for you to be a member in good standing.

Do I Need a Lot of Technical Skills to Build a Home Page?

Yes and no. Greater skill and knowledge enables you to create your site faster and perhaps better than people who have less. However, Tripod includes tools and help that make it easy for even a novice to create a Web page. This book will also help you, regardless of the knowledge you have. Also, page editors like FileMaker Home Page or Adobe PageMill enable you to visually design and publish your Web page. However, a good page builder is always trying to learn more in a quest to create better pages.

Tripod also has plenty of help pages. Forums such as the Page Slave Pod are filled with people and information about building Web sites. So if you don't know it yourself, there are plenty of places to learn. We have also tried to pack into this book tons of help for people building pages—from a complete HTML reference, listings of Java applets, and pointers to pages that help you learn various Web skills.

Do I Need Any Special Tools to Build My Home Page?

Tripod includes everything you need to build a page right on its site. However, by employing other tools, you can create a more advanced page. This book identifies many types of tools that will help you build great pages.

Three tools you should consider using are a graphics production tool, a Web page editor, and an FTP program. A number of shareware and low-cost graphics tools can help you prepare great graphics for your site. Tripod includes a Web page editor, but you might also want to use a higher-end editor that enables you to build a page visually instead of by typing in the specific HTML tag codes that make up a Web page. Chapter 3, "Using the Tripod Filemanager," covers some of the more popular Web editors. An FTP program is what you use to transfer pages, graphics, and other materials from your home computer to your Web site. Tripod includes the ability to transfer items to your site directly from the Web, but a full-fledged FTP program like Fetch (Mac) or CuteFTP (Windows) will include more power and capability.

Most people first use the built-in editing tools to create their pages. Then, if they decide to invest more time and energy, they turn to the types of outside programs previously described for more power and capability. Nearly every known Web page building tool, and FTP tool is useable with Tripod; however, FrontPage 97/98 users should look into the Tripod Premium membership that supports FrontPage extensions, as the normal free version does not.

How Much Space Do I Get for My Home Page?

Tripod initially offered just 2 megabytes of space per home site. After upgrading thc service and hearing from members, Tripod desperately wanted more space to add images, sounds and multimedia on its Web site. Tripod responded by increasing the amount of space available for building pages to 11 megabytes.

If 11 megabytes isn't big enough, you can upgrade to the Premium Membership, which offers 22 megabytes of space. Tripod might even raise the amount of space again. Still, 11 megabytes is a lot of space to use when building pages—it's more than enough to build pages that include lots of imagery, sounds, and more. It is the equivalent of nearly 1,500 typewritten pages. You could write an epic novel with the space Tripod gives you.

Can I Have My Own Domain Name?

Many people want their own domain name. A domain name is the Web address—like `www.tripod.com` or `www.lycos.com`—that, when typed in, instantly sends people to your Web site. Tripod does not give members their own domain names—that costs money, and your page wouldn't be free if Tripod did that. If you develop a page that is so spectacular and important that you must have your own domain, you will have to move it to a site you pay for and enable the domain.

How Much Time Does It Take to Build a Web Site on Tripod?

Because building pages requires you to sometimes collect and construct a lot of content, you need to spend time writing text, processing imagery, and building the layouts. Even though many people worry that a Web site might take a lifetime build, that's not usually true; only large-scale sites with complex layouts take long periods of time to design and build. By using the built-in tools and keeping things simple, you should be able to construct a nice page in just a few hours. If you already have great Web skills, that will help speed things up.

However, after you get your first few pages up, you will likely want to add more, not to mention jazzing up your existing pages. That can take hours, but building pages is an investment. The more you put into your work, the more you will get out of it.

In short, it takes as much time as you are willing commit to build a Web site. That could indeed be a lifetime.

Can Tripod Process Web Forms on My Free Home Page?

Forms enable you to gather information from people who visit your site. For example, if your site was dedicated to your favorite rock band, you could have a form on which people could pick their favorite song or album by that band from a list.

Tripod offers a simple but capable forms-processing script that you can use to have any form's contents emailed to you. With some useful design and the built-in forms processor, you'll be accepting forms in no time. One thing you can't do is offer secure forms processing that is primarily used for accepting orders. Tripod does not allow member sites to engage in commerce.

NOTE

For more on building and using forms, see Chapter 8, "Developing Forms on Tripod."

Can I Add Java Applets, Dynamic HTML, and RealAudio to My Home Page?

Yes. Your home page on Tripod can support Java applets, Dynamic HTML, and many other advanced forms of Web technology. It can also support RealAudio or RealVideo as downloadable files. Almost every Web technology that you can put on a Web page or offer for download is fair game with your Tripod home page. This book covers many of these technologies and how they work on Tripod.

NOTE

Special effects are covered in Chapter 9, "Adding Special Effects to Your Tripod Pages," graphics in Chapter 10, "Adding Graphics to Your Tripod Pages," and multimedia in Chapter 11, "Adding Multimedia to Your Tripod Pages." These items are also covered in other areas throughout the book.

Are There Other Special Effects I Can Add?

Tripod includes several special effects that are covered in Chapter 9, "Adding Special Effects to Your Tripod Pages." They include a custom guest book that people can use to leave you messages, an answering machine application that lets people record messages onto your site, and a Web counter that tells you and others how many people have visited a page on your site.

Does My Page Have to Have Advertising on It? Can I Accept My Own Advertising for My Site?

Just like free network television, Tripod supports itself and is able to offer free home pages by selling advertising on Tripod. Tripod does its best not to let the advertising get in your page's way. By using special pop-up windows to serve ads, Tripod avoids changing your site in any way.

If you really don't want the ads to show up on your site, you can upgrade to the premium membership and, for $3 above that premium membership cost, Tripod will remove the advertisements from your pages.

Because Tripod needs to sell advertising to exist, members are not allowed to sell ad space on their sites.

Can I Make Money from My Tripod Home Page?

One of the rules of Tripod is that you can't engage in commerce. In fact, Tripod does not offer the security systems needed for accepting secure forms and credit cards. However, Tripod does offer you the chance to set up associate stores with their sponsors that could lead to some money for you. Associate store programs pay you a commission for each sale you send to the sponsor. For example, Tripod and CDNow have set up the Cosmic Credit program in which you recommend CDs to your page's visitors. If someone clicks through your link and orders a CD, you earn credit at CDNow. If you earn more than $100, you can actually receive that as cash.

Tripod even has Pods set up for small businesses and people who are selling things on the Web. For small businesses and entrepreneurs, there is the Small Biz Pod. People who like to shop at thrift stores and antique shops can find help in the Second Hand Pod. Many small businesses do have simple home pages on the service. They usually include contact information, a description of the business, and what it offers. Many people put their Tripod home pages on their business cards or other advertising. Although larger businesses might want to build an enormous Web site and pay thousands of dollars to do so, millions of small businesses can't afford to do that. With a free home page, even the smallest businesses can set up on the Web.

One of the best ways your page can help your business or professional career is by demonstrating your expertise. Many people set up Web sites that contain writings or tutorials. For example, someone who is an expert on building computer networks might build a Web site that is devoted to just that. Perhaps someone in need of a network will visit the site and, seeing all the information, hire the site's creator to build an office network.

So even though you can't just set up shop on Tripod, you can find interesting ways, such as associate programs or putting up a page about yourself and your business, that can help you combine real business with interesting content.

How Do I Make My Site Famous?

After anyone builds a Web site—whether it's on Tripod or not—the most important thing people want to do is promote the site so that the 100 million plus people that have access to the Web will flock to it. There are many ways to make your site well known; first and foremost is to build a site that is interesting to other people.

After you've built your site, you can help improve its odds of showing up on search engines by inserting keywords that will help search engines list your page. You'll also want to find sites similar to yours and ask to trade links with them. Tripod also offers special help to promote your page. By aligning your page with a Pod, you can help promote your site to other Tripoders. Poderaters might even pick your site as a featured pod site. In addition, because Tripod is owned by Lycos—one of the best and most popular search engines on the Internet—it has a special offer to help you list your site on Lycos.

NOTE

For more information on promoting your site, see Chapter 12, "Attracting Visitors to Your Tripod Pages."

What's the Difference between Premium Membership and Regular Membership?

Tripod knows that not everyone is content with just 11 megabytes of free Web space. That's why it created the Premium Tripod membership. As of this writing, Premium membership offers you several advantages over the free Web site:

- A personal chat room
- 22 megabytes of Web space
- Your own tripod.net email address which will forward any mail to it on to your regular email
- A monthly newsletter featuring free goodies and sneak peeks at Tripod content and services
- The ability to enable Microsoft FrontPage extensions to your Web site. These extensions work only with the FrontPage Web design tool and offer special features for your site. If you have the program you should consider the Premium membership.
- Access to a special image library that helps you add great graphics easily to your site.
- 20% off Tripod apparel

The Premium membership is just $3 per month. For $6.00 per month, you get the Premium membership plus removal of all ads from your Web site.

Will My Tripod Pages Ever Expire?

If you violate any of Tripod's rules—such as posting pornography or copyrighted material—your site will be removed quickly. However, if you remain a member in good standing, your site should remain up for quite a long time. Tripod pages never expire, although it makes sense to upgrade over time. Updating your site will keep things fresh so that people will continually return to the site. If all goes well, people will be visiting your site for years.

This All Sounds Great. Is There Anything Else I Should Know?

The rest of this book will guide you through all the possibilities and knowledge you need to build the world's best Tripod homepage. The sooner you work through this book, the faster you'll be able to start building your first site or begin improving the site you already have started.

Oh, and most of all, have fun!

CHAPTER 2

Getting Started with Tripod

Tripod, which was born in 1992 as an interactive media company created and maintained by young people for young people in transition from college to the workplace, has evolved into a leading Web community. Programmers, designers, editors, customer service representatives and business associates of Tripod work to maintain a community of Web pages that have been built by Tripod's approximately 2 million members. Tripod offers original content, personal publishing tools, and community-building opportunities.

Tripod's home page (`www.tripod.com`), shown in Figure 2.1, is a portal to an incredibly wide variety of member pages, which are organized according to content. Browsers can easily navigate through the material on the homepages and find members with similar interests. Tripod enhances the sense of community among its members by coordinating chat sessions on popular issues and encouraging interest groups to post interactive bulletin boards. Its communities are interactive domains in which members can discuss and promote their personal interests. Tripod's site also provides its members with original content and links to up-to-date news, stocks, and sports.

This chapter walks you through the steps to becoming a member and explains the basic contents of Tripod's site. It will also introduce Tripod's services and terms of membership and will assist you in navigating through the site. Much of this information will be covered later in the book. We don't want to bog you down with too much detail here.

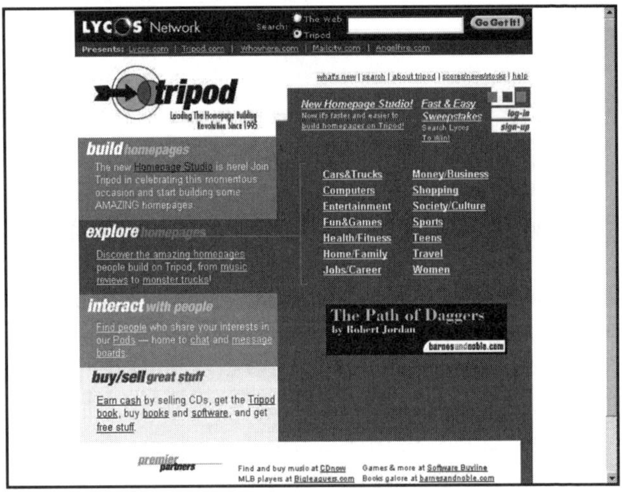

FIGURE 2.1
Tripod's home page.

BECOMING A MEMBER

Becoming a Tripod member is easy and, in case you forgot, free. It involves a straightforward application process, which we will walk you through.

1. Go to `www.tripod.com` and click sign-up (or go straight to `www.tripod.com/planet/membership/`

signup). This provides you with a membership application (see Figure 2.2).

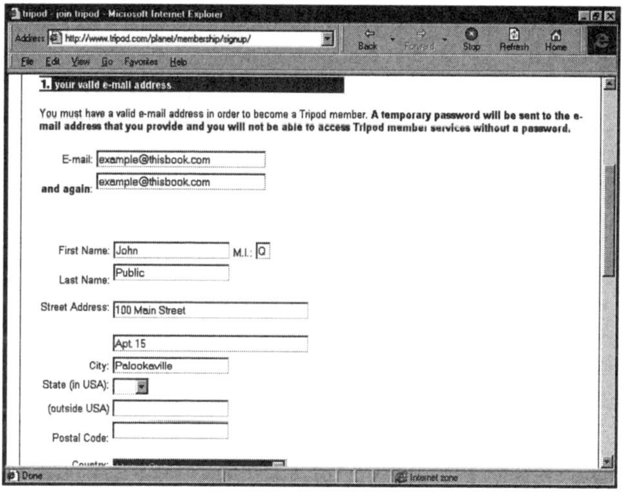

FIGURE 2.2
Tripod's Membership Application page.

2. Type your email address in the box at the top of the application.
3. Tab over to the next box and enter your email address a second time.
4. Tripod requires that you submit the following personal information: name, address, city, state, zip, country, gender, and date of birth. The date of birth information will help you access Tripod's site if you lose your password. After you have completed and submitted the form, Tripod will send a temporary password to your email address.
5. Enter a member name of your choosing. This name will appear in your homepage URL. Letter, numbers,

and underscores are valid characters. Tripod will ask you to resubmit your application with a new member name if your first choice is taken. You also have the option of receiving a free email journal that includes news features, events and information about Tripod.

6. Click the submit box and wait a few moments to assure that you have entered all the mandatory information.

Tripod will confirm your membership immediately. After you have properly completed the process, Tripod places a cookie, or tracking device, on your browser to give you easy access to Tripod's entire site.

Within 48 hours, you will receive an email with a temporary password that Tripod has chosen. Every time you log onto the Tripod site, you must resubmit your member name and password.

TIP

If you would like to change your password, sign on and go to `www.tripod.com/service/change_passwd`.

As soon as you become a member, you are eligible to begin joining Pods. Click the box next to the subject names of the Pods of your choice at `www.tripod.com/bin/signup/signup`.

Members can personalize their Pod membership after submitting their Pod selections or by going to `http//:www.tripod.com/service/pod_central/pod/join_pods` (see Figure 2.3). Members are asked interesting questions related to the Pod topic. For instance, if you are part of the Cooking Capers Pod, you might be asked what your best dish is. Your answers will be added to your membership profile. If you prefer to not have your answers added, uncheck the box underneath your response. Members may also request a monthly email newsletter for each Pod.

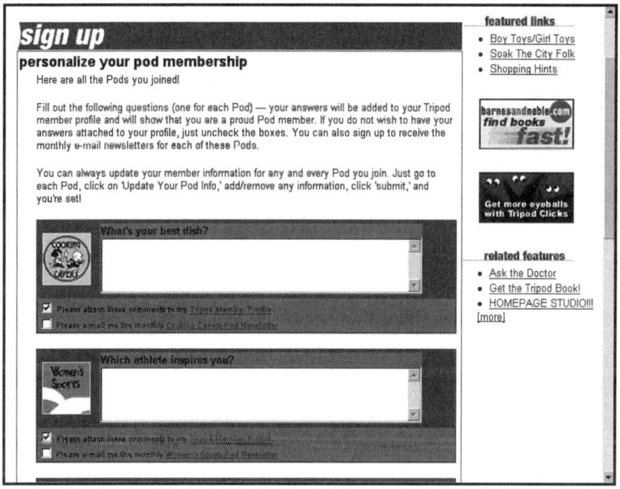

FIGURE 2.3
Personalize Pod Membership page.

To update your Pod membership information, go to the page for that particular Pod, click Update Your Pod Info, edit your profile, and click submit.

HELP!

Now that you are a Tripod member and will be building a Web site, what kind of help does Tripod offer? To advance to Tripod's Help page, click Help on the homepage or go to `http://help.tripod.com/`.

Tripod's Help System provides members with up-to-date assistance on all aspects of the site (see Figure 2.4). Help menus for membership support and homepage building cover practically every question a new member could have. The Help Page is also linked to informational pages on Chats, Conferencing, and Pods. Members can use a search engine for assistance in locating help.

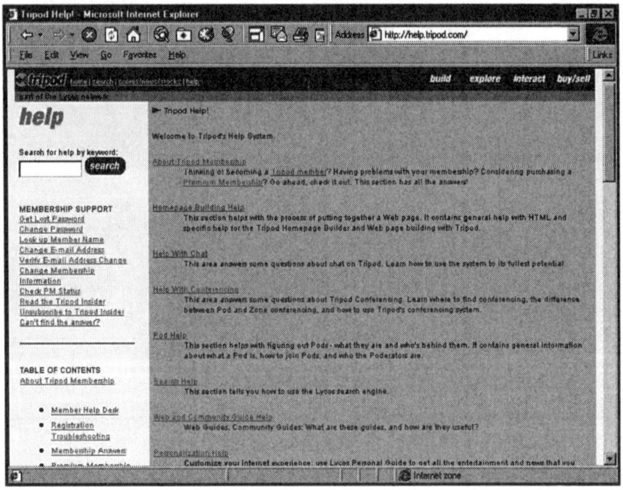

FIGURE 2.4
Tripod's Help System.

TRIPOD'S COMPONENTS

Tripod's site is divided into four main sections: Build, Explore, Interact, and Buy/Sell. These areas are all accessible from the main page. All of these segments—plus the General information—are listed on the Site Map page (`www.tripod.com/tripod/map`), as shown in Figure 2.5. Users can also find the Site Map page by clicking the Site Map icon on the About Tripod page.

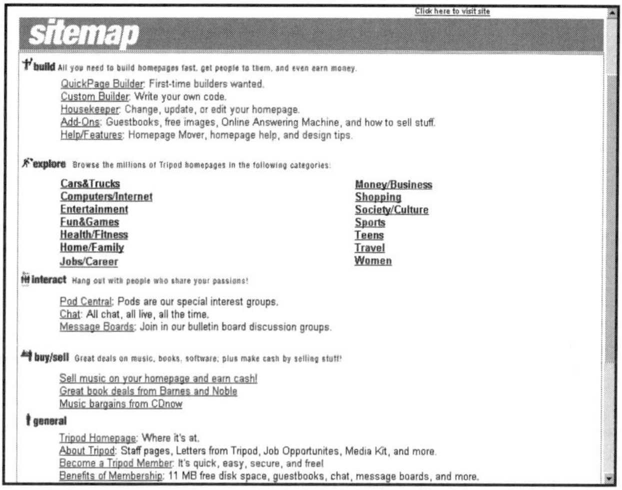

FIGURE 2.5
Tripod's Site Map.

BUILD

The Build section—also referred to as Homepage Studio (`www.tripod.com/build/`)—includes all the tools needed for registered Tripod members to build their own Web site (see Figure 2.6). You can build your own site, customize your site by writing your own code, update or change your homepage, and add free graphics. The Build section is linked to a Help/Features page with design and technical tips and building ideas. (Homepage Studio is covered in more detail in Chapter 5, "Homepage Studio QuickPage: Build by Topic," and Chapter 7, "Homepage Studio QuickPage: Build by Design.")

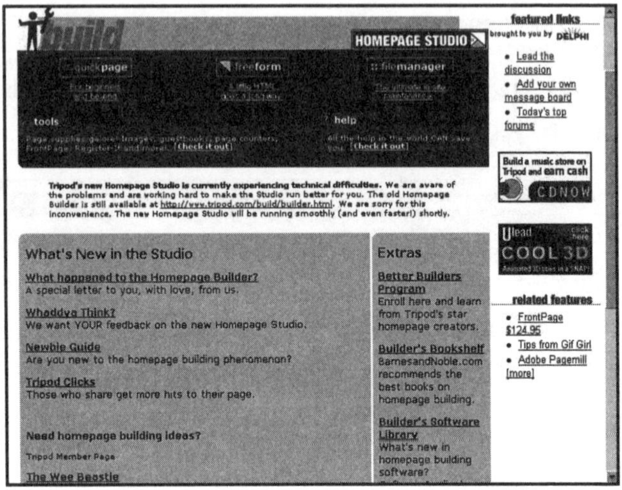

FIGURE 2.6
Tripod's Build page.

QuickPage

Homepage Studio's QuickPage (see Figure 2.7) enables you to build your site by using one of two types of templates: Build by Topic and Build by Design. These templates require no knowledge of HTML or even any layout ability.

To advance to QuickPage (`http://209.185.181.170/servlets/HPStudio?xfile=/hpstudio/quickpage/index.xtl`), click the QuickPage icon on the Homepage Studio page, enter your member name and password (if you are already a member).

Build by Topic

The Build by Topic templates (covered in detail in Chapter 5) offer designs that fit the desired topic. For example, the Photo Album template looks like an actual photo album, and the Patriots Fan Page Builder template includes banners that utilize the NFL team's logo, photos of players, and so on.

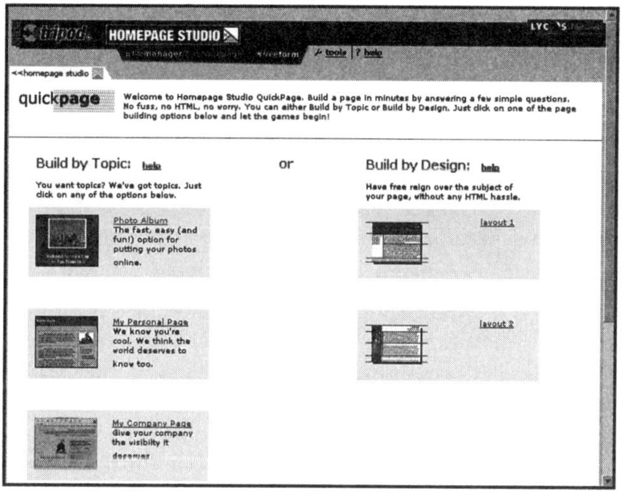

FIGURE 2.7
Homepage Studio's QuickPage.

The Build by Topic templates include:

- Photo Album
- Personal Page
- Company Page
- Patriots Fan Page
- Recipe Publisher
- Cdnow Store
- Homage to Evil
- My Most Embarrassing Moment
- Celebrity Page Builder

Build by Design

If you would rather not be limited by Tripod's Build by Topic templates, but aren't ready to build a page from scratch, you might prefer to use one of the two Build by Design templates. Build by Design offers two basic layouts, which are covered in more detail in Chapter 7.

FREE FORM

For seasoned Web site builders, Tripod offers Free Form, located at `http://servlets.tripod.com/servlets/FreeFormEditor` or by clicking Free Form at the Build page. Designers can edit a page or build a new page by adding HTML code into the Page Editor box (see Figure 2.8). Free Form has set up the basics to make it as easy as possible. The text inside the box tells you what to write and where to put it.

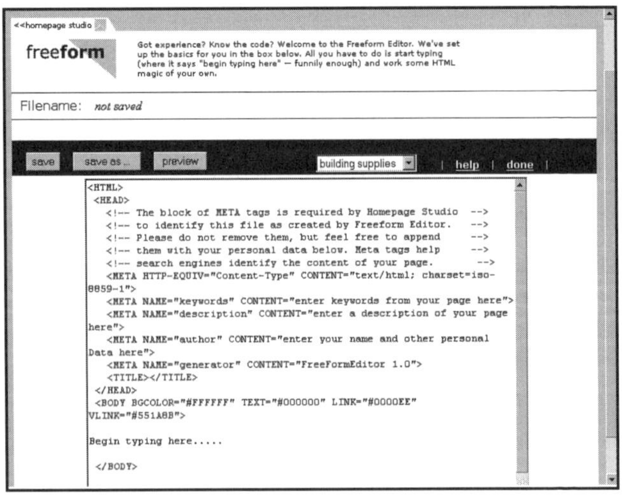

FIGURE 2.8
Free Form page.

You can use the Building Supplies drop-down box to edit specific aspects of a page such as the color palette, guest book or links. After creating a new page or editing a previous page, builders submit their changes and can view their customized design. Tripod offers the option to new page designers to become an affiliate of a Web store, submit pages to Lycos, or sign up as a Pod member.

FILEMANAGER

The Filemanager (`http://build.tripod.com/servlets/HPStudio?xfile=/hpstudio/filemanager/index.xtl`) makes it easy for Tripod members to keep track of their home page-related files (see Figure 2.9). To check the configuration of files on your site, click the Filemanager on the Build page. Here you can view, edit, move, rename, copy, delete, or convert files. Tripod members can review the number of files and directories of their site and see how much disk space they have remaining.

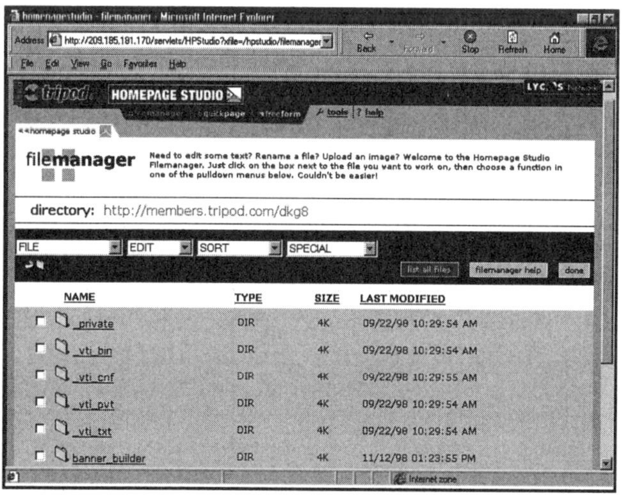

FIGURE 2.9
The Filemanager page.

NOTE

The Filemanager and the transfer of files are covered in more detail in Chapter 3, "Using the Tripod Filemanager."

Tools

Tripod offers a variety of page-building tools that will help add some zip to your site. To advance to the Tools page, click Tools on the Build page or go to `http://build.tripod.com/hpstudio/tools/index.html`. The Tools menu provides everything from free images to banner building templates. Some of these are described below in more detail.

Media Library

Tripod has a bank of free images that you can add to your Web site. To preview animated images, audio and video clips, click Media Library or go to `http://209.185.181.170/servlets/HPStudio?xfile=/hpstudio/medialibrary/index.xtl`.

Banner Builder

Banner Builder, which is covered in Chapter 12, "Attracting Visitors to Your Tripod Pages," enables you to build a promotional banner without additional software by using any of several templates. Banner Builder can be found at `http://homepager.tripod.com/build/banner_builder`.

The Banner Builder Exchange program, also covered in Chapter 12, enables you to display your banner on other member sites in exchange for displaying their banners on your site. Click Banner Builder/Exchange or go to `http://www.tripod.com/build/clicks`.

Better Builders Program

The Better Builders Program will help you learn more about the Web and page building. For more information, or to sign up for the Better Builders Program, click Better Builders Program or go to `http://www.tripod.com/build/better_builders/`. Better Builder members can place a Better Builder logo on their site, receive a newsletter with page building tips, receive awards, and join special chats and Pods.

Web Site Garage

The Web Site Garage will give your site a tune up. Tripod members can access services that will optimize search engine registration and speed up your site's load time. The Web Site Garage is located at `http://Websitegarage.tripod.com`.

The Web Site Garage includes services in the areas of Web Maintenance, Web Site Promotion and Analysis, and Consulting.

Maintenance Services, which you can purchase collectively for $24.99 per month, include:

- **Tune Up** Tune Up enables you to run performance diagnostics on your entire site. You can try a free one-page tune up or pay $9.99 per month for continuous service.
- **Browser Snapshot** The Browser Snapshot ensures browser compatibility by seeing your site in 18 different browsers, platforms, and screen sizes. The cost is $9.99 per month.
- **GIF Lube** GIF Lube speeds up your site by optimizing your images. The cost is $9.99 per month.

Web Site Promotion and Analysis options include Register-It, Press Release, and Hitometer.

- **Register-It** Register-It provides comprehensive registration with as many as 400 search engines, directories, and award sites. The cost is $39.99 per year for one URL, $59.99 per year for two URLs.
- **Press Release** This is a service of use for business sites only. Broadcast your press release to the media through Business Wire for $99.99 per release.
- **Hitometer** This service enables you to analyze your site's traffic with a customizable tracking tool. The cost is $4.99 per month for one URL.

Finally, under Consulting, is the Performance Registration Package, which is most likely to be used by business sites. A diagnostic check, search engine, and award site registration as well as a report outlining the steps needed to improve site performance costs $399.99 per year for one URL.

Web Site Post Office

The Web Site Post Office enables members to create mailing lists to keep in touch with their site's visitors. You can create a targeted mailing list by customizing the demographic information visitors leave behind. Mailing lists and newsletters not only enable you to gather information about your visitors, they also foster a feeling of community and enable you to immediately notify your visitors concerning updates, changes, news, and so on.

The more your visitors feel like they are part of your site, the more likely they are to keep coming back. The free version of Web Site Post Office enables you to do this.

There is also a commercial version that enables you to customize messages, send specific messages based on demographics, and segment your mailing list by demographic data. This service costs $9.99 per month and is most useful for commercial sites or sites with extremely heavy traffic and large mailing lists.

Click Web Site Post Office at `http://websitepostoffice.tripod.com/` for more information.

Explore

Want to check out the sites of fellow Tripod members? Explore `www.tripod.com/explore/`. The Explore page is where you can begin browsing for member sites through categories and more specific subcategories (see Figure 2.10). For example, if you are searching for information on a car, you might click the Cars & Trucks category and then the subcategory of Cars, or select a site from the Top Car and Truck Sites on Tripod. Browsers can explore home pages by topic, rate the page, and find Tripod members with mutual interests.

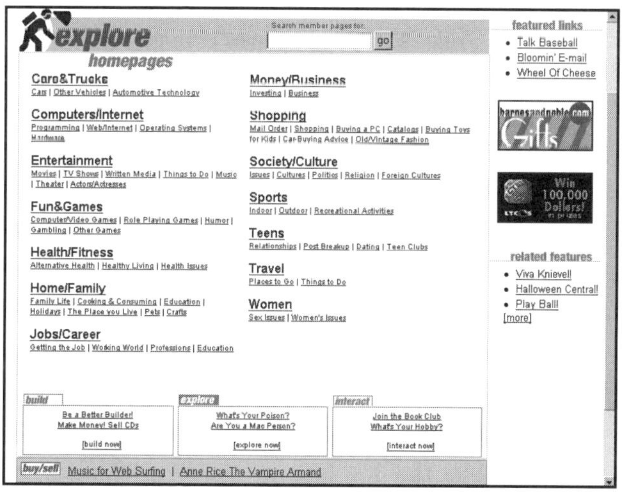

FIGURE 2.10
Tripod's Explore page.

INTERACT

Interact (www.tripod.com/interact/) is where members can interact with other members of the same interest groups or Pods. A list of Pods and the schedule for chat topics and sessions are listed on the Interact page. Tripod also offers Pod members a bulletin board to post messages or comments.

POD.CENTRAL

Members join Pods based on the theme, topic, or interests discussed in the Pod. Members can send content suggestions for new Pod communities to Tripod for consideration. Pods are created in response to member interest and assist members in finding one another.

Members can join as many Pods as they want. Tripod only requires that you register as a Tripod member and have an interest in the Pod community theme. Members may access all Pod activities such as chats and message boards.

To access Pod.Central, go to www.tripod.com/pod_central/ or click Pod.Central on the Interact Page (see Figure 2.11). From this page, members can search for Pods by subject or alphabetically. If you search by subject, you will advance to a page listing all Pod titles, Pod chats, and Pod message boards relating to that topic. If you search by title or alphabetically, you can access a list of Pod Publishers.

Pod Publishers are members of Pods who have created home pages about the particular theme or interest of a Pod they have joined. Pod Publishers are eligible for additional recognition. Their home pages may be selected by Tripod for the Best of Pod Awards or member page spotlights.

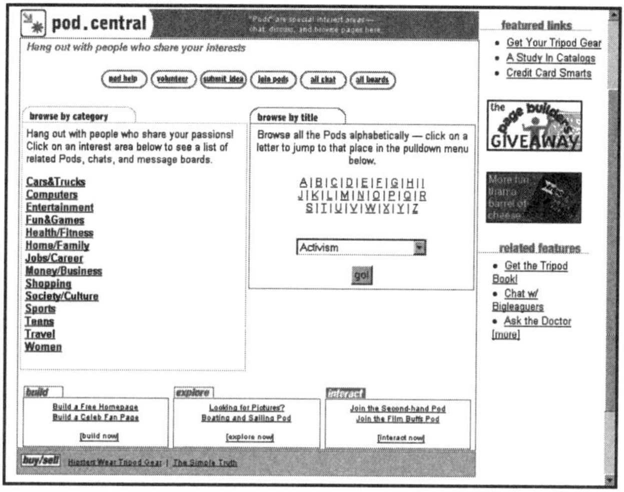

FIGURE 2.11
Pod.Central page.

Members must submit the Web address of their homepage to be recognized as a Pod Publisher. The form needed to submit a URL is accessible on any Pod by clicking the "Add me to this Pod" graphic and following the instructions.

CHATS

Members can advance to the Chat page (`http://chat.tripod.com/`) by clicking the Chat icon on the Interact page. Chats are live discussions among Tripod members related to a particular Pod topic or issue. On the Chat page, browsers can view the schedule for today's and tomorrow's chat sessions. The listing includes the dates, times, and Pod topics of the live chats (see Figure 2.12).

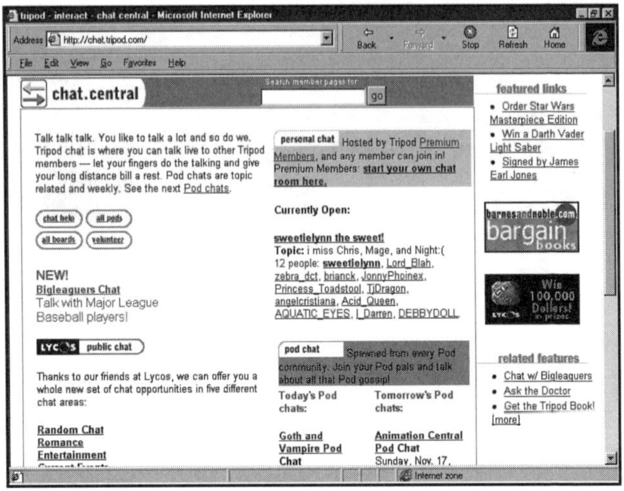

FIGURE 2.12
Tripod's Chat page.

Using Chat

The Tripod chat area also contains Lycos chats. To use the Lycos chat, you must create an account with Lycos; your Tripod member name and password will not work in one of the Lycos public chats.

To enter the Chat area, click the Chat link in the Interact area on the Tripod homepage, and choose the chat you want to join. You can choose from the list of Currently Open chats or one of Lycos public chats in five different chat areas. You can also see the other chats that are available in the near future in the Pod chat area. This will allow you to chat with other members of your Pod or join the Pod if the topic interests you.

To enter one of the open chat rooms, click the link above the Topic. Enter your member name and password, and click the Submit button to enter the chat area.

After you are in the Chat room, choose to whom you want to send a message from the drop down menu (the default setting is "everyone in the room.") Write your message in the box below and click Send. To read the other messages, click Refresh or the Tripod Chat graphic. (Using the Refresh button to view the message is for anyone who is not using the Netscape browser. Tripod uses a special Java applet that can only be used with Netscape now.) You can also choose the Review button to read chat transcripts.

To exit the chat, click the (surprise!) Exit button. If you choose, you can go to another chat room without having to re-enter your member name and password. If you need help using chat, click the Help button.

If you want to send a private message, choose the desired name from the drop-down menu, write a message, and hit Send. A note appears in bold indicating that your message was sent. If a private message is sent to you, it appears in bold letters and is labeled as such.

Premium members can create a private chat room from the chat.central page.

You can also find out who is in each chat room from the chat homepage. Clicking a name results in a member profile. Names are also listed in the section below the message box in the actual chat room. This list of names is updated throughout the chat as people enter and exit the area.

If there is someone on the chat that gets under your skin, you can use the Chat Bozo Filter to keep from seeing that person's messages. In the message section, type **/bozo** or **/ignore**, and the person's name and click Send. For example, if the Bozo's name is mic, type **/bozo mic** into the message box and click Send. If you decide to view the Bozo's rantings later, change **/bozo** to **/unbozo**. (The program indicates when you have successfully ignored someone and how to receive their messages again.)

One thing to remember is that when you ignore someone, you are not able to read his or her member profile. Although you do not receive messages from this person, he or she is still able to read your public messages.

Lycos chat

To use the Lycos chat area, enter the chat page from the Tripod home page. At the chat.central page, you can click one of the five categories under the Lycos Public Chat headline. If this is your first time using a Lycos chat, you must sign up.

Click the Create Account button under the First Time Users heading, fill out the form, and click Submit. At the Welcome page, choose the software you want to use. The Chat Client Options are listed near the bottom of the page, and the descriptions help you make the best choice based on your computer. Click the Enter Now button to log in to the chat.

MESSAGE.BOARDS

Message.Boards are bulletin board discussions moderated by volunteers or Poderators. Volunteer Pod leaders select a Pod topic to be discussed and post it on the message board page (`www.tripod.com/planet/conferencing`). To view a listing of Pod message boards, click Message.Board on the Interact page. Members can browse through message board postings by looking through the alphabetical listings of Pod topics (see Figure 2.13).

After selecting a Pod message board of interest, members choose from a listing of message board topics. Although you must be the member of a Pod to post on a Pod's message board, you can join as many Pods as you want. After selecting a message board topic, click its title to read other Pod members' opinions about the particular issue. You can learn more about Pod members by clicking their name and reading their profile.

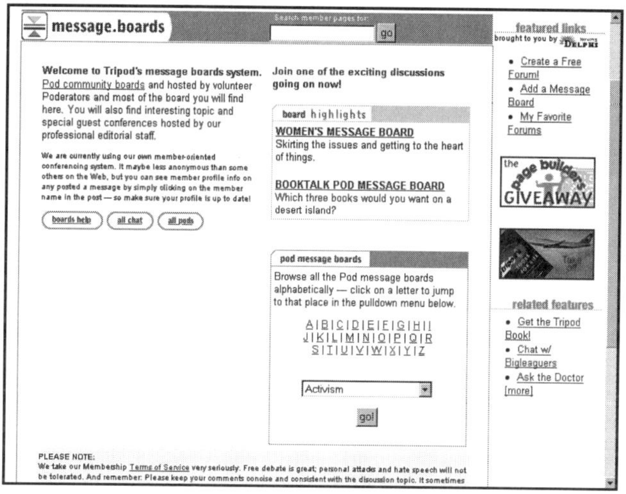

FIGURE 2.13
Message.Board page.

Poderators are encouraged to keep their message boards clean and interesting. A new or exciting message board is selected periodically to be a featured message board and two significant message boards are listed under Board Highlights on the Message.Board page.

PODERATORS

Poderators are volunteers who build and maintain Pods and keep Pod members focused on the particular theme or issue. Poderators ensure that Pod members are informed of new Web sites and industry news and are responsible for updating the main Pod page. They generate a sense of community among Pod members by helping members of the community interact with one another.

To become a Poderator, fill out the online application at `http://www.tripod.com/pod_central/poderator/`. Tripod asks that Poderators be 18 years old or older, have an expressed interest in a Pod topic, a basic knowledge of HTML, the ability to dedicate a few hours a week to a Pod site, and inventive ideas to improve a Pod community.

Buy/Sell

Browsers can shop online through Tripod's Buy/Sell page (`www.tripod.com/buy_sell/`), as shown in Figure 2.14. Shoppers earn savings at a number of stores linked to Tripod's sites or earn shopping credits through an online affiliation with a store. Stores such as Barnes & Noble offer Tripod members shopping discounts if they add a store link to their homepage. If consumers buy products through their page, they earn money or receive a store credit. For more on affiliate stores, see Chapter 9, "Adding Special Effects to Your Tripod Pages."

Tripod offers direct links to get animation or multimedia objects; to order T-shirts, mugs, or hats customized with personal photographs; and purchase Tripod products such as books and T-shirts. There is also a link to a free shop page. This page includes links to free magazines, newsletters, catalogs, and memberships.

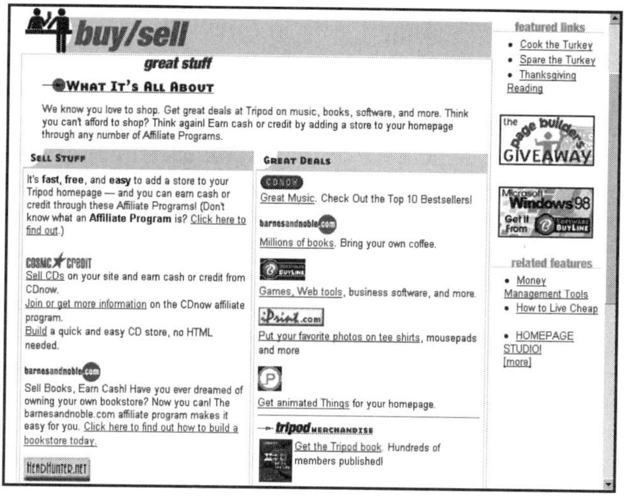

FIGURE 2.14
Tripod's Buy/Sell page.

GENERAL

Tripod's site also contains general information about the benefits of membership, how to log in, links to the newest sites, and help information. Members can stay informed of new opportunities by clicking What's New (`www.tripod.com/whats_new`) on Tripod's home page. The What's New page lists new Web publishing tools, promotions, programs, features and games, pages, and pods.

To search for member profiles, click Search on Tripod's Home page or go to `www.tripod.com/search/`. The search engines enable you to search for members or Web sites on Tripod's site or the World Wide Web.

TRIPOD SERVICES AND CONDITIONS OF USE

Although this book highlights some terms and benefits of Tripod membership and covers premium membership in detail in Appendix A, "Premium Membership: Tripod's First Class Services," you should read Tripod's detailed Terms of Service agreement at `http://www.tripod.com/planet/membership/signup/tos.html` before becoming a member.

The basic Tripod membership is free. To become a member, simply use one of the Sign-Up links and submit all required information (as covered earlier in this chapter), including a legitimate email address and an original member name and address. You are only eligible for one Tripod membership per email address. If multiple users have the same email address, you must request special permission to be allowed more than one membership for the address.

Tripod Premium membership, which includes an additional 11 MB, costs $3 per month. For more information on Premium membership, go to `http://www.tripod.com/planet/membership/premium/`.

Web Page Guidelines

Tripod encourages the exchange of opinions and ideas on the community Web site but has defined a set of regulations by which members must abide. Tripod is not responsible for the viewpoints of members that are voiced in the membership area or on any of the personal home pages of the communities. Web pages are not reviewed by Tripod before they are uploaded onto the site, but Tripod does have the right to remove any sites that publish copyrighted material, pages exploiting children, grossly offensive material, the promotion of illegal activity, and abusive material. Members are responsible for monitoring and maintaining their pages. Tripod is not responsible for any undesirable changes to the site.

Rules for Online Conduct: Tripod Surveys, Chatrooms, and Message Boards

Tripod reserves the right to refuse to publish electronic mail or postings that threaten or abuse, are racially offensive, advocate criminal activity, contain obscene content, or advertise commercially. Tripod wants you to express yourself—that's what building a home page is all about. That doesn't mean you can throw civility and decency out the window.

Privacy

All member information remains confidential and will not be forwarded to a third party without member consent. In other words, when you become a Tripod member, you needn't worry about Tripod selling your name and contact information to another company. None of us like to get spammed, and Tripod says that it does not do anything to cause this.

CHAPTER 3

Using the Tripod Filemanager

Tripod gives you 11MB of disk space to create your home on the Web. (Unless you're a premium member, then you get 22MB of disk space.) That's a lot of space! You can build more than just one Web page with a few graphics in that kind of space. This chapter shows you how to get your files into your disk space, how to move them around, and gives you a few tips on managing your Web site.

After you've built your first page, or few pages, you'll want to update that page to keep it fresh by adding new information or graphics. Before you know it, you'll have a messy home on the Web! Every time you look at your main directory, you'll see a long list of files and you can't remember what half of them are or which graphics are used on your main page. Aagh! You need a housekeeper, and Tripod provides one for you. Tripod's Filemanager lets you upload, delete, copy, rename, edit, and move files. It can even help you reorganize your closets, er, subdirectories.

UPLOADING FILES

The greatest Web site in the world won't be seen by anybody if it's just sitting on your C drive. You need to copy the files from your hard drive to Tripod's servers. That's called uploading.

> **TIP**
>
> Confused by techno-babble? Look it up on NetLingo at `http://www.netlingo.com`. NetLingo is an online dictionary of technical terms related to the Internet and the World Wide Web.

Generally, uploading and downloading (copying files from a server to your hard drive) uses File Transfer Protocol, or FTP. Tripod gives you a couple of different ways to upload, or FTP, your files to their servers. You can use the Filemanager, an FTP program like CuteFTP or Fetch, or you can use your browser if you use Netscape Navigator 2.0 or higher (or something comparable).

USING THE TRIPOD FILEMANAGER

The Tripod Filemanager is probably the easiest way to upload your files. Point your browser at `http://www.tripod.com/build/` and click the Filemanager link. It'll be on the right side of the black bar across the top of the screen. Provide your Tripod member name and password when prompted.

TIP

If you've forgotten your password, go to `http://help.tripod.com` and look under Membership Support Center in the left column. Click Find Lost Password for more information on how to get your password back. If your password just isn't working, remember that Tripod's member names and passwords are case-sensitive. Make sure that your Caps Lock key isn't depressed and try again.

After you've logged in, you'll see a listing of your main directory. You might already have subdirectories if you've used any of the Homepage Studio's Build by Topic templates (see Chapter 5, "Homepage Studio QuickPage: Build by Topic"). Figure 3.1 shows a sample main directory listing.

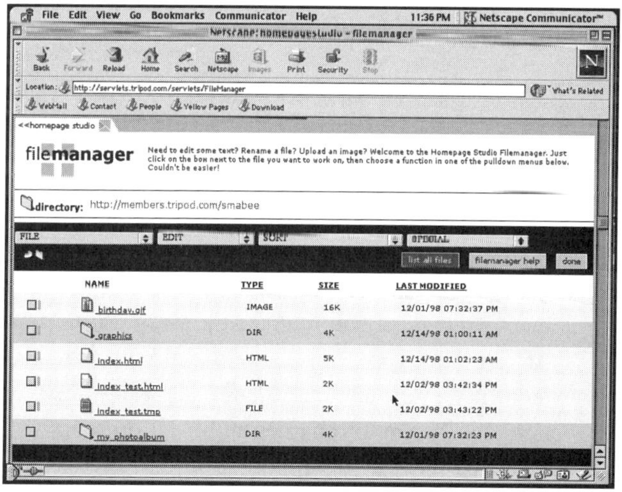

FIGURE 3.1
The Tripod Filemanager shows you all the files and subdirectories in your main directory.

Follow these simple steps to upload your files:

1. Select Upload… from the File pull-down menu. The file upload window will open for you (see Figure 3.2). You can use this window to upload up to four files at a time.

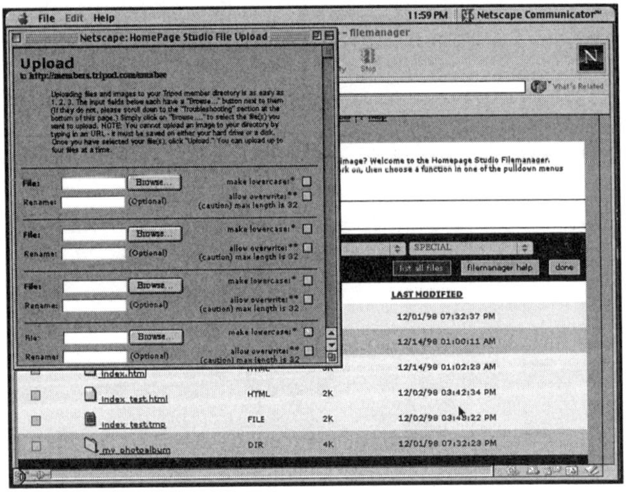

FIGURE 3.2
The File Upload Window lets you select up to four files to upload.

2. Click the Browse… button and look through your hard drive until you find the file you want to upload. If you want, you can rename the file at this point by entering a new name in the field labeled Rename. You don't have to rename the file if you want its name to stay the same, only using lower-case letters. Just check the box labeled Make Lowercase. You might also want to check the allow overwrite box. You'll be able to edit a file, or replace a file with a newer copy, at a later date.

A ROSE IS A ROSE, BUT NOT ALWAYS.

Tripod's servers recognize many different file types, but only if they're named correctly. Files that end in .htm or .html are recognized as text files containing HTML code. HTML files are "served," or sent to your browser, differently from the files ending in .gif or .jpg, which are graphics formats. Tripod's servers won't recognize files with "illegal" file names. Always use numbers, letters (upper- or lower-case), _, or -. Never start a file name with a dash or a period. File names are also case-sensitive: index.html is different from Index.html, which is different from index.HTML.

3. When you're done selecting files to upload, click the Upload button. Tripod does the heavy lifting for you. When it's done, a new window will open telling you if Tripod has been able to upload the files (and the names of the files uploaded).
4. Click OK to return to the file upload window. You can close the window by clicking Cancel or you can select more files to upload by clicking Browse....

That's it! Pretty simple, huh? If you want to upload files into subdirectories, navigate to the subdirectory using the File pull-down menu. When you're in the right subdirectory, follow the steps outlined above. For more, see the "Creating Subdirectories" section later in this chapter.

Using a Graphical FTP Tool

You can easily use another FTP tool instead of Tripod's Filemanager utility. Many FTP programs enable you to do all the same things you can do with Tripod's Filemanager. A popular program for Windows users is

CuteFTP. Let's step through downloading, installing, and uploading a file using CuteFTP. (Macintosh users should check out a freeware program called Fetch. Fetch works similarly to CuteFTP and can be found at `http://www.dartmouth.edu/pages/softdev/fetch.html`.)

NOTE

Some programs, like CuteFTP, are known as shareware. Shareware programs let you try out the software before you buy it. If you like the software and want to keep using it, you should send the developers some money. Most shareware is reasonably priced around $15-20. If you use shareware, sending the developers money has a couple of advantages. First, you'll know when there are upgrades to the software to correct bugs. Second, you might get a cheaper price on "commercial" versions of the software if a big software developer eventually buys it. Last, but not least, if you pay your shareware fee, you receive a registration key that makes the dialog box that asks you to register go away.

Downloading and Installing CuteFTP

Downloading and installing CuteFTP is easy. Simply perform the following steps:

1. Go to `http://www.cuteftp.com`.
2. Enter your email address in the Quick Download box and click Download.
3. The software should automatically begin to download. If it doesn't, follow the Click here link.
4. After the software has finished downloading, navigate to the folder on your C drive which contains the software and run the install program.

The first time you run CuteFTP, you'll see that there are a lot of sites included in the program. These are usually software libraries that contain interesting programs and popular games. You can explore these sites later. First, let's use CuteFTP to upload some files to Tripod's servers.

Uploading Files with CuteFTP

Perform the following steps to upload files with CuteFTP:

1. Open the CuteFTP program.
2. Click the Add Site button on the opening screen as shown in Figure 3.3.

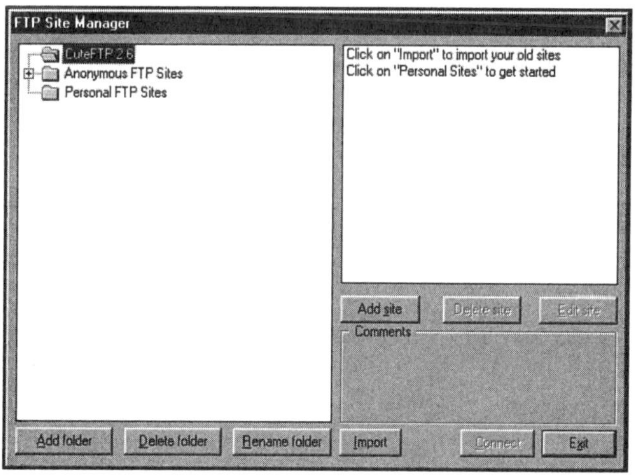

FIGURE 3.3
CuteFTP already has some sites "bookmarked" for you. Let's add Tripod to the list of sites.

3. Position the cursor in the Site Label field and type **Tripod** and press the tab key. Place the cursor in the

Host Address field and type **ftp.tripod.com**. Press the Tab key again.

4. Having tabbed to the User ID field, type in your member name and press Tab. Now type your password. You won't actually see your password, just asterisks in place of the characters.
5. Press the Tab key four times or until the cursor is in the Initial Remote Directory field. Type **/**.
6. When your screen looks similar to Figure 3.4, click OK. If you have all of your Web site files in one place on your hard drive, you can set the initial local directory to something like C:\mywebsite or click the button to browse to the folder you want before clicking OK.

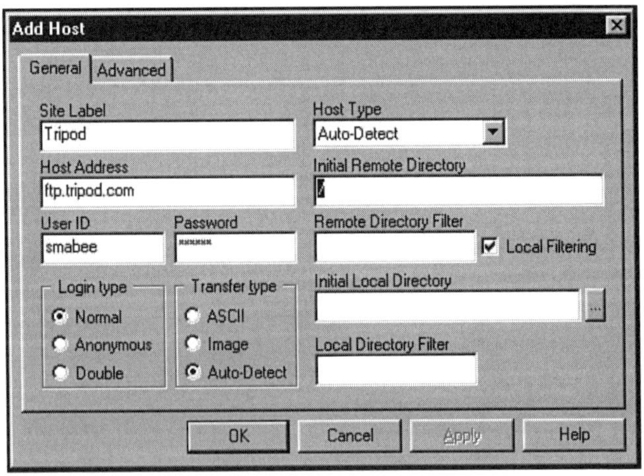

FIGURE 3.4
Setting up CuteFTP is as simple as filling in a few fields.

7. You should now see Tripod as a site available in the box on the right side of CuteFTP's window. If it's not

already highlighted, click it and then click the Connect button at the bottom of the window.

8. You'll see a new window as CuteFTP tries to connect to Tripod. After you're connected, you might see some login messages. If you're interested, you can read them, otherwise, just close the window by clicking the Close button in the top-right corner of the window.
9. After connecting, you'll see either a directory listing of your C drive or the initial directory you set up on the left side of the window. On the right side of the window, there will be a directory listing of your Tripod main directory.
10. Take a moment to run your cursor over the tools in the toolbar at the top of the window. Make sure you know where the Upload button is. It's the button with a picture of a folder, a file, and an upward-pointing arrow.
11. Select a file in your local directory and click the Upload button. You might see some messages that are similar to the login message scrolling by in the top part of the window. After a moment, your Tripod main directory should reflect the addition of the new file.
12. When you're done uploading files, click the Close button in the top-right corner of the window to exit CuteFTP.

That's all there is to it! The difference between using Tripod's Filemanager and CuteFTP is that you can upload to and download from many different servers using CuteFTP. If you think you'll be FTPing files to two or more servers, you might want to consider using CuteFTP. Don't forget to pay the shareware fee!

Using a Web Browser

If you're using Netscape 2.0 or higher (or a comparable version of Microsoft Internet Explorer), you might be able to upload files using your Web browser. Versions of Netscape Navigator prior to 2.0 do not support using FTP to upload, so make sure your browser supports uploading before trying the following steps.

Using a Web browser to upload files (see Figure 3.5) is quick and easy. But that's pretty much all you can do through a Web browser. You can't manage files in your Tripod disk space using a browser. If you want to move, delete, or rename files, you'll need to use an FTP program or Tripod's Filemanager.

1. From your browser's File menu, select Open Location.
2. Type in the following URL: **ftp://[*membername*] @ftp.tripod.com** (use your member name instead of [*membername*]).
3. When prompted by your browser, enter your password. You'll see a listing of the files and subdirectories in your main Tripod directory. You can upload a file by dragging and dropping a file into the Navigator window. Or you can select Upload file from your browser's File menu and select a file.

TIP

If you have problems entering your password while uploading a page using your browser, try typing the following URL in step 2: **ftp://[*membername*]:[*password*]@ftp.tripod.com**. Use your own member name and password. Remember, member names and passwords are case-sensitive. Always check your capitalization if you have problems.

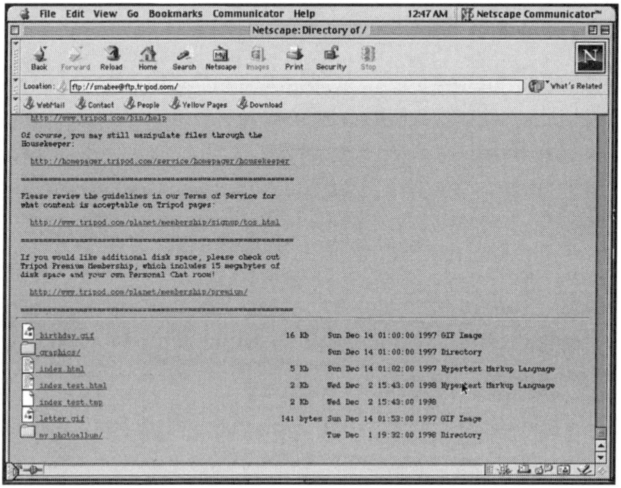

FIGURE 3.5
You can upload files to Tripod's servers using some Web browsers.

If you uploaded a finished HTML document (and any graphics used on the page), it is immediately viewable by going to your member Web space.

Although many Internet-related acronyms sound scary or complex, you can see that actually doing stuff on the Internet is pretty easy. You've just learned three different ways to FTP files.

MANAGING FILES

As your Web site grows, you'll probably want to do more than just upload new pages or files. The rest of this chapter focuses on using Tripod's Filemanager to do more than upload files.

EDITING FILES

From time to time, you might want to update your Web page(s) with new information or graphics. You can do that using Tripod's Filemanager and either the QuickPage editor or the Freeform Editor.

First, point your browser at `http://www.tripod.com/build/` and click the Filemanager link. It'll be on the right side of the black bar across the top of the screen. Provide your Tripod member name and password when prompted.

When the listing of your main directory appears, select the checkbox to the left of the file you want to edit. If you created your page using QuickPage, selecting Edit from the Edit pull-down menu takes you straight to the Homepage Studio. If you choose Edit With…, you can then select either the Freeform editor or the QuickPage editor. If you choose the Freeform editor, Tripod converts your file from a QuickPage file to a regular HTML file. If you do this, you won't be able to use QuickPage with this file again.

If you created your page with the Freeform editor or any other HTML editor, choosing Edit opens the Freeform editor. Remember, you cannot edit regular HTML files with QuickPage.

NOTE

QuickPages contain special formatting that regular HTML files don't have. You can convert QuickPages to regular HTML if you want full control over the HTML code. However, you can't convert HTML files to a QuickPage. Make sure you really want to convert the file! Better yet, make a copy of the file before converting it. Then, if you don't like writing HTML, you still have the QuickPage version. Also, QuickPages can only "live" in your main directory. Don't move them to subdirectories or they'll lose the special information that makes them easy to edit.

After your page has opened with the appropriate editor, you can edit the page in the same place you created the page. Don't forget to save often. Click Done from either the Freeform editor or QuickPage to exit the editor. The next page that appears in your browser will tell you how much space you have and how much space you've used (see Figure 3.6). There are also some links that will help you promote your updated page.

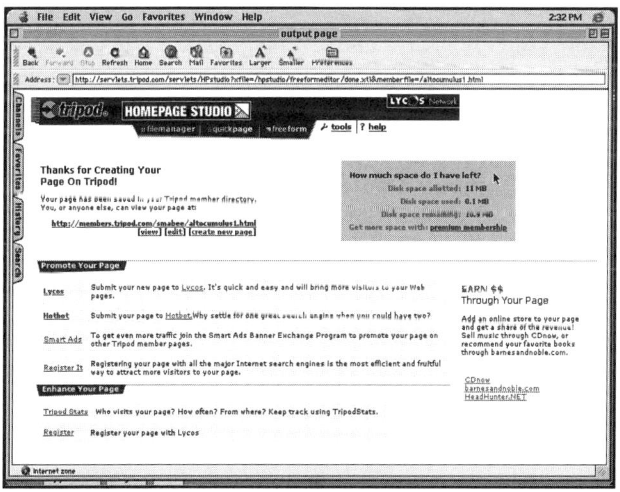

FIGURE 3.6

Tripod updates you on the status of your disk space when you're done creating or editing a file.

Deleting Files

Occasionally, you might want to delete a file. Maybe you put up the file before it was complete or maybe you don't want to use a particular graphic anymore. That's pretty easy, too. Again, start from the Filemanager. Point your browser at `http://www.tripod.com/build`, click the Filemanager link, and enter your member name and password if prompted for them.

After you see your main directory listing, select the checkbox to the left of the file you want to delete. Then select Delete... from the Edit pull-down menu. Confirm that you want to delete the selected file by clicking OK in the delete window. If you don't want to delete the file, simply click Cancel.

You should be sure that you want to delete a file before clicking OK. After you've deleted a file, Tripod cannot recover it for you.

The Kitchen Sink—Or Everything Else You Can Do in the Filemanager

Here's a quick list of other actions you can take using the Tripod Filemanager. You'll find that the Filemanager is pretty easy to work with, so we won't go into a lot of detail.

File Menu

Create a new page Just what it says. You can create a new page using either a QuickPage template or the Freeform editor.

View You can use the View option to see the file the way your visitors will see it. This feature is useful to check for missing graphics or to make sure the file looks the way you intended.

Open Directory This feature shows you a listing of the files in the directory you've selected.

New Subdirectory You can create a new subdirectory inside the current directory.

Select All You can use this feature to select all the documents in your directory.

Clear All This feature "unchecks" all the boxes you've checked. Don't worry, it doesn't delete your files.

TIP

It's easy to get lost moving through the directory structure of your main Tripod directory. There is a quick (and easy) way to get back to the main directory. Directly under the FILE pull-down menu there is an image of an arrow curving to the left and a yellow folder. Clicking that image will take you up one directory level.

Edit Menu

Copy Copy makes a duplicate of the file you selected and gives it a different name. This is a useful feature if you want to edit a file, but aren't sure if you'll like the changes. Copy the file and make your changes in the new file. If you like it, you can rename it with the original document name. If you don't like your changes, you still have the original document intact.

Rename This feature renames a file. This is useful when you're reorganizing your site or just making updates to files.

Move Use this feature to move files between subdirectories, from your main directory to a subdirectory, or from a subdirectory to your main directory.

Sort Menu

The Sort menu enables you to change the view of your main directory. You can view a list of all the files alphabetically by name, type, size, or the last modified date. You can also select to view a subset of all the files. If you only want to work with images you have in your directory, select List Images from the pull-down menu. You can also display the HTML files, subdirectories, or other file types. If you've selected to view only a subset, you return to a full list of files by selecting List All.

Special Menu

Member stats If you're wondering how much space you have left, this is the place to find out. Selecting Member Stats… from the pull-down menu opens a window that contains information about your disk usage.

Promote Select the checkbox to the left of the file you'd like to promote and select Promote… from the pull-down menu. Fill in the requested information (people you'd like to tell about your page, your email address, etc.) and click Send. If you change your mind, just click Cancel.

Organizing Your Web Site

After you have created a bunch of Web pages, it might be difficult to decide what pages you should update or delete if you can't tell what they are. You need to organize your Web site.

You can organize your Web site the same you way you would organize files on your hard drive. Most people organize files by putting related files together in subdirectories that have a descriptive name.

Let's say you have a relatively small Web site—say, one page about you, another page about your hobby, and a few small graphics. You might be able to organize your Web site by simply creating a subdirectory called graphics and moving all your graphics files there.

If you have a large, complex Web site, you might need to organize differently. Let's say you have a page for each member in your family, a collection of your favorite recipes, and a photo album of pictures from your vacation to the Bahamas. Creating a graphics subdirectory probably won't help you clean up too much. Instead you might want to create three subdirectories named family, recipes, and Bahamas vacation. Then you can put all the files related to your family members in the family subdirectory and so on. If necessary, you can create graphics subdirectories for each new subdirectory.

When you move files from your main directory into subdirectories, you might also have to clean up your Web pages as well. Let's say that you had all your HTML files and graphic files in your main directory. If you decide to clean up your main directory (by moving all your graphics files into a separate directory just for graphics), then Web browsers won't be able to find the images until you change the HTML files that "call" the graphics. If you created your Web pages using QuickPage, just edit the file and tell QuickPage where to find the graphics. If you wrote the HTML yourself, you'll need to change your source code to include the subdirectory name. For instance, your original HTML might have looked like this:

```
<IMG SRC="my_picture.jpg">
```

You must edit it to look like:

```
<IMG SRC="graphics/my_picture.jpg">
```

As you can see, reorganizing your Web site after you've built lots of pages might take some time and work. It pays to consider your Web site's organization before you start building pages like crazy.

Creating Subdirectories

Like many other actions in the Filemanager, creating subdirectories is simple. Start at the Filemanager. You know how to get there, right? If not, see the instructions in the previous sections about uploading files to Tripod and using the Tripod Filemanager.

When you see your main directory listing, select New Subdirectory… from the File pull-down menu. Enter a name for the subdirectory and click OK (see Figure 3.7).

To navigate to subdirectories, select the checkbox to the left of the subdirectory and select Open Directory… from the File menu.

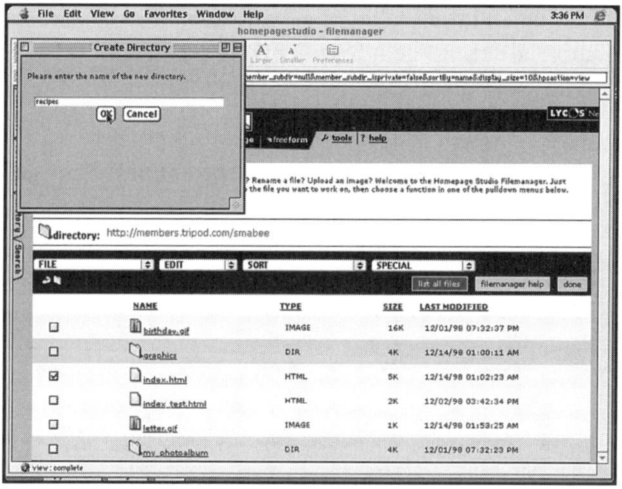

FIGURE 3.7

You can use the "new subdirectory" feature of the Filemanager to organize your Web site.

NOTE

If you start creating a lot of subdirectories, you might begin to wonder how much of your disk space they take up. Most directories only take up 1.5K of disk space. For comparison, an average HTML file takes up 2–4K of disk space, and small graphics files can take up 15K of disk space. Many graphics will be larger than 15K. If you're running out of space, the culprits are probably the files inside the subdirectories. Consider deleting old files or becoming a Premium Member for $3 per month and receiving more disk space.

Moving Files between Directories

After you've created new subdirectories, you'll need an easy way to move files into the directory. You could go through all the bother of downloading files to your hard drive, deleting them from Tripod's server, and then uploading them again into the right directories. But why would you do that when you could just move them?

To move a file, check the box to the left of the file and then select Move... from the Edit menu. Select the directory to which you want to move the file and click OK (see Figure 3.8). If you change your mind, you can move the file back to its original location.

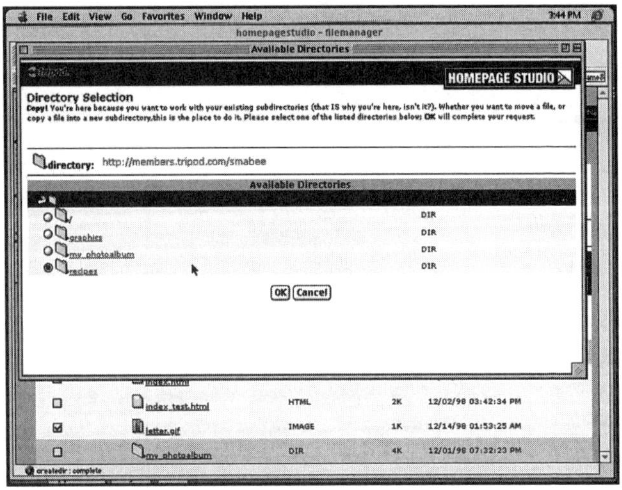

FIGURE 3.8
Moving files between directories is as simple as point and click.

TIP

If you need help on a topic that didn't get covered here, you can always click the Filemanager help button (it's on the right side of the screen underneath the pull-down menus) or point your browser at `http://help.tripod.com/`.

PART II

DEVELOP YOUR POD

CHAPTER 4

Web Page Design—The Basics

Web page design—those three words can sound a little intimidating if you've never created a Web page before. But don't let the semantics get in your way. Designing a Web page simply requires that you proceed one step at a time. It's like most accomplishments in life—planning a party, completing a course, building a sandcastle, painting a room, even tackling a mountainous pile of laundry—it looks like a lot of work, but the job gets done easily if you proceed one sock at a time.

The steps to designing a Tripod Web page can be organized into four piles:

- Web site blueprint
- Page layout and design fundamentals
- HTML and HTML editors
- Tripod's Web page tools

This chapter addresses each category and eliminates the Web page design intimidation factor. So, let's stop staring at the syllabus and get started. Web page design can be easy, fun (even if you aren't the "artsy" or "techie" type), and rewarding.

Creating a Blueprint

OK, forget about your computer for a minute and grab a pencil and paper. The first step of Web design is to conceptualize your Web site. In other words, pinpoint why you are creating a Web presence. What's the main idea? The plot? The unifying theme? Sounds like an English class, but it's true. You have to come up with an idea, and try to envision any tangents you want to include. If it helps, brainstorm—just write down everything that comes to mind. You can cross ideas off later or even trash the page and start over. In the meantime, let's look at an example.

Let's say you want to build a Hot Wheels site (it could happen!). You could put pictures of all your Hot Wheels on one gigantic Web page—after all there's no limit to how long a Web page can be. Well, you *could* do that, but there are some major drawbacks to the enormous one-page-fits-all approach. Mainly, gigantic pages take a long time for surfers to download, and that's bad. It's a fact that if Web surfers have to wait more than 10 seconds to load a page, you've lost them.

Here's a better approach to creating your Hot Wheels Web site. You can create a main Hot Wheels page that welcomes viewers and provides links to other Hot Wheels pages that you've created (as you'll see later in this chapter, that's easier to do than it sounds). If you've surfed the Web, you've run into this multipage arrangement. It's a very common arrangement, because it works. Using this technique, you could have a main Hot Wheels page that links to pages that incorporate the tangential ideas you came up with while brainstorming. For example, maybe you want a Hot Wheels Corvette Web page, an Antique Hot Wheels page, a Hot Wheels For Sale page, and a page listing links to other Hot Wheels Web Sites on the Internet. With those pages in mind, you have the makings of a Web site.

Now, return to your pencil and paper. Draw rectangles representing your main page and tangential pages. If you want, you can even draw arrows emanating from the main page (also called the *home page*) to the tangential pages (some sites go multiple levels deep, with tangential pages leading to their own tangential pages). Next, list the contents of each page, and make sure you include all the topics you want to cover. Fortunately, Tripod gives you 11MB to work with, so you have room to create a number of ancillary Web pages. Returning to the Hot Wheels example, the Hot Wheels site could consist of the following five Web pages (see Figure 4.1 for a sketch of the Hot Wheels Web site):

Web Page	**Page Contents**
Main page	Welcome viewers Site description Links to other Web site pages Daily Hot Wheel picture
Corvette Page	Pictures of Hot Wheel Corvettes Facts, prices, and other information
Antiques	Pictures of Antique Hot Wheels Facts, prices, and other information
For Sale	Pictures of Hot Wheels for sale Facts, prices, and other information Email address
Other Links	Page of links to other Hot Wheel sites Site descriptions following each link

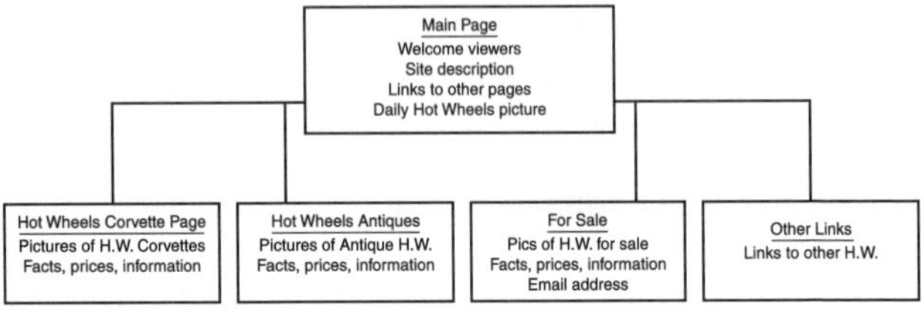

FIGURE 4.1
A sketch of the Hot Wheels Web site.

Sketching a blueprint helps you visualize how your Web site will present information. The preceding table, combined with a sketch of the Web site as shown in Figure 4.1, results in a fairly detailed *site map*.

At this point, if you've used your pencil wisely, you're well on your way to designing your Web site. In fact, after you complete your brainstorming and sketching, you've met your first milestone; your Web site's big picture is in focus. Your next step is to zoom in on the pages.

Reviewing the Fundamentals of Web Page Layout and Design

This section starts with a rule—*keep your Web pages clear, clean, and simple*. Sounds obvious, but it's worth stating. One of the beauties of the Web is that you can use as many pages as you need to present your information without wasting a single tree. Plus, the old adage is true—a picture is worth a thousand words. So, instead of describing where the latest UFO sighting occurred—"Go to the end of Carroo Street, take the third dirt lane toward the corn fields…"—you can show a map to the UFO landing pad instead, (See Chapter 10, "Adding Graphics to Your Tripod Pages," for tips on obtaining and using Web graphics.) There's simply no reason to clutter up your Web pages, as demonstrated in Figure 4.2. With that rule adequately emphasized, let's move on to some more concrete concepts of page layout.

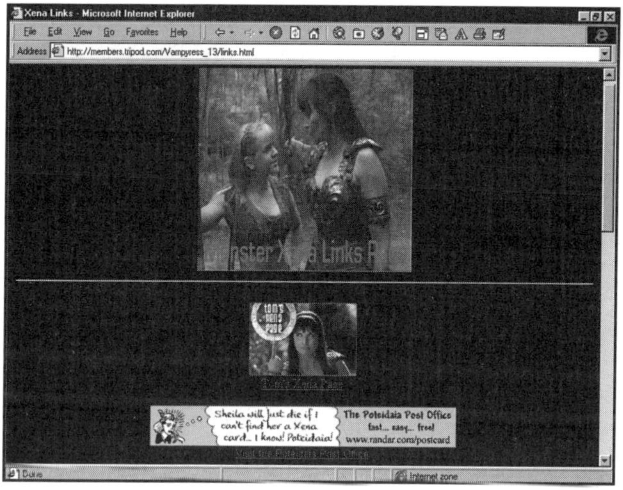

FIGURE 4.2
A prime example of a simple Web page—you probably guessed what this site's about almost instantly. (By the way, you can bring Xena to your own computer screen by visiting `members.tripod.com/~Vampyress_13/links.html`*).*

To make the Web page design job easier, Web pages can be analyzed as consisting of a few basic components. This chapter calls the basic components the *fundamentals of page layout*, which is just a fancy way to say "parts of the page." The fundamentals are so basic, that you'll have these concepts mastered in no time. In a nutshell, the parts of a Web page include:

- Title area
- Link area or menu bar
- Main body
- Footer

Figure 4.3 shows a very useful Tripod site that clearly implements the basic elements of a page. The HTML 4 Rookies (`members.tripod.com/~larrydoz/html4rookies.html`) Web site provides loads of HTML information, so visit the site and bookmark it. You'll return to this site later in the chapter, and you'll probably find yourself returning to this HTML site as a reference after you've put this book aside.

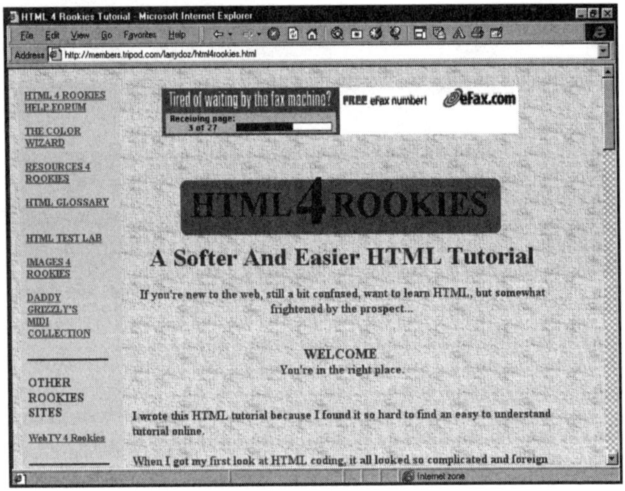

FIGURE 4.3
The HTML 4 Rookies page clearly implements the basic parts of a Web page.

Let's take a closer look at each part of a Web page.

Title Area

Most Tripod sites have a title area. Usually, the title appears centered at the top of the Web page. Generally, the title takes up about one-quarter to one-third of the browser window. Most often, people render their Web page title as a graphic to add more pizzazz to their page.

Notice in Figure 4.3 that, although the title consists mainly of text, the words *HTML 4 Rookies* appear stylized and on a green background. So, even though it looks like text, it's actually a graphic. (If you don't believe it, open the page, and right-click the title. Your shortcut menu will offer you graphic-related menu items, such as Save Picture As.)

Figure 4.4 shows another example of a graphical title element. On the Your Daily Freebies (`members.tripod.com/~SJEWELRYS`) page, the title appears top-center, and it's obviously a logo-type graphic.

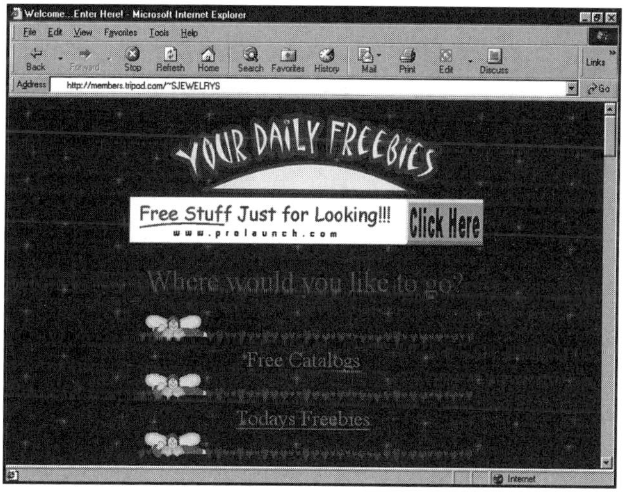

FIGURE 4.4
The Your Daily Freebies page shows an appealing graphical title at the top of the Web page (a visit to this site can turn out to be not-so-quick after you start to see the number of free items listed—you'll be amazed).

LINK AREA

The next main area of a Web page is the links area. As discussed earlier in this chapter, you can divide your Web site into a number of pages. Therefore, you'll have to provide an easy way for viewers to move from one page to the next and back again. The easiest way to provide smooth navigation among your Web pages is to create a links area. Your best bet is to show the list of links on each Web page in your Web site—consider your links menu to be a handy travel guide for viewers. If viewers get lost or access a page they don't want to see, they can turn to the comfort of your links area and move on. The G.A.B.S. (Gaithersburg Area Brewers Society) page makes good use of a links menu. Figures 4.5 and 4.6 show two pages from the G.A.B.S. (`members.tripod.com/~G_A_B_S`) Web site. Notice the main menu section appears along the left edge on both pages.

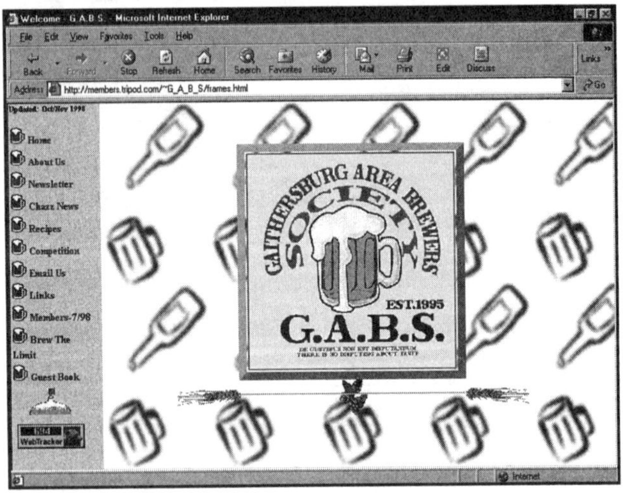

FIGURE 4.5
Making good use of a links menu keeps viewers around longer and helps them to find the information that interests them.

FIGURE 4.6
This site maintains a consistent placement of the links menu—on the left of the screen—throughout the site.

Links menus can be placed anywhere on your page—left, right, top, bottom, wherever. Just try to place the menu in the same area on each page or at least in a predicable area. For example, some Web pages (like the HTML 4 Rookies site shown earlier in Figure 4.3) provide a links menu on the main page in one form, and then consistently use another links menu style on all ancillary pages. Figures 4.7 and 4.8 show a couple of HTML 4 Rookies pages that are linked to the HTML 4 Rookies home page. Notice the ancillary pages' links menus appear consistently across the top on each page, and the home page shows the links menu along the left edge of the page. Regardless of the approach you use for your links menu, your goal should be to ensure that the links menu is easy to find and instantly recognizable.

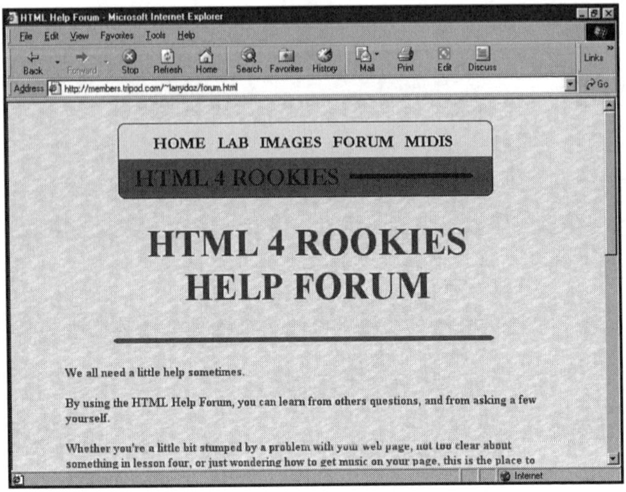

FIGURE 4.7
Using an identifying links menu on ancillary Web site pages.

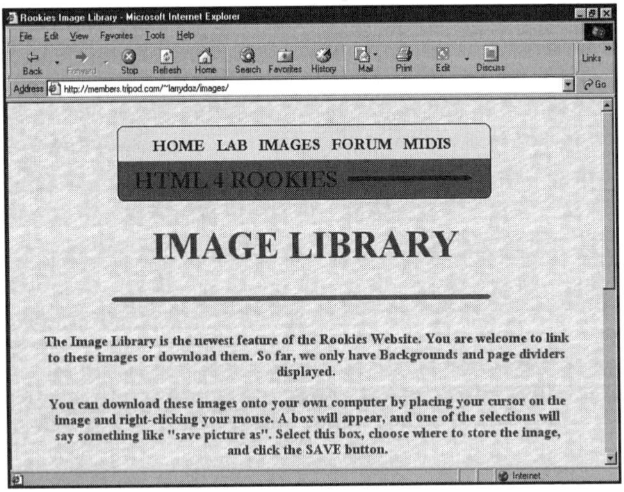

FIGURE 4.8
This site keeps its links menu consistently across the top of the page.

After you get comfortable with the basics of page design, you might consider using frames to create a links menu. The G.A.B.S. site shown in Figures 4.5 and 4.6 uses frames. See Chapter 6, "Popular Topics and Outstanding Tripod Examples," for more information regarding advanced Web page design using frames and other advanced techniques.

Main Body

Not surprisingly, the *main body* is the core of a Web page. The title quickly tells readers what the page is about, the links menu keeps viewers grounded, and the main body provides all the fun. The main body can contain text, tutorials, images, graphics, or lists of links. Generally, the main body takes up the bulk of your page. You should dedicate at least 60 percent of your Web page to the main body. When designing the main body of a Web page, remember the rule emphasized at the beginning of this section—keep it simple. Furthermore, try to use elements that break up the text. You can use spacing, graphics, images, rule lines, and headings to visually organize your Web page.

Figure 4.9 shows some impressive quilts Bonnie has made (`members.tripod.com/~Bonquilt/photo1.htm`). Notice her use of a title and her clean presentation of text and graphics. At the bottom of the page, Bonnie presents a single link named Return and a simple footer. (Footers are described in the next section.) The Return link takes you to Bonnie's home page. If you wander around Bonnie's Web site, you'll notice she consistently provides navigational links along the bottoms of her Web pages; this gives viewers a predictable spot to turn to when they want to move along.

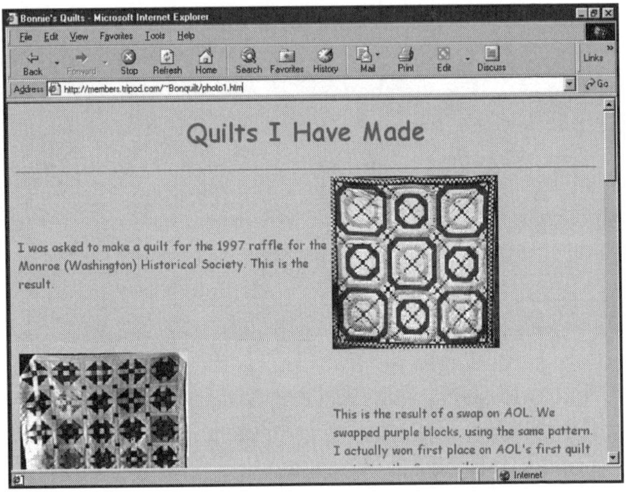

FIGURE 4.9
Keeping it simple in the main body of a Web page.

FOOTER

The final Web page layout element is the footer. Not surprisingly, the footer appears at the bottom of the page. If you keep your eyes peeled, you might notice that many Tripod Web pages include an area at the bottom of the page that provides information concerning the Web page. This brief information is the footer. A footer can include a copyright date and symbol, author's name, email link(s), acknowledgments, and often (on Tripod sites) a link to the site's guestbook. Tripod's home page (`www.tripod.com`) provides a prime example of the effective use of a footer (see Figure 4.10).

For a good look at creating a personal home page that successfully uses a title, bottom-align links menu, and a footer element, return to Bonnie's site and check out the About Us Web page (`home1.gte.net/mbh535/page2.htm`).

Click links on the menu bar, and you'll see how easy it is to navigate among this site's Web pages. It's clear, simple, informative, and straightforward—an admirable accomplishment.

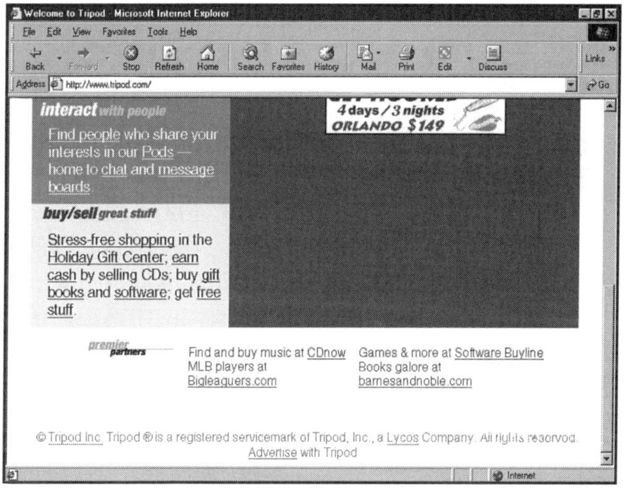

FIGURE 4.10
Tripod's home page and its affiliated pages make good use of the footer element.

OTHER ELEMENTS

In addition to the basic page layout elements, Web pages can also contain many other elements. These include dates stating when the page was last updated (often included in the footer), visitor count, buttons denoting what tools were used to create the Web page, Web forms, Tripod's voting banner, and other Web page additions. Don't overwhelm yourself by trying to add everything at once. Like most creative projects, the most interesting pieces evolve over time.

The Web site groundwork is established, and you're now ready to dig in and design your Web pages. Roll up your sleeves and put down your pencil, because the next phase is the hands-on phase of Web site development.

Using HTML and HTML Editors

After reading this far into the chapter, you're ready to apply your page-layout knowledge to actual Web pages. This is where the fun part begins. You'll get a quick review of HTML (Hypertext Markup Language) and an introduction to a couple of HTML editors. Oh—*HTML* and *HTML editors*—now there's some potentially intimidating terminology. Never fear—it's another case of semantics. *HTML* isn't for programmers, it's more of an elaborate yet somewhat-cumbersome, command-ridden word processing program. Following is a quick (as in rapid) review of basic HTML. Then you'll see what HTML editors are and how they can make your Web designing life more comfortable.

Getting the Skinny on HTML

This section provides enough HTML detail to get you started and to let you see that HTML isn't a technology reserved for brain surgeons. There are lots of HTML resources around these days, so we won't try to reproduce a primer on HTML here. A good dictionary-type resource for HTML is *HTML: The Definitive Guide*, 2nd edition, by Chuck Musciano & Bill Kennedy.

Basically, HTML consists of tag sets that instruct browsers how to treat elements in a text document. To format text, you enclose text within a tag set. Here, check this out:

```
<B>Browser--I command you to bold this text.</B>
<BR>
<I>Browser--Italicize these words.</I>
```

The preceding examples are fairly self-explanatory. The <B>…</B> tags instruct the browser to display all text between the tags in boldface. Likewise, all text between the <I>…</I> tags should appear italicized. And finally, the <BR> tag between the sample lines of text instructs the browser to add a line break (similar to hitting your Enter key). You can test this sample in a moment, but first you'll need to add the shell tags that appear on every HTML page:

```
<HTML>
<HEAD>
<TITLE>This text appears in the title bar of a Web
page</TITLE>
</HEAD>
<BODY>
</BODY>
</HTML>
```

The <HTML>…</HTML> tags define to the browser that everything contained between the tags constitutes an HTML page. The <HEAD> section contains header information, including the <TITLE> element. As described in the example, the <TITLE>…</TITLE> tags create the text that will display in the title bar of viewers' browsers. Finally, the <BODY>…</BODY> tags define the start and end of the body of your HTML page.

Now, it's time for you to put all of this together. First, open a text editor, such as Notepad or WordPad. Then, copy the following HTML into a blank document:

```
<HTML>
<HEAD>
<TITLE>This text appears in the title bar of a Web
page</TITLE>
</HEAD>
<BODY>
<B>Browser--I command you to bold this text.</B>
<BR>
<BR>
<I>Browser--Italicize these words.</I>
</BODY>
</HTML>
```

After you enter the text, save the file as basic.html on your hard disk. Close the file, open your browser, and navigate to basic.html on your hard disk. Your page should display similar to the page shown in Figure 4.11.

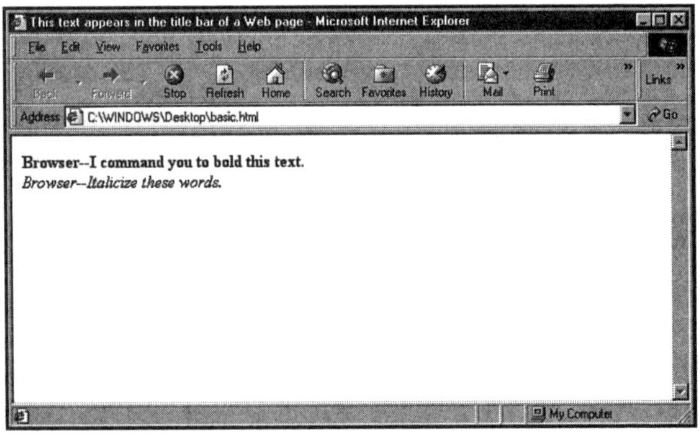

FIGURE 4.11
Viewing basic.html.

Sure, it's not the most exciting Web page, but nonetheless, you just created a Web page. Frankly, you've mastered the basic concept of HTML. Of course, it gets a little more complicated—HTML's twist lies in the fact that there are quite a few tags you can use. Fortunately, two things work to your advantage:

- You don't need to memorize all the HTML tags if you have a handy HTML reference.
- Tripod provides a link (on the very bottom of the `www.tripod.com/build` page) to a Barnes and Noble listing of handy HTML references.

Now that you know that HTML consists mostly of text and tags saved in a file with the .html extension, lets move on to looking at a couple of HTML editors popular among Tripod members.

Freeform

Tripod offers a standard HTML editor called Freeform. Basically, Freeform is an online version of a Notepad-like application. The benefit of using Freeform is that you don't have to upload your pages to Tripod because they are automatically uploaded when you are done working on them. The easiest way to learn how to use Freeform is to play around with some HTML and Freeform features.

1. Open your browser if necessary, and navigate to `www.tripod.com/build`.
2. On the Homepage Studio page, click the Freeform link, enter your Tripod username and password, and then click Submit.

   The Freeform HTML editor page appears, as shown in Figure 4.12. Notice the toolbar on the Freeform editor above the HTML window. The toolbar provides buttons to Save, Save As, Preview, Select Building Supplies, Help, and Done. Let's use the building supplies to apply background and text colors.

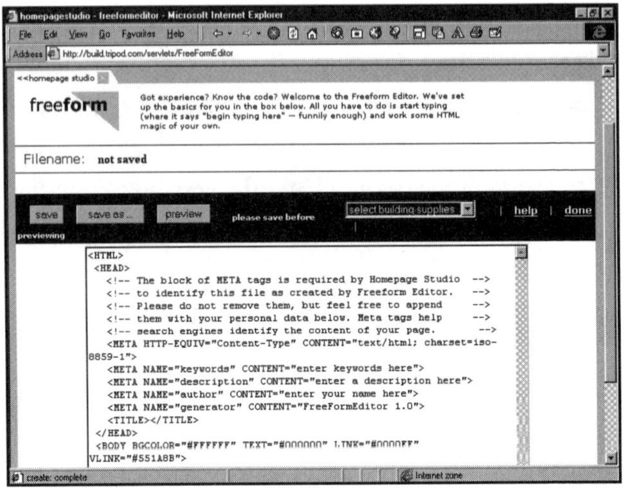

FIGURE 4.12
The Freeform HTML editor.

3. Click the Select Building Supplies drop-down list button, and then click Color Palette.

   When you create Web pages, you can assign colors to the background and text using hexadecimal color codes. There's no need for you to run out and take a math course to learn how to find the hexadecimal number for red. Instead, you can use the Color Palette to tell you what number you need to provide in your HTML.

   Most browsers also recognize common color names in HTML code, such as red, blue, black, and so forth. Furthermore, the HTML 4 Rookies page provides a handy Color Wizard Background Maker on `members.tripod.com/~larrydoz/colors.html`. Not only is the Color Wizard fun to play with, but it's also very helpful in obtaining hexadecimal numbers.

4. On the Color Palette, click a black color square.

The small text box displays the hex number for black, #000000.

5. In the Freeform HTML window, find <BODY BGCOLOR="#FFFFFF". Replace "#FFFFFF" (the hex color for white) with **"#000000"** (the hex color for black). The code should now look like <BODY BGCOLOR="#000000".

Your page is formatted to have a black background. Now, let's change the text color to green.

6. In the Freeform HTML window, find <BODY BGCOLOR="#000000" TEXT="#000000". Replace TEXT="#000000" with **TEXT="#009900"**. The code should now look like <BODY BGCOLOR= "#000000" TEXT="#009900".

Your page is now formatted to have green text on a black background.

7. Click OK to close the Color Palette.

Now that you've slightly customized the default HTML code in Freeform, save your work.

8. Click the Save button.

The Directory/Filename window opens (see Figure 4.13). By default, Tripod assumes the first page you are creating is your home page. You can change the file's name if you desire, but for this exercise, keep the index.html name, as shown in the filename text box.

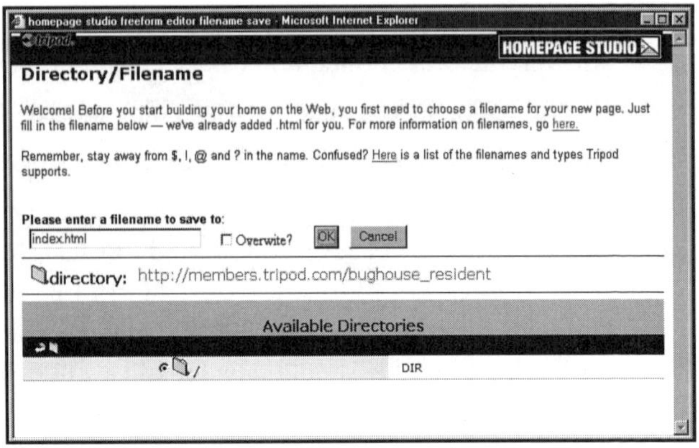

FIGURE 4.13
The Directory/Filename window.

9. In the Directory/Filename window, click OK.

The Freeform window reappears. Notice the filename area above the Freeform toolbar now shows that you are working on /index.html. Home pages are almost always named default.html or index.html. It's best to stick to this convention.

Now, let's add a graphic and some text to our Web page.

10. Click the Select Building Supplies drop-down list, and click Media Library.

The Media Library window opens.

11. In the Media Library window, click the Images link.

A directory of images appears.

12. In the Categories list, click AnimSport, and then click Basketball.

A selection of basketball-related graphics appears, as shown in Figure 4.14.

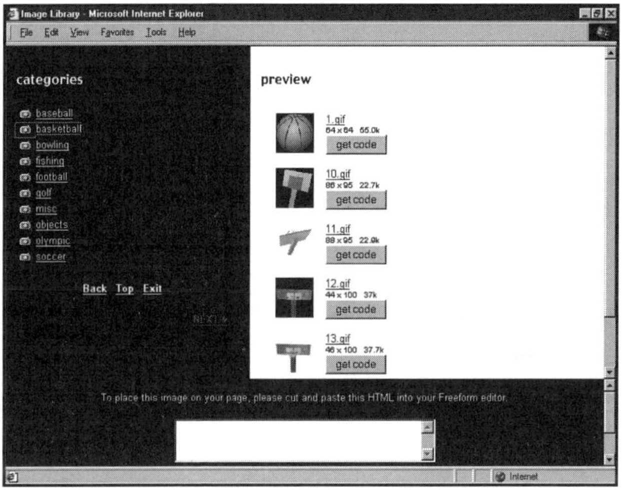

FIGURE 4.14
Viewing available graphics.

13. Click on the Get Code button associated with the top basketball graphic.

The code necessary to insert the graphic onto your Web page appears in the text box below the graphic images.

14. Highlight the code, and click Edit | Copy.

15. Close the Image Library, display Freeform, select the Begin Typing Here… text, and click Edit, Paste.

The code referencing the image replaces the Begin Typing Here…. text on your HTML page. Notice the <IMG> tag contains attributes that identify the source of the graphic (SRC=), as well as the graphic's width and height.

16. Click after HEIGHT="64" (before the **>**), and type **ALIGN=LEFT><IMG SRC="/imagelib/Sports/**

basketball/1.gif" WIDTH="64" HEIGHT="64" ALIGN=RIGHT>.

This aligns the image along the left side of the page and adds a second copy of the image aligned to the right side of the page.

17. After the image tags, type **<CENTER><H1><B> The Green Lizards<B> </H1></CENTER>.**

    This code creates a heading that is centered on the page.

    Now let's create a link to the Team page. For this exercise, the Team page is a fictitious page that you haven't created yet. If you were to actually create this Web site, you would also have to create the team page and save it as team.html in the Directory/Filename window.

    If you make a mistake while editing your HTML code, click your browser's back button to undo the last change.

18. After </H1>, enter **<CENTER><P><B>Get to know the <A HREF="team.html">Team</A></B> </P></CENTER>.**

    The <A HREF=>…<A> tag is called an *anchor tag*. Anchor tags are used to create hyperlinks. All you need to do is supply the address of the Web page within the anchor tag to create a hyperlink. If the Web page is part of your Web site, you only need to specify the document's name. (Make sure the capitalization matches; Team.html is different than team.html on Tripod's server.) If the Web page is located on another area of the Internet, you must provide the entire Web page URL, such as

<A HREF="http://www.tripod.com/build">The Tripod Build Page<A>.

At this point, your HTML code should look similar to the code shown in Figure 4.15.

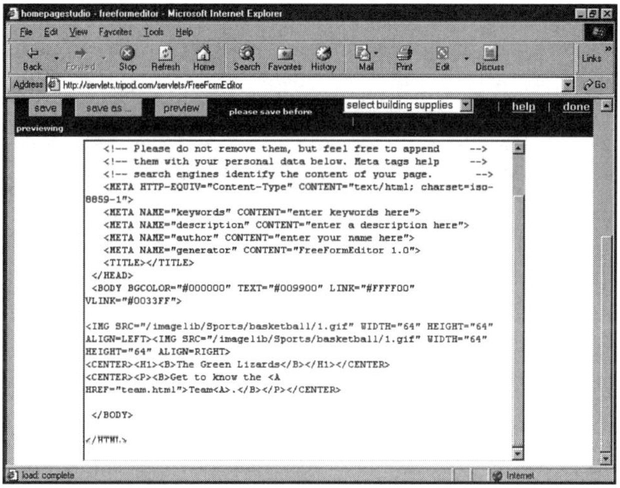

FIGURE 4.15

The code for the sample Web page.

You are now ready to preview your Web page. You should save and preview your page often so you can make changes and alterations along the way.

19. Click Save, and then click Preview.

The Web page displays. Your page should look similar to the page shown in Figure 4.16.

20. Close your browser window, and click Done in the Freeform window.

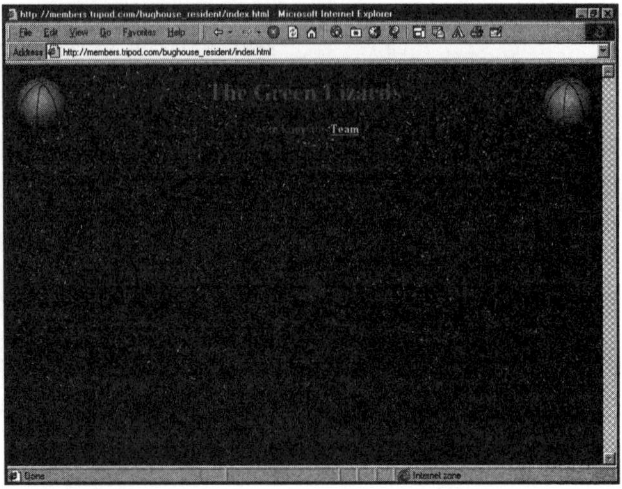

FIGURE 4.16
The fruits of your HTML.

The page you created is automatically published on the Tripod server, and anyone can view the site if they know the site's address. After you complete the page, you should register your site with search engines, as explained on the summary page that appears in Figure 4.17. Notice the page also provides a summary of the resources you have available on the Tripod site.

As you can see, creating a Web page in Freeform leaves a lot of the work and a lot of creative freedom up to you. To get the most out of this HTML editor, you'll want to have some quality HTML resources handy and take frequent visits to the Tripod's Tools page (more about the Tools page later). Notice there is a Tools link at the top of the Freeform Web page. Also, experiment with the other gadgets available in Freeform's Select Building Supplies drop-down list. Finally, you might decide to use another HTML editor, such as a graphical HTML editor like FrontPage, to create your Web pages, and then use Freeform to edit your pages after you've published the pages to the Web.

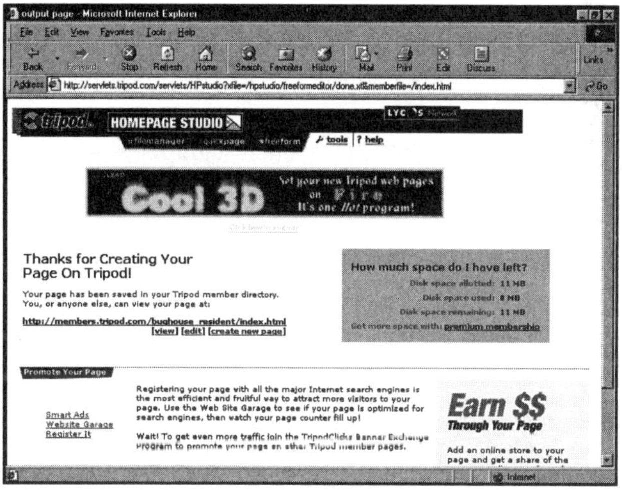

FIGURE 4.17
Wrapping up a creation session. You can return to a page for further editing at any time.

For example, let's say you noticed that you misspelled a word. You could open the page in Freeform, make the textual change, save the change, and be on your way—without having to upload the Web page (if you use HTML editors other than QuickPage or Freeform, you have to upload your pages to Tripod's server).

To return to a page you've worked on, visit the Homepage Studio page (`www.tripod.com/build`), click Filemanager, and click the check box next to the name of the file on which you want to work. Then, click the Edit drop-down arrow, and select Edit With. A pop-up window appears. Select Freeform in the pop-up window, and click OK. The file will open in Freeform. See Chapter 3, "Using the Tripod Filemanager," for more detailed information regarding Tripod's Filemanager feature.

FrontPage

If Freeform seems a little too technically inclined for you, you might want to purchase Microsoft's FrontPage HTML editor. FrontPage offers a graphical interface for Web developers. When you work in FrontPage, you don't need to know all the HTML commands; instead, you use basic Windows-type menu and toolbar commands to create your Web pages. FrontPage is like a desktop publishing program that creates documents containing HTML code. Figure 4.18 shows the FrontPage interface.

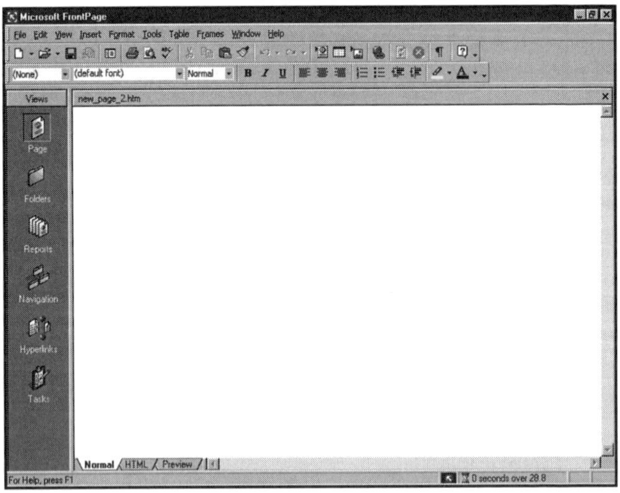

FIGURE 4.18
Viewing FrontPage's interface.

As of this writing, Tripod supports only FrontPage Web sites created with FrontPage98 or later versions. Figure 4.18 shows the FrontPage 2000 interface.

To create a Web page, you simply use the menu commands and toolbars to add and format page elements. For example, to add a picture to the page, click Insert, Picture. Navigate to the picture, and insert it onto the page. To add text, type text directly on the page, and use the formatting toolbar to change the text's size, font, and style.

Figures 4.19 and 4.20 show a Web page being built. Figure 4.19 shows the graphical interface of the page, and Figure 4.20 shows the HTML. When you use FrontPage, you can do most of your page designing using the graphical interface. Most likely, you'll only forage into the HTML source code if you want to tweak the code a bit.

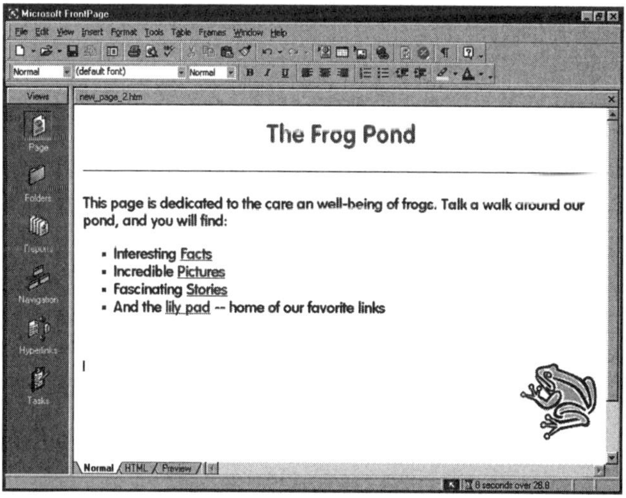

FIGURE 4.19
Viewing a Web page in FrontPage's graphical view.

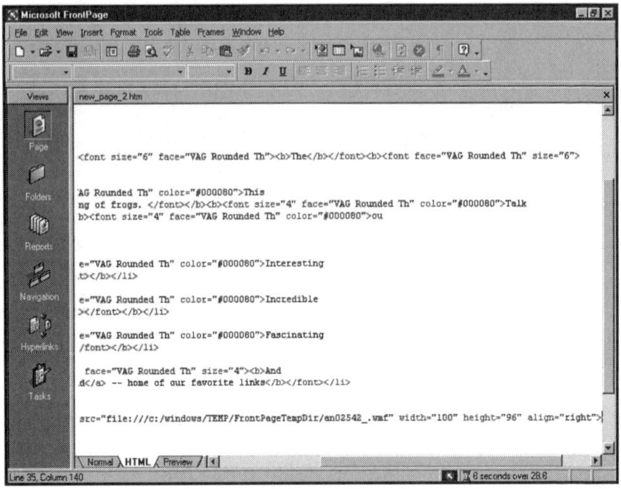

FIGURE 4.20
Viewing a Web page in HTML source code view. To change views, click the tabs along the bottom of the FrontPage window.

After you create your Web pages in FrontPage, you will have to publish, or upload, your Web pages to Tripod's server. To publish your FrontPage Web pages on the Tripod site, click File, Publish Web in FrontPage menu bar. When you are prompted to provide the location where you want your pages to be published, enter **http://members.tripod.com/*your member name***. Follow the prompts to enter your Tripod member name and password, and then your site will be uploaded to the Tripod Web server.

There are many FrontPage resources available at most bookstores and on the Web. For some of the best information on the Web, go straight to the source for FrontPage information—Microsoft's FrontPage Web site at `www.microsoft.com/frontpage`.

Checking Out Tripod's Tools Page

Tripod offers a number of tools to members. Visiting the Tools page is a worthwhile venture for anyone interested in creating Web pages. The Tools page is located at `build.tripod.com/hpstudio/tools/index.html`. You can also access the Tools page by clicking on any tools link you see on the Tripod site. Figure 4.21 shows the Tripod Tools page.

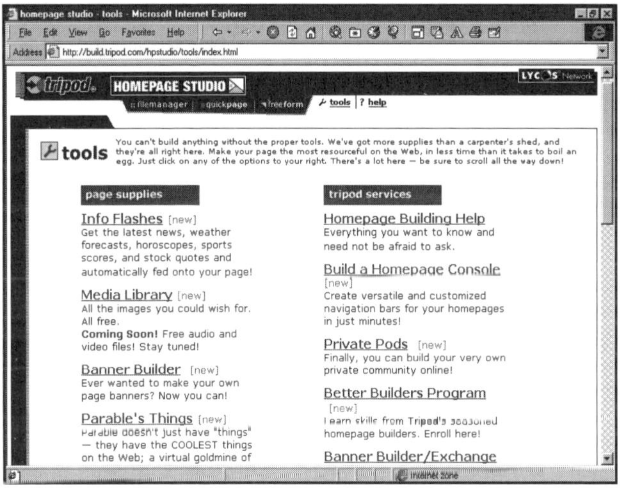

FIGURE 4.21
Tripod's Tools page provides a wealth of Web page information and add-on elements.

The Tools page is divided into two categories: page supplies and Tripod services. Following is a quick rundown of the supplies and services links provided on the Tripod Tools Web page.

First, let's look at the page supplies. As you'll notice, some of the links on the Tools page are included on

Freeform's Select Building Supplies drop-down list. The page supplies links include the following:

- **Media Library** Here's an area where you can get images and image-placement HTML code for your Web pages. This feature was visited earlier in the chapter while using Freeform.
- **Banner Builder** This tool enables you to create your own banners for your Web pages. You can choose from six banner templates, ranging in complexity from static text to triple-animation, and then you can modify the templates to create personalized banners.
- **Parable's Things** This link takes you to loads of cool multimedia Web page *Things* (really—they're called Things!). Things are cool animated, clickable, mouse-sensitive, audio-accompanied graphics. So, even if you don't use any Things on your Web page, you should visit Parable's Things to see what things are all about. Parable's Things come from ThingWorld (`www.thingworld.com/home.asp`). Thingworld's home page is shown in Figure 4.22.
- **Cool Links** Did you ever wonder how people add those graphic links to other pages? You can easily add link buttons to selected Web pages using the Cool Links site. At the time of this writing, you can add button-like graphical links to CDnow Search Box; barnesandnoble.com Search Box; Lycos Search Box; GIF Girl's Web Design Tips; Chank's Free Rockstar Fonts; Tyler's Mad Crib (for Teens); Tripod's Internship Database; Ask Evel Knievel; Ask the Doctor; and Tripod Members' Recipe Book. Not only does this tool provide the graphic, but it also provides the necessary HTML code.

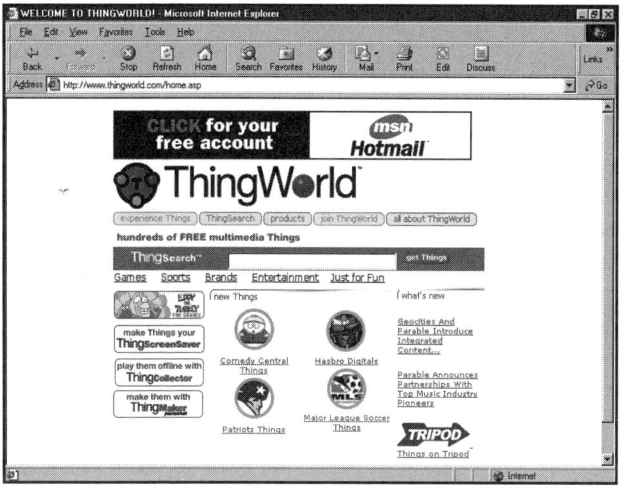

FIGURE 4.22
Take a break and visit ThingWorld for some Web page entertainment and ideas.

- **Lycos Picture and Sounds** This tool links you to Lycos' collection of free graphics and sounds. There are over 40,000 graphics here, so you should find at least a couple of graphics that you can use on your Web pages.
- **Earn Money on Tripod** Did you know that you can earn money from your Web page? It's a new trend in Internet marketing. All you have to do is to become an affiliate for companies offering an affiliate program. The Earn Money on Tripod tool describes how you can become an affiliate for CDnow, Barnes & Noble, and HeadHunter.NET. Your end of the bargain entails providing a link on your page to a site that offers the affiliate program. Each time someone clicks on the company's link that appears on your page and purchases services or products from the

linked site, you get a kickback. Not bad. Learn how to become an affiliate by clicking the Earn Money on Tripod Tools page link.

- **Guestworld Guestbooks** Here's a way to keep in touch with who is visiting your Web site. When you add a guestbook link to your site, you enable viewers to provide feedback quickly and easily. Many Web pages on Tripod take advantage of this tool. To see how guestbooks work, click on a few guestbook links on Tripod sites. If you like what you see, click the Guestworld Guestbooks link on the Tools page to learn how to add a guestbook to your Web page.
- **Page Hit Counter** Of course, you've seen all kinds of counters. Counters are those small elements, usually appearing near the bottom of Web pages, that show you how many people have visited the site. Use the Page Hit Counter tool to create the HTML code you need to add a counter to your Web page.
- **Online Answering Machine** Learn how to activate and use Tripod's answering machine service. The answering machine service enables people to send private messages to you at any time.
- **Gif Girl** GIF is the most common form of graphic files found on the Web. This tool links you to a site that contains lots of helpful articles about GIFs and Web design in general. Take some time to read through these informative articles. The more you know, the greater success you'll experience as a Web designer.
- **Chank's Fonts** Let's just say, this link takes you to a site that starts out by stating, "Meet Mister Chank Diesel, Tripod's Travelling Font Salesman." Chank is a successful fontist, who has created fonts for Disney,

Taco Bell, Tanqueray, and others. Now, Tripod enables you to get in on the font action, as well. Chank has taken handwriting samples from rock stars, and turned the samples into fonts. Those fonts are free for you to download and use as you wish. Chank offers other interesting links on his page, so check out his other links while you're downloading the rock star fonts.

The Tripod services links include the following:

- **Homepage Building Help** Here's a link for you—it takes you straight to the Homepage Building Help pages. This area is packed with answers to your Web page design issues.
- **Build a Homepage Console** Tripod's new Homepage Console is a customizable navigation bar for your homepage. You can select the number of buttons, the coloring and the labeling. Choose links to Tripod areas such as Build, Today's News, Search or just about any place else under the Tripod sun.
- **Private Pods** Now you can create your own private pod. Private pods enable members to create private homepages with private chat and private message boards. The creator of a private pod creates a member list and maintains complete control over who can view its contents. Keep in mind that you must still abide by Tripod's general rules within a private pod. Certain Tripod employees have access to all private pods so they can verify that members aren't violating Tripod's rules. For more on creating a Private Pod, see Chapter 5, "Homepage Studio QuickPage: Build by Topic."
- **Better Builders Program** You can join Tripod's Better Builders group for Web designers. At this

time, a logo, contacts, and a biweekly newsletter are the main benefits of becoming a member. But the program promises more benefits in the near future, including chat groups, message boards, award programs, and more.

- **Banner Builder/Exchange** This combines the Banner Builder described earlier with an exchange program. You can use this link to exchange banners with other Tripod members. For more information, see Chapter 12, "Attracting Visitors to Your Tripod Pages."
- **Website Garage** Here's a Web developer's friend. This page enables you to run diagnostics on your Web site. For example, you can see what your page looks like in 18 different browsers. This is important because not everyone uses the same browser you're using and browsers tend to interpret HTML tags in various ways. You can also optimize your GIF images (which will make the download faster). There are lots of other under-the-hood types of tools on this page—don't miss it!
- **Register-It** You need to register your page with Web search engines if you want people to find your site. Register-It is one of the most popular means of registering your page.
- **Web Site Postoffice** This tool enables you to create your own mailing list to keep in touch with Web site visitors. Also, you can create a mailing list based on specified demographics. Using a mailing list, you can send emails to multiple recipients at once with ease.
- **TripodStats** This tool provides the HTML code necessary to add the Tripod Stats tool to your page. Tripod Stats keeps you posted on who visits your

page, how often, and where they come from. You can use this tool to find out page views by the day, week, or hour. You can also tell what domain and region viewers are coming from.

- **Homepage Mover** This tool enables you to create a mirror site for your Web page. A mirror site is a copy of your original site, that it is duplicated elsewhere on the Web or server. Mirroring a site is often done if a site is too busy and viewers are having a hard time accessing your site. A mirror site provides a second site they can attempt to access.
- **Microsoft FrontPage Enabler** You might want to work on your Tripod Web pages in FrontPage. This tool enables you to do just that.
- **Page Building Columns & Features** Now here's some helpful reading. This link takes you to a site that links to the columns and features presented on Tripod's site.
- **Feeling Claustrophobic?** When you first start designing your Web page, 11MB seems like a lot. But, you can eat up those 11MB in a hurry if you're not careful. Tripod offers Premium memberships to members who want to up their ante to 22MB of server space. The cost is minimal, and the instructions and benefits appear after you click the Feeling Claustrophobic? link. See Appendix A, "Premium Membership: Tripod's First Class Services," for more information on Premium Membership.
- **Builder's Bookshelf** Barnes & Noble offers a directory of books you might want to collect for your Web design reference library. Click this link, and Barnes & Noble presents a list of resources organized in best-selling order.

After reviewing the Tripod Tools page, you can see that Tripod offers a nice batch of Web page supplies and services. Be sure to check the Tools page frequently to keep abreast of new additions to the tools family. Most of all, take advantage of Tripod's tools as much as possible. Not all Web page designers have access to such a concise, helpful collection of resources—you just happened to luck out by being a Tripod member!

See, It's Not That Difficult

As mentioned at the beginning of this chapter, the aim of Chapter 4 is to demystify the Web page creation process. Clearly, there's nothing magical or outlandish about Web page design. It's simply a matter of planning, creating, and refining. With a little time, patience, and willingness to learn, you can create suitable (and more-than suitable) Web pages. For more advanced Web page design topics, refer to later chapters in this book. For example, Chapter 6, "Popular Topics and Outstanding Tripod Examples," presents some advanced Web page design techniques, and Chapter 10, "Adding Graphics to Your Tripod Pages," explains how you can create and gather your own Web graphics.

However, if you are still nervous, have no fear. Chapter 5, "Homepage Studio QuickPage: Build by Topic," covers Homepage Studio's new QuickPage. HTML? You don't need no stinkin' HTML!

CHAPTER 5

Homepage Studio QuickPage: Build by Topic

Building home pages with Tripod has always been an easy process, even for those who are inexperienced. With the new Homepage Studio and the improved QuickPage, it is even easier. How easy? We're going to show you.

QuickPage offers two options: Build by Topic and Build by Design. The Build by Topic option includes topic-driven layouts—such as My Photo Album or My Company—that provide the foundation for well-designed sites. Users simply follow a series of numbered steps through the page-building process.

The Build by Design option includes two basic layout templates and 12 coordinated styles—such as Jungle or Romantic—that ensure an attractive combination of fonts, colors, and background. There is also a Clip Art Library with more than 10,000 images.

In this chapter, we'll cover QuickPage's Build by Topic option and check out some new additions such as Private Pods and the Newbie Guide. Chapter 7, "Homepage Studio QuickPage: Build by Design," explores the Build by Design option.

Build by Topic

Build by Topic enables you to build your site based on a number of templates. These templates include Photo Album, My Personal Page, My Company Page, Patriots Fan Page (for fans of New England's NFL football team), Recipe Publisher, CDnow Store, Homage to Evel (as in Knievel), My Most Embarrassing Moment, Celebrity Page Builder, and Dawson's Creek Page.

Building a Patriots Fan Page

To show you how easy the Build by Topic templates are to use, we decided to build a Patriots Fan Page (because we're Patriots fans).

1. Start by going to the Patriots Fan Page Builder at `http://homepager.tripod.com/templates/patriots/thingindex.html` (see Figure 5.1).

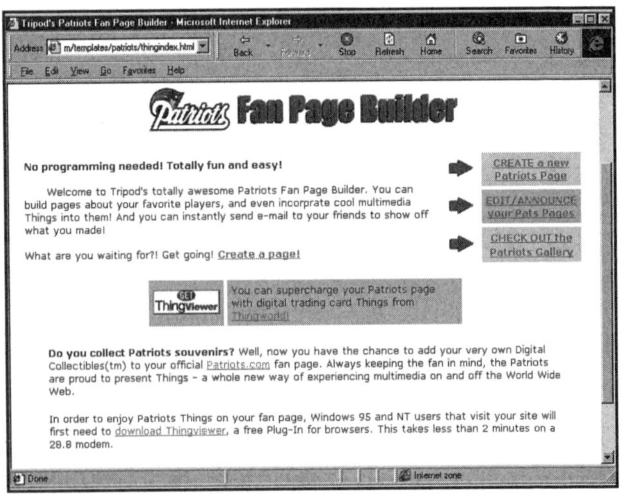

FIGURE 5.1
Starting a Patriots fan page.

This page welcomes you to the Patriots Fan Builder, which enables you to build pages about your favorite players and incorporate multimedia Things. Before we start building the Patriots Fan Page, let's talk about some Things.

Things, in this case, are multimedia objects you can place on your page. They are available at Thingworld (`www.thingworld.com`).

2. At the Thingworld homepage, click the Patriots logo on the left side. You automatically begin installing ThingViewer.
3. Click Yes when asked if you want to do so (assuming you want to view Things).
4. To make sure you have downloaded the correct version, follow the directions and right-click the sample Thing.
5. Because we're getting ready to build a Patriots page, let's look at Patriots Things. Follow the link to the Experience Things page (`http://www.thingworld.com/experience/index.asp`). This gives you the opportunity to check out all kinds of Things. Go ahead, look around. Things react when your mouse moves over or clicks on them, so give them a test. Pretty cool, huh?
6. Let's go find the Patriots Things by clicking the Patriots logo. This takes you to Patriots Things (you expected maybe Cowboys Things?) at `http://www.thingworld.com/experience/patriots.asp`.

After you see the sample Patriots Thing, roll your mouse over it. Now click it. That gives you an idea how Things can spice up your Patriots page, or any other page for that matter. Here you can also search the database, go to the Patriots gallery, or get a Patriots or other branded screen saver. Before you return to the Tripod building process, visit the Patriots gallery by clicking that link.

Wow! It's Terry Glenn and Drew Bledsoe. Rolling the mouse over the cards makes the players move. Clicking them offers information about the players (see Figure 5.2).

If you decide to use Things rather than the photos that Tripod supplies, you must take the Thing. This is a simple process.

1. Right click on the Thing you want to take.
2. Select Save Scene
3. Select a location to save the file on your hard drive.

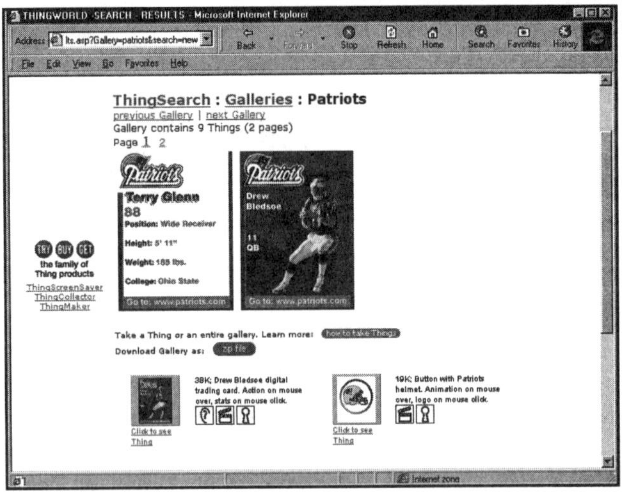

FIGURE 5.2
It's Patriots Things!

Okay, enough about Things. Back at the Patriots Fan Page Builder, click Create a new Patriots Page to start the fun.

1. To start your page, choose one of the many Patriots photos or one of the Patriots Things. Things are cool, but we're going to start with a photo. Any visitor can view a photo, but your visitors must download ThingViewer to see Things in action.
2. Scan the thumbnails for the photo you want, and use the pull-down menu to select the desired photo (see Figure 5.3).
3. Click Start my Pats Page.
4. When prompted, enter your user name and password.

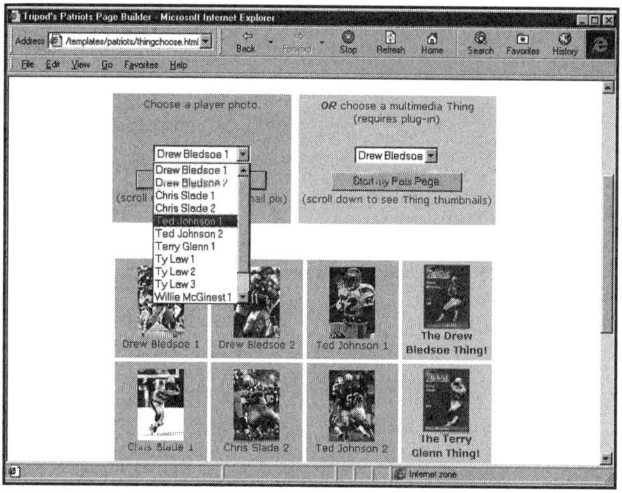

FIGURE 5.3
Patriots photos and Things for the taking. We're taking a photo of linebacker Ted Johnson.

After you've picked a player, it's time to start building your page. This example is about that nasty Patriots linebacker, Ted Johnson. Tripod's QuickPage walks you through the process of building this simple page.

After completing Step 1 (picking a player), you are asked to enter a title. As Tripod says, make it dramatic. Because Johnson has to sit out for the season due to a torn biceps tendon, we went with "Ted Johnson, One-Armed Runningback Wrecker."

Step 3 asks you to choose a Patriots logo banner for the top of your page. Use the pull-down menu to click the option you like best.

Step 4 is completed for you with vital statistics for your player.

Step 5 gives you the opportunity to rant and rave about your player. The offered headings are "Best Game" and "Ted Johnson rules because:" You can change these headings and, because Ted had just been injured when we built this page, we changed the first one to "I'm Sad Because:" and added the text "Ted's done for the season!" We kept the "Ted Johnson rules because:" heading and added in the text box "even with one arm, he's better than any middle linebacker in the NFL!!!"

Step 6 provides a pair of football-related links (Patriots.com and NFL.com) that you can change if you want to. We kept them and, in the third box, added ESPN SportsZone.

Step 7 offers the same choice of banners for the bottom of our page as was presented for the top. We picked the same one as before (logo two). Click Build My Patriots Page. Doing so saves the page to the Tripod member directory. Scroll down to preview your page (see Figure 5.4).

You can also send the URL of your new page to your friends by clicking on Send the URL and filling in the desired email addresses (there's a limit of five).

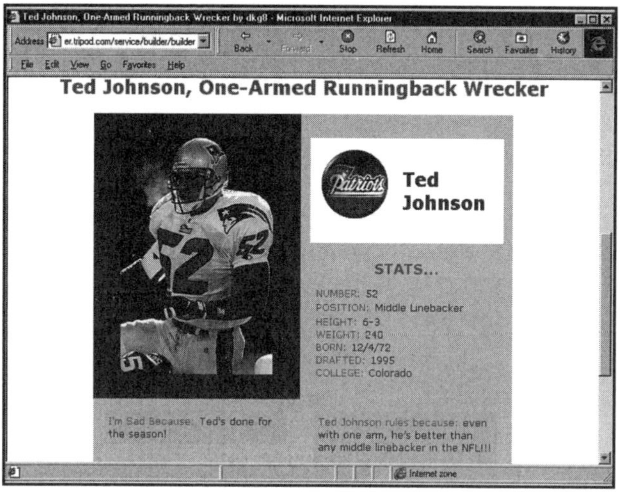

FIGURE 5.4
A preview of our Ted Johnson page (minus the banners).

If, after looking at the preview, you want to make some changes, click on the link that says Click here if you want to edit or change this page. Make the desired changes to the text or banner logos, and then click Build My Patriots Page.

The preview page also tells you what the URL for your page is. Looking at the preview is fine, but go see it on the Web! Click on the URL, and there it is your page is on the Web!

Is that simple enough for you? As previously mentioned, there are several other Build by Topic templates, all of which are just as easy. QuickPage is a great way to get a page up on the Web quickly. Of course, we know you'll want to do more and, as you grow more comfortable, begin to create your own designs. All the information you need to do this is found throughout this book. Chapter

6, "Popular Topics and Outstanding Tripod Examples," covers popular types of sites, and Chapter 7 includes the Build by Design templates.

More Build by Topic Examples

To get an idea how some of the Build by Topic templates look after they have been put to use, check out the following examples.

Recipe Publisher

Do you have a great recipe that you want to share with the world? The Recipe Publisher enables you to put your concoction in a category and indicate the serving size, preparation time, ingredients, and directions for your culinary masterpiece. This example shows Cheater's Lasagna, found at `http://members.tripod.com/CVSurfer/mycookbook/SuperSimpleLasagna.html` (see Figure 5.5).

CDnow Store

Music is one of those things that draws passionate feelings among fans. With the CDnow store, you can introduce your favorite artists, songs, and albums to your Web page visitors, and you can even make a little money if people follow your links to CDnow and buy records. Grrrl Punk is really great, so our example is, of course, riotgrrrlpunk's CD Store, found at `http://members.tripod.com/riotgrrrlpunk/cdnow/my_cdnow_store.html` (see Figure 5.6).

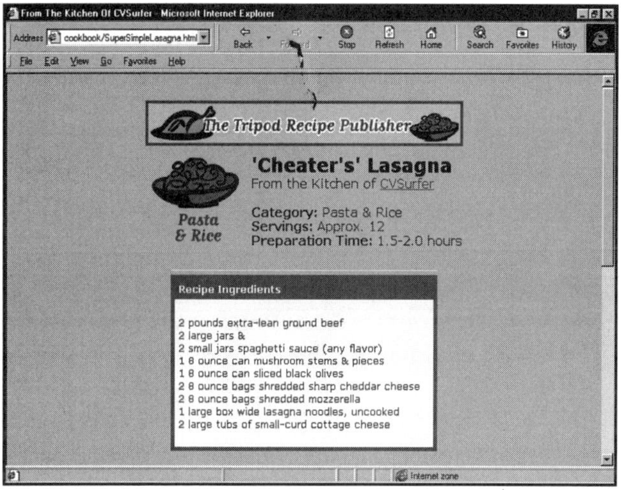

FIGURE 5.5
Mmmmm. Cheater's Lasagna sounds good.

FIGURE 5.6
All the grrrl punk you need.

Homage to Evel

Evel Knievel has lived through death-defying stunts. Now he lives in cyberspace thanks to Tripod's Homage to Evel template. Visit `http://members.tripod.com/funkmessage/evel/Evel_1.html` to see Evel in all of his star-spangled splendor (see Figure 5.7).

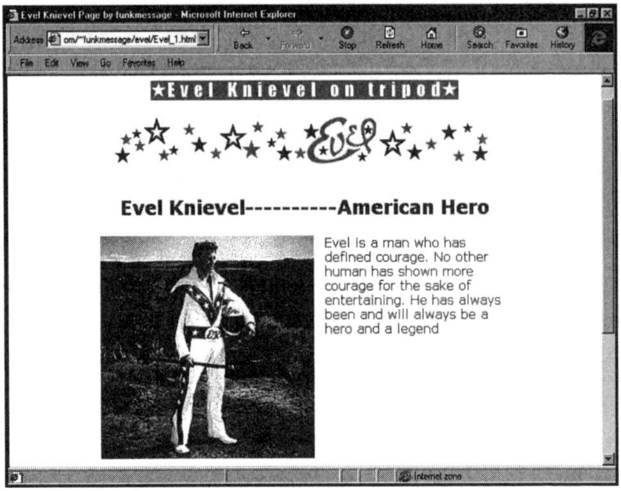

FIGURE 5.7
The man, the myth, the legend—Evel Knievel.

My Most Embarrassing Moment

What good is a truly embarrassing moment if you can't laugh at it and share it with the world? We're not sure how this happened, but go to `http://members.tripod.com/RHTurcott/embarrass/Embarrass_1.html` for an example of a *really* embarrassing moment (see Figure 5.8).

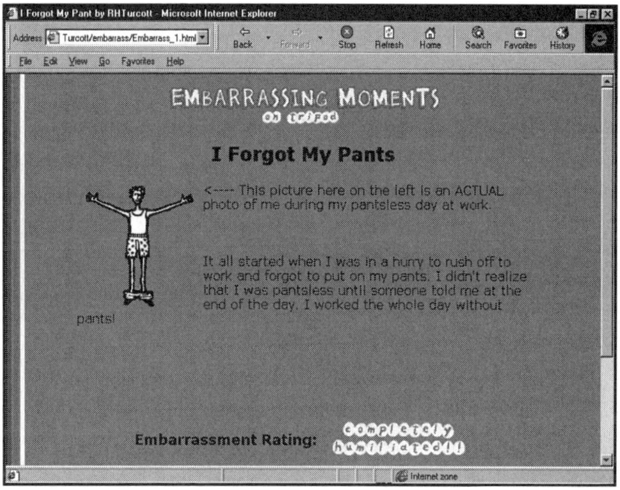

FIGURE 5.8

If you've done something embarrassing, why not tell everyone about it.

CELEBRITY PAGE BUILDER

The Web is overflowing with celebrity tribute sites. We like the one located at `http://members.tripod.com/~baboo57/celebrity/Gwynn.html` (see Figure 5.9) because it is a tribute to a worthy subject that hasn't been beaten to death by media exposure (hello, Leonardo!).

DAWSON'S CREEK PAGE

One of the hottest television shows among young people is Dawson's Creek. If you love Dawson's Creek, you can build a page dedicated to your favorite Dawson's creek cast member(s) or actor(s).

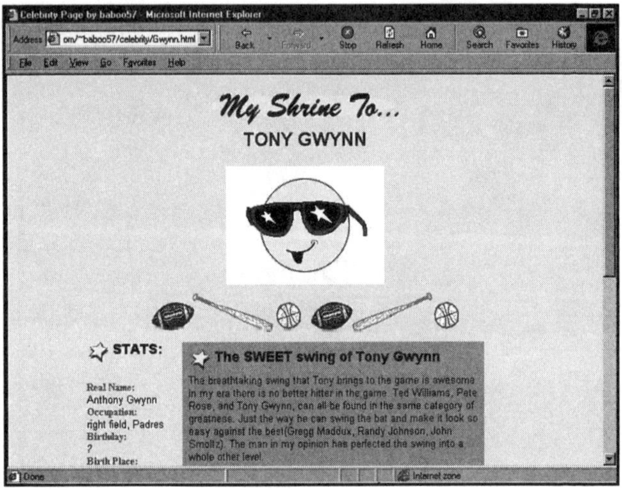

FIGURE 5.9
A shrine to San Diego Padres baseball star, Tony Gwynn.

WHAT'S NEW IN THE STUDIO

The revamped Homepage Studio offers a number of new features in addition to QuickPage. You can build private pods, check out the Newbie Guide (if you are new to page building), and, if you are a WebTV user or just like the old Homepage Builder, you can use that instead.

PRIVATE PODS

Even though many people want to build home pages that deal with a favorite topic, they never say anything about themselves. However, some people could care less about building the best fan page; they want to build pages about themselves or family members, and enable those people to communicate with one another, get updated addresses, or phone numbers. However, many of those same people are hesitant to go splashing their address, phone numbers, and other personal information all over the Internet for anyone to see. They're doomed, right? Wrong.

Private Pods use Lycos' new Private Webs technology to enable you to build a site that includes personal chat and a personal message board to which only you and the Private Pod members have access. After a page is created, the builder can invite other members to join via an automated email system. There is no need for visitors to remember new passwords or usernames: The Private Webs technology does all the work by matching Tripod member names to a database of the private Web pages, chat rooms, and message boards that each member can access.

If, for example, you want to post a list of all the current addresses of your extended family without making it accessible to everyone with a Web browser, a Private Pod is the thing for you. It is also a good way to post information you want to only be available to your group, club, or association.

Private Pods are listed in the Listing Index, which allows you to visit the public page (if there is one) of any Private Pod site. You can build a public page for your Private Pod that then asks for people to log on to visit the chat, message, or other private areas of the site.

Creating Private Pods

To build a Private Pod, you simply create a private directory, build the pages for the Private Pod, and create a member list.

Go to the Private Pod page at `www.tripod.com/interact/private_pods/` and click Create/Edit a Private Pod (and log in if you haven't already). Here is where you are asked to create your private directory by entering your Private Pod name, choosing whether or not you want a public front page, and placing it in an available directory (see Figure 5.10).

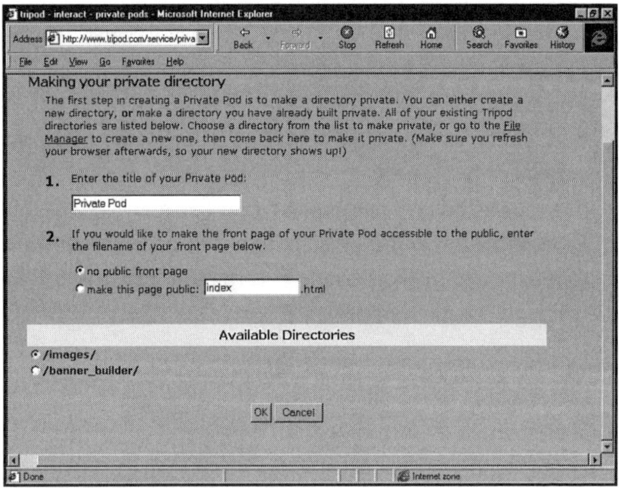

FIGURE 5.10
Creating your Private Pod.

At this point, your chosen directory is private and it is time to build the pages for your Private Pod (Figure 5.11).

As usual, you have three choices: QuickPage Templates, FreeForm, or your own HTML editor. (Tripod provides the necessary code for the third option.) Choose your weapon, and off you go.

The Private Pod administrator, who can be reached by clicking the Menu link, enables you to do a number of things to your Private Pod by clicking on the desired choice.

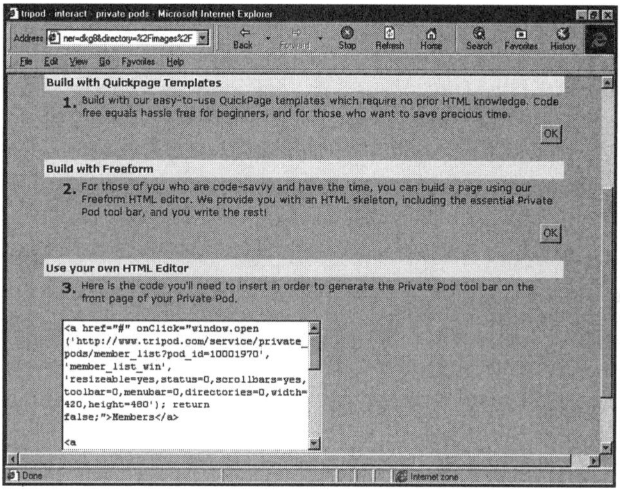

FIGURE 5.11
It's time to build your Private Pod pages.

- Click Edit Your Pod to change the title, change the public front page, make your private directory public, or build more Pod pages.
- Click List Your Pod to list your Private Pod in the index.
- Click Promote Your Pod to find out how to, well, promote your Pod.
- Click Add Pod Members to allow Tripod members to access your Private Pod.
- Click Remove Pod Members to remove a member or view Tripod members' profiles.
- Click Invite Pod Members to invite non-Tripod members to join your Private Pod.
- Click Help to get help.

Not surprisingly, these options are self-explanatory and Tripod walks you through the process. However, because you might be just building your Private Pod, the next sections cover Add Pod Members and Invite Pod Members.

Adding Pod Members

So you've decided to add members by clicking on the Add Pod Members option. At this point you are asked to enter member names of people you want to invite. If you can't remember someone's member name, Tripod asks you to enter his or her first name, last name, city, state, or country and let the search engine do the work. The more of this information you can provide, the better your chances are of finding what you're looking for. Click Add New Members and you're all set. Don't forget to let your lucky new friends know that they can now enter your private pod by logging in.

Inviting Pod Members

Surprisingly enough, not everyone is a Tripod member. To invite someone who is not a Tripod member to visit your Private Pod, click on Invite Pod Members or just go to `http://www.tripod.com/service/private_pods/invite?pod_id=10001970`. From here, you can send that person an email invitation. How does this work? Well, it asks them to become a Tripod member. This is obviously not hard for someone to do and, as you know by now, doesn't cost a cent. Being a member doesn't mean someone has to build a home page, but it does enable him or her to access your Private Pod. Of course, these new members just might catch the page-building bug and build a Private (or public) Pod of their own.

Don't Be Afraid!

We covered the basics of page building in this chapter and the previous one. Why stop there? You can build a build a better page—a faster, stronger page; you have the technology. In fact, we are willing to wager that, as you learn the basics, you become more eager to learn about page building. We're pretty sure you didn't buy this book just to learn about using QuickPage's Build by Topic feature. Keep reading, keep learning, and keep building. It's just starting to get fun!

CHAPTER 6

Popular Topics and Outstanding Tripod Examples

It is amazing what you can do with a little creativity, 11 free megabytes, and Tripod's page-building tools. Whether you are an HTML master or someone who runs away screaming at the first hint of code, Tripod enables you to put your thoughts on the Web for, potentially, the whole world to see. And let's face it, no one builds a Web page with the idea that they'll be the only one to see it.

With that thought in mind, making the best site possible is important. You'll get out of it what you put into it. If you're reading this book, you are obviously interested in building the best site possible. We hope this book gives you more than enough information to make it possible for you to do this. However, there is one more thing that will help you improve your site-building abilities—stealing!

Okay, not stealing. Gathering ideas from other sources, however, isn't stealing and doesn't hurt. The best thought is original thought, but sometimes the thought process needs a little kick-start. This chapter is intended to do just that—kick start the thought process by showing you some of the most popular types of pages, what you should include on those pages, and examples of some of the best of Tripod's sites.

The point isn't to rip off other people's work. Visit some of these sites, study them, and learn from them. Or don't. No matter how great a site is, you might just see something and say "I'm *never* doing that!" But keep in mind, Steven Spielberg didn't get where he is today by never seeing another movie. Don't be afraid to be influenced; then you can use those influences to create your own style.

The point of this chapter isn't to cover the technical information on tasks like adding photos of your favorite celebrity or including files to download; that's the rest of the book. This chapter deals with the nontechnical basics of what kind of content your site should have and where you can find it.

By the way, if your site is spectacular but isn't mentioned here, don't be offended. This is but a small sample.

Fan Pages

America—the world, even—is fascinated by celebrities. Tabloid newspapers and television shows make a living on the public's lust for information about the famous, whether they are musicians, actors and actresses, models, athletes, or even politicians. However, as a fan you don't need to peddle the gossip that the tabloids handle, you just need to provide information. For example, people don't always have the time to visit every entertainment site on the Web to hear the latest about Jennifer Love

Hewitt. That's where fan pages come in. If you can provide the latest about someone like Jennifer Love Hewitt—her new movie, her next project, a great magazine article you just read—then all of those Love fans will beat a path to your Web site.

Don't limit your potential sites to individual celebrities. For example, instead of just a Jennifer Love Hewitt site, you could have a "Party of Five" site that includes information about episodes, the cast, and so forth.

Some things to consider when building fan pages:

- **Photos** Who wants to visit a Cindy Crawford site with no photos? Of course there is the question of copyright infringement, which is mentioned throughout this book. Celebrities generally have publicists who might provide photos for you. Other than those, many photos you come across might be owned by the photographer or the publication. In many cases, as long as the photos are used in a positive way and are not altered, the celebrities are happy for the free publicity. Be warned, however, the best way to be safe is to find out who owns the copyright to the picture, ask permission from the relevant party or parties, and give credit.
- **Layout** Obviously you want to let visitors know immediately about your site's subject. An appropriate title and header is a good start and a well-placed photo and accompanying text about the site's subject is a nice addition. From there you can branch off to other areas of your site, such as news, more photos, biographical information, links to other sites, and so on.

- **Content** Keep things fresh. Nobody wants to return to a site to look at the same old photos and read the same old news. To keep your visitors loyal, add new photos and keep the news fresh. For example, if your subject is an athlete, you should include information on his or her latest game.

You probably know a lot about your topic if you are going to take the time to build a Web page. However, you can always learn more. One place to search for news on any topic is NewsBot (`www.newsbot.com`). Type in the appropriate name or topic and search for recent articles on the Web. You can always make a habit of checking the newsgroups by heading to Deja News (`www.dejanews.com`) and searching for your topic.

If you are doing a site on an actor, actress, or a movie or television series, a good place to start is the Internet Movie Database (`www.imdb.com`). This site has a database of movies, television shows, and stars that is unsurpassed. If the IMDB doesn't have it, it will probably have a link to a fan site that would be informative.

Other places to check out are E! Online (`www.eonline.com`), Ain't It Cool News (`www.aint-it-cool-news.com`), Hollywood Online (`www.hollywood.com`), and of course, the various network sites that are home to your favorite television shows.

For musicians, some excellent news sites are Addicted to Noise (`www.addict.com`), Wall of Sound (`www.wallofsound.com`), Rolling Stone Online (`www.rollingstone.com`), MTV Online (`www.mtv.com`), the All-Music Guide (`www.allmusic.com`), and the Ultimate Band List (`www.ubl.com`), which has news, reviews, and links to tons of fan sites like yours.

When it comes to sports, all the major sports leagues have their own Web sites, as do the individual teams. The same goes for colleges. For more general information, check out ESPN SportZone (`www.espn.com`) and CNN/SI (`www.cnnsi.com`). To find the newspaper that covers your favorite team or athlete, go to the Columbia Journalism Review's Newspaper Finder (`www.cjr.org/database/papers.asp`) and search for the city or, if you know it, the name of the paper.

One final tip on fan sites—fill a niche. **Some pages are able to cover every aspect of a subject, and some subjects are able to be covered completely.** It depends on the breadth of the topic, your specific interest, and how much time you want to spend working on your page. To remedy the dilemma, you might want to focus on one area of a subject. For example, instead of doing a site dedicated to a band that covers all aspects of that band, you could focus on live performances and build a concert archive that includes a list of songs, venues, dates, and reviews of the band's live performances. Or you could focus on an artist's lyrics and what they mean to you.

Here are two Tripod Fan Pages worth checking out.

A.S.'s Tribute to Mark McGwire

In the summer and fall of 1998, with Michael Jordan headed toward retirement and the NBA suffering through its first work stoppage, American youths needed a new hero. That person was St. Louis Cardinal slugger Mark McGwire, who hit a major league record of 70 home runs in 1998 and spawned even more tribute sites. One of those sites is A.S.'s Tribute to Mark McGwire (`members.tripod.com/msgtgumby`).

The site (see Figure 6.1) includes a profile, career statistics, a home run chart that gives the opposing pitcher and team, date, and distance of McGwire's 70 home runs, a game-by-game breakdown of McGwire's record-breaking season, information on McGwire's charity work, and plenty of photos and downloads.

This site incorporates a clean, simple design and just about every bit of McGwire-related information you could possibly want. The home run chart and game-by-game coverage of the season are nice additions, as is spotlighting McGwire's extensive charity work.

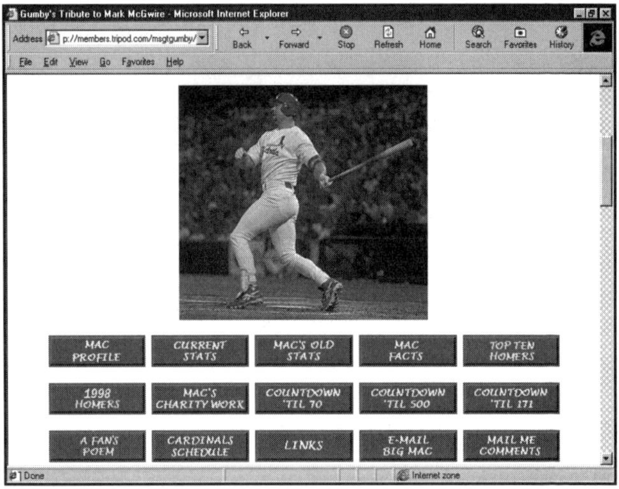

FIGURE 6.1
Mark McGwire's spectacular 70-homer season has spawned numerous fan pages.

ERIC'S BLUES ROOM

Eric's Blues Room (`members.tripod.com/~grebs_eric/page8blues.html`) isn't quite as extensive as the aforementioned Mark McGwire page, but Eric clearly loves the blues and lets you know it with his guided tour of top blues sites, his nice use of photos of his favorite blues artists, and his enthusiastic writing. Don't be afraid to let everyone know exactly how you feel.

Eric also picked a topic that would enable him to continue to build this site forever. For now, he's keeping it simple (see Figure 6.2).

FIGURE 6.2
The blues obviously makes Eric very happy.

Expertise or Hobby Pages

You've got to be an expert at something, right? It might be stamp collecting or it might be computer software. Share that information. Chances are good that there is somebody else out there like you.

Your main page should introduce the site's topic and your background (i.e., I began collecting stamps when my grandfather made me aware of it as a 10-year-old). As with any page, include a graphic or photo (like a big stamp) that makes the topic of your page clear.

From the homepage you can build out to the different pages.

Expertise pages can be very precise (early 20th century American stamps) or very broad (Stamp Collecting, although that's probably a bit too broad). It should contain informational articles written by yourself, links to similar sites, possibly a Barnes and Noble associate store to sell books on the topic, and a timely news area.

Your own input, because you are the expert, will carry your site's content. These articles can be instructional, if your expertise lends itself to that, or simply informational. Try to update your articles on a regular basis based on the amount of time you have, and don't make them too long. If you have photos, adding them to support your story will help break up the text and illustrate the stories.

Now if you want to talk about experts, the following site is run by one.

DMG Ice: Serious Gameboy

Not surprisingly, there is a seemingly endless number of sites dedicated to computer and video games. DMG Ice's Serious Gameboy site (`http://members.tripod.com/cgb001/`) covers all things Gameboy in the hopes of informing and educating the casual game player when it comes time to make a purchase. News, reviews, previews, editorials, game help, rumors—it's all here (see Figure 6.3).

DMG Ice (sounds like a rapper) also has a chat room, message boards, and plenty of downloadable files. This site is an example of the breadth of coverage you can devote to your topic with some time and devotion.

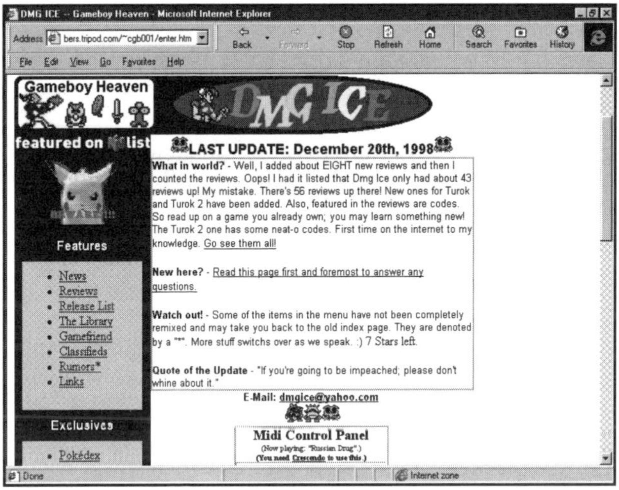

FIGURE 6.3
DMG Ice offers all you need to know about Gameboy video games—and then some.

Review Pages

The expertise site, depending on the topic, will often contain reviews. However, if you just want to share your opinion (everyone has one!), you should consider a review site. That way, you don't have to get involved in all the research required of a fan site or the knowledge base required of an expertise site. Pick a reviewable subject—movies, music, books, whatever—and let everyone know what you think.

For example, you can stay on top of the latest popular music releases and rate them on any number of scales. Try to make your rating system interesting—we've all seen enough of the 1–5 stars or the simple 1–10 scale. If you rate hard rock records you could go from Blows the Windows Out (that's good if you're rating rock) to Put Me Into a Coma (that's not so good) with a few gradients in between like Only Slightly Heavier Than Hanson or Darn Wimpy. Don't leave it at that, though. Write a few hundred words on the record to tell people why it was darn wimpy or put you into a coma. Have fun with it, just keep your language clean. Not only will Tripod frown upon profanity, it just makes you sound stupid.

It is essential that you keep your reviews up to date. Nobody wants to read a review of an old Korn record when they've just released a new one. Of course, you can archive those old reviews for new visitors or for a Best of the Year announcement. You can also ask for visitor feedback and visitor's ratings.

Although you know your reviews will be the final word, you might want to link to other review sites. A news area is a good idea to let people know what's ahead.

With that in mind, let's go to…

Ste5en's Book Reviews

Ste5en's Book Reviews (`http://members.tripod.com/~Ste5en/index.html`) is an excellent example of how to keep something as potentially overwhelming as book reviews to a manageable size.

First, he focuses on a specific genre: science fiction and horror. This is a good idea for any review site. Other examples are foreign films or rap music. Doing so ensures that your visitors will have at least some interest in the latest reviews. A site that reviews all popular music might entice someone with a review of Snoop Dogg's latest one week, but turn them off by reviewing Metallica's latest the next week. At Ste5en's (see Figure 6.4) we don't have to worry about looking for a science fiction review only to get bogged down with self-help books.

The reviews are broken down by author and kept very short—a couple of paragraphs—and include numerical ratings from 1–10. Also included are links to science fiction sites.

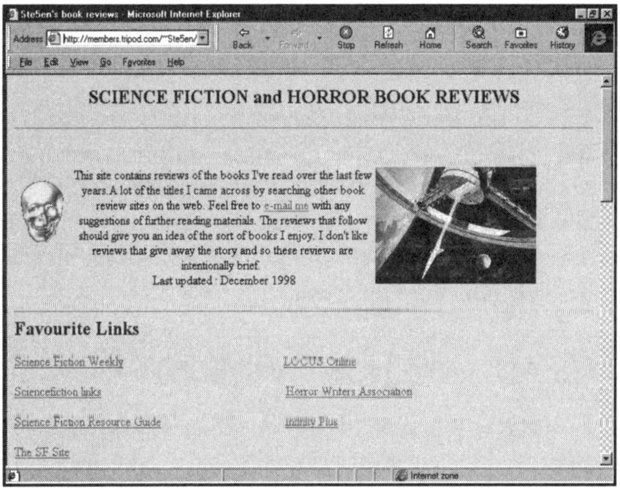

FIGURE 6.4
Dig the spinning skull (and of course the reviews) at Ste5en's Book Reviews.

PORTALS

What used to be referred to as link sites are now called *portals*. Portals act as hubs that send people to sites dedicated to the topic. Although sites like Lycos and Yahoo! act as portals, smaller, more specific portals can attract significant traffic.

Building a good portal involves a lot of searching and constant updating. Today's excellent Puff Daddy fan page might be gone tomorrow, only to be replaced by a better site elsewhere. Search the Web for the best sites, organize them on your site, provide a summary, and even consider ranking the various sites.

You should keep the links on one page, unless your topic is easily divided into subcategories. For example, if you wanted to do a pro sports portal, you could divide your site into general sites, NFL sites, NBA sites, NHL sites, and MLB sites.

Your portal should alert people as to when the site was last updated (you should do this as often as possible) and note which links are the most recently added. You should also have a forms page that enables people to submit links for consideration. (See Chapter 8, "Developing Forms on Tripod," for more on forms.)

Justin's Approved Heavy Metal Web Pages

Just in case you thought metal was dead, Justin's Approved Heavy Metal Web site (`http://members.tripod.com/~JustinHarvey/links.html`) proves otherwise. Metal has morphed into so many subgenera that it is hard to keep them straight sometimes. Justin's site sends metalheads everywhere off to the sites of lesser-known bands such as HammerFall and legends like Black Sabbath.

You might not like metal, but Justin's site illustrates what a strong knowledge of a topic can do for a site. If you're looking for metal sites, Justin's site is a great jumping off point (see Figure 6.5). You can provide the same service in your area of interest.

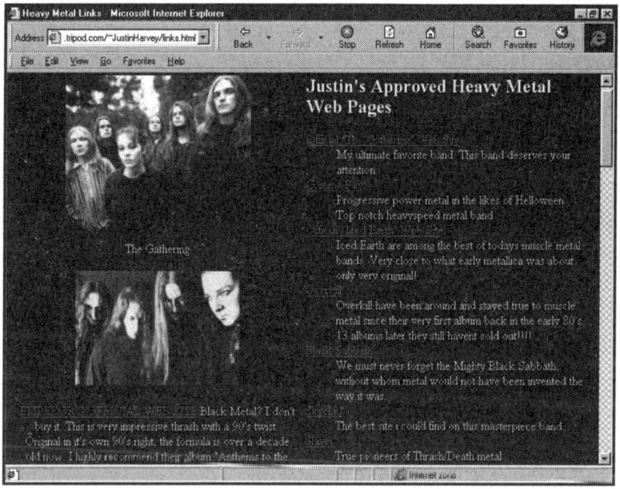

FIGURE 6.5
Long live metal—Justin's site is an example of a portal or link site.

FAMILY PHOTO ALBUM PAGES

The Web enables you to keep far-flung members of the family connected. Pictures you take of the baby this morning can be available to grandma across the country this afternoon. Tripod even has a Photo Album template available in its QuickPage Builder (`http://servlets.tripod.com/hpstudio/quickpage/index.html`). For more on the Build By Topic templates, see Chapter 5, "Homepage Studio QuickPage: Build by Topic."

Getting pictures on the Web involves scanning in traditional photos or directly uploading them from a digital camera. Neither is inexpensive, but the price of digital cameras has been falling and will likely continue to do so. (For more on either option, see Chapter 10, "Adding Graphics to Your Tripod Pages.")

Your family site needn't stop at photos. You can include family news, links to related sites (such as dad's company Web site or son's college Web site), holiday greetings, and a calendar of important events (birthdays and anniversaries, etc.). Any private information, such as private schedules, phone numbers, and addresses can be kept private through the use of Tripod's Private Pods (`http://www.tripod.com/interact/private_pods/`). This only allows select people access to the private area. For information on adding Private Pods, see Chapter 5.

Pages about Yourself

Enough about them, how about you? If there's anything you know about, it is you. Who knows if anyone else is interested? Still, a Web site about yourself is a good way to express your feelings, interests, and opinions. It can be a combination of a family page, expertise page, and, of course, a fan page. (You are your own biggest fan, aren't you?)

Your personal site should include a biography and picture of yourself; a photo gallery of friends, family, pets, and whatever else interests you; accomplishments; your own writings on topics of interest; and links to Web sites that cover the interests and topics that make you unique.

If you want to sell yourself to potential employers, you can even include an online résumé. An online résumé is especially useful if you are involved in the Web, computer, or graphics industry. This enables you to display samples of your work. If you are looking for a Web design job, your site already serves as a résumé.

Keep in mind that if you want to show off your online résumé, you should probably keep it away from your personal pages. Even though it might be cool that you like to dress up gothic on the weekends, a potential employer might not find the black clothes, black lipstick, and black nail polish such an attractive trait.

Your résumé should include the usual résumé stuff (experience, education, contact information, and so on). But remember, your contact information will be out there for all to see. The Private Pod option would require the potential employer to get the password.

For more on résumé writing, go to `http://members.tripod.com/~Transitions/c.html`. For an example of an online résumé, visit `http://members.tripod.com/~Giusti/Resume`.

Instructional Pages

Although an expertise site might offer a lot of information, a how-to site is instructional. How to sites can include everything from recipes (see Chapter 5 for information on Tripod's Recipe Builder template), to building a deck, to computer programming. You should make sure you really know what you are doing before you design a site to tell somebody else how to do it.

Among the items you should include on your instructional site are fresh instructional articles to keep people coming back, an archive of past articles, illustrations (if applicable), examples, and links to other sites of interest. Remember, no matter how much you know, your visitors will appreciate your offering other options. If your site is well done, they will keep coming back. You could also include a Barnes & Noble associate store for people who need more information than your site can supply.

Here is an example of one of Tripod's most popular instructional sites.

HTML 4 Rookies

The name says it all. HTML 4 Rookies (`http://members.tripod.com/~larrydoz/html4rookies.html`) is the site to visit if you are in search of understandable HTML help (see Figure 6.6).

The site includes seven basic lessons, select topic tutorials, and advanced topics such as forms and frames. The site is easy to navigate and also includes links to other helpful sites.

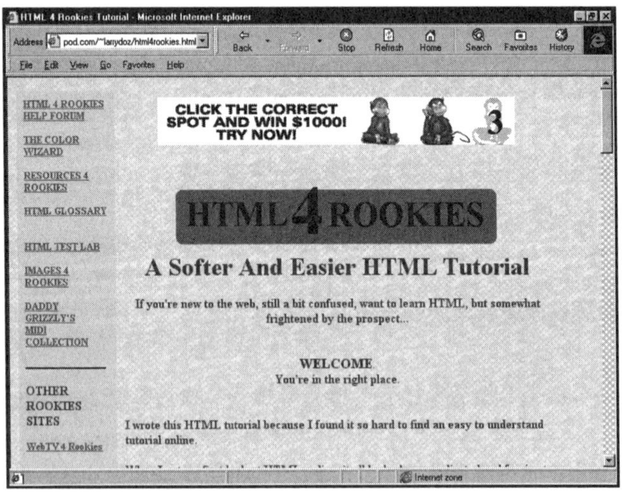

FIGURE 6.6
The HTML 4 Rookies site grew from the creator's difficulty in finding an understandable tutorial on the Web.

Travel Pages

Do you travel? Have you visited exotic places? If so, sharing those experiences can help enhance the experiences of other travelers. A travel site, however, is not just a chronicle of your trip (although that is fine, too); it is a site that offers information such as recommended hotels, restaurants, activities, modes of transportation, and everything else you might need to know on a vacation. Check out sites like Travelocity (`www.travelocity.com`) or Expedia (`www.expedia.com`) to see what top-level travel sites offer. Think about things that you wish you had known when planning your trip. For example, we were glad that we knew about how the locals adhered to the jaywalking law when we visited Seattle; thus, we didn't go darting across the street as we might have at home. The quirky things about an area are what your visitors need to know.

The Wanderer's Guide to Japan

Here is a site (`http://members.tripod.com/GlennH/wa_japan.htm`) that covers almost all of the aspects mentioned. The Wanderer's Guide to Japan offers plenty of information on cities, beautiful pictures of people, and attractions, and information on "Interesting Problems" and "Those Hard To Describe Daily Sites" (see Figure 6.7).

If nothing else, check out the hilarious street sign on the front page.

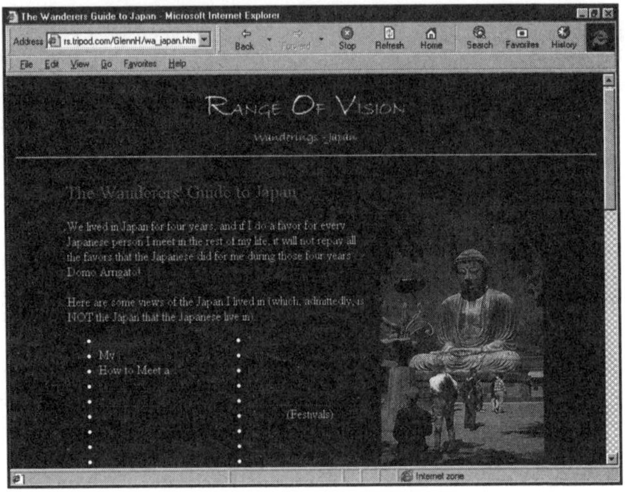

FIGURE 6.7
The Wanderer's Guide to Japan might just make your trip a better one.

BUFFALO, NY ON THE WEB

Here is another site (`http://members.tripod.com/bflo`) with a very specific interest—Buffalo, New York. If you don't care about Buffalo and western New York, you probably won't care about this site. But if you do, watch out! The Buffalo Chamber of Commerce should send a letter of thanks because this site covers Buffalo—from Arts and Entertainment to Schools to Sports—with a blanket of links. One would expect links to the obvious, like the Buffalo Bills official homepage. But Buffalo, NY on the Web also links to the Buffalo Jills (the Bills cheerleaders), the Gamblers (lacrosse), and numerous other sites in a number of categories.

This is a combination portal and travel site. Even though most link-oriented sites stick to Web pages, this one also has a list of Buffalo-related news groups, such as alt.sports.hockey.nhl.buffalo-sabres and rec.music.artists.ani-difranco (for the Buffalo-based indie rock darling). Again, a specific site for a specific interest. If you're shufflin' off to Buffalo, shuffle here first.

Small Business Pages

Businesses are moving to the Web in droves. Even companies that don't know what to do with their Web site have a Web site because, well, you know, you've gotta have a Web site! Putting your business on the Web does not mean you are enabling electronic commerce, it simply means that all of the information about your small business that is available in the real world is now available on the Web.

You should include background, information about your products or services, client information (with links if possible), contact information, articles about your company (feel free to leave out the negative ones), and pricing or rates.

Lucid Thought

Lucid Thought (http://members.tripod.com/~Lucid_Thought/index) is a small business offering writing, editing, and research in the areas of business to business, copywriting, public relations, and Web content. This site gets to the point, refusing to succumb to the temptation to overwhelm the message with all sorts of bells and whistles.

A simple design and an unobtrusive color scheme enable the business to get its point across quickly and effectively (see Figure 6.8). The site covers all the bases (including the important aspect of making contact information readily available on the front page) and offers an impressive list of clients (ESPN, Goldman Sachs, Dow Jones News Service) and testimonials from satisfied customers.

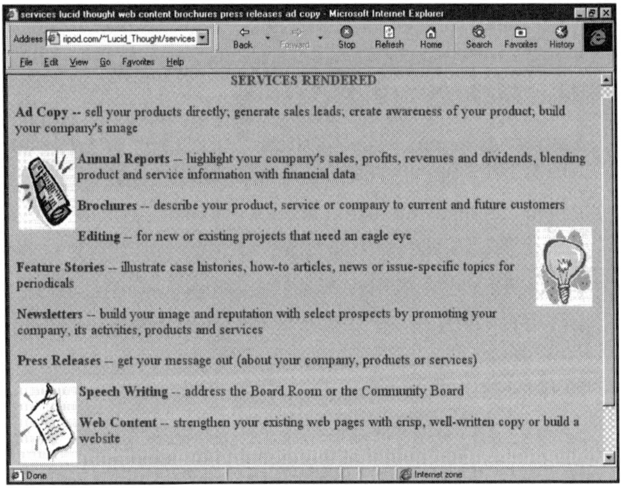

FIGURE 6.8
Lucid Thought is a simple, effective small-business Web site.

Let's Get Our Hands Dirty

There you have it—a variety of Web site types and topics and examples of how it has been done. As you move forward with your Web site, visiting other outstanding sites is a great way to find inspiration. You might also find examples of what not to do. Study and learn.

Knowing and doing, however, are two different things. Now that you know about some types of sites, you probably want to go from concept to reality. Keep reading. The following chapters cover layouts, forms, special effects, graphics, multimedia, and more.

CHAPTER 7

Homepage Studio QuickPage: Build by Design

You might have already built some Tripod member pages using the Build by Topic templates covered in Chapter 5, "Homepage Studio QuickPage: Build by Topic." Or maybe the Build by Topic templates just don't fit your needs. Don't worry, you still have options. Tripod's Homepage Studio QuickPage also offers Build by Design templates. The great part about working with these templates, as is the case with the Build by Topic Templates, is that you can build great pages without knowing HTML.

Build by Design Templates

Enter the Homepage Studio QuickPage by linking from the Build page or by going directly to `http://servlets.tripod.com/hpstudio/quickpage/index.html`. If necessary, enter your Tripod username and password. If you know what you want your page to look like, move on. If you aren't sure, you might consider skipping ahead to the Content Collection section of this chapter.

You can build a page in about half an hour using these templates. It's best if you have any images or other pages you've created that you want to link to already uploaded to your disk space. You have 11MB of disk space, so don't worry about running out of space.

You can upload files using Tripod's Filemanager. Go back to Chapter 3, "Using the Tripod Filemanager," to refresh your memory about using the Filemanager.

Layout 1

The two layouts are very similar. You can see them on the right side of the QuickPage screen (see Figure 7.1). The advantage to using one of these two layouts rather than the Build by Topic templates is that you have control over the subject matter of your page. It's difficult to describe your summer vacation using the Build by Topic Photo Album. However, the Photo Album template is a nice way to share pictures from your vacation.

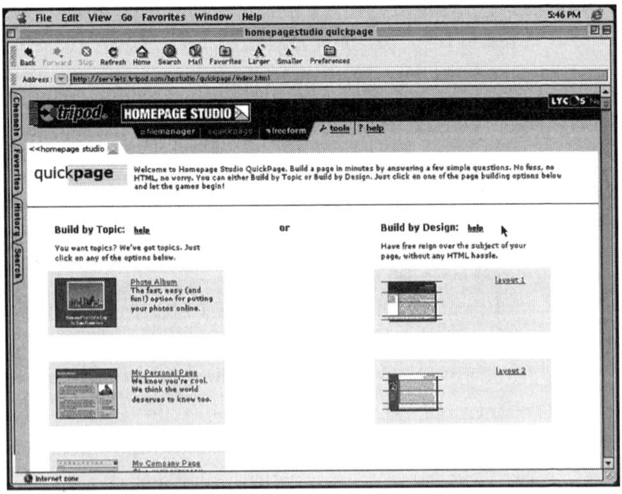

FIGURE 7.1
The two Build by Design templates are very similar.

Layout 1 divides the page into three horizontal strips. The top and bottom strips run the entire width of the screen. The middle strip is divided into two columns. The top and bottom areas are ideal for header- and footer-type information. If you're considering building an online resume, you might want to use the top area for your contact information: name, street address, email address.

You can use the left column of the middle area to provide highlights about your work experience and skills. The right column is split into two more horizontal strips. You might want to use the first one for a detailed work history and the second for your educational background.

Additional information, like the date you last updated your resume or a link to your personal page, can go at the bottom of the screen.

Layout 2

The second Build by Design template divides the page into four rows or strips. As in Layout 1, the top and bottom rows run the entire width of the screen. The two rows in the middle of the screen are both split into left and right columns.

You could build a fan page using this template. You could display a banner of an actor's name at the top of the page. You might put a picture of the actor in the left column of the second row and a brief biography in the right column.

Demographics, for example, the actor's name, age, and recent work, could be placed in the left column of the third row. Additional information about recent work or achievements, upcoming roles, or reasons why you're a fan could be placed in the right column.

Your contact information or a guest book could go in the last row. If you put a guest book on your page, then other fans can share their thoughts with you.

Working With QuickPage's Build by Design

The first thing to remember about working with QuickPage is the first, ubiquitous rule of any computer work: Save often! The main template screen displays four buttons that enable you to: save your work (Save); preview your work (Preview); quit working (Done); and go to a help screen (Help). You need to save your work before you can preview it, and you should definitely save your work before quitting.

Almost every time you want to add to or edit part of your page, a new browser window will be opened for you. Don't panic, Tripod closes them for you when you're done. Don't navigate between windows on your own and you'll be fine.

Getting Started

Working with the layouts follows the same process no matter which one you choose. To get started, click the layout of your choice from `http://servlets.tripod.com/hpstudio/quickpage/index.html`.

The next window you see will ask you to choose a directory in which to store your file and a name for your file (see Figure 7.2). If you haven't created a Tripod page yet, you should probably name your file index.htm or index.html and save it in your member directory.

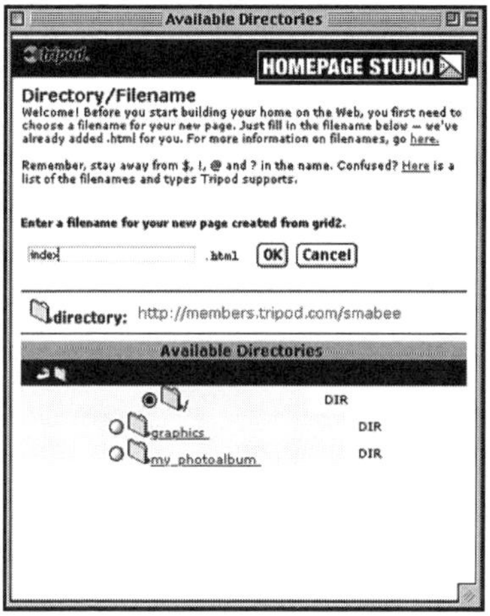

FIGURE 7.2
To get started building a page by design, you need to name your file and save it in a directory.

TIP

When naming files on Tripod, don't use characters such as !, @, ?, or $. These are reserved characters that have special meaning for the server.

The default page on Tripod server is an index.html or index.htm file. If no page name is included in the Uniform Resource Locator (URL), then it either displays the default page or a listing of all the files in the directory. These two URLs—`http://members.tripod.com/membername/` and `http://members.tripod.com/membername/index.htm` (or index.html)—point to the same page. It's nice to have a default page in your member directory because then the URL you hand out (or register with search engines) is shorter, and visitors can't see the contents of your directory.

Building the Page

After you've named your file, Tripod will take you into the Homepage Studio (see Figure 7.3). The studio shows you a sample of the layout and then a pasteup of your page. A pasteup shows you the different areas of your page. Each area has drop-down menus with all the content options.

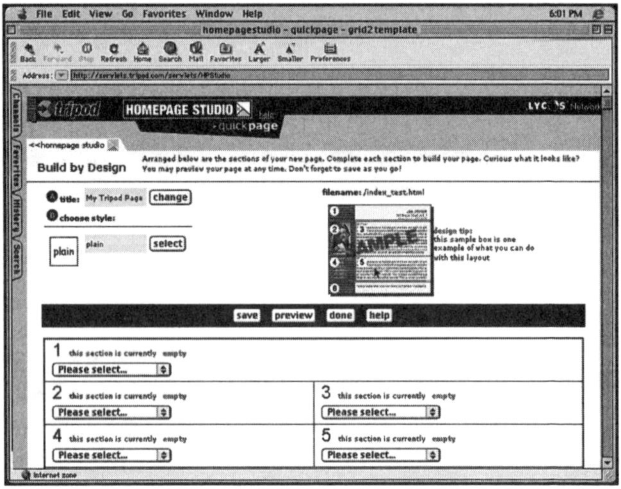

FIGURE 7.3

The Homepage Studio is a work area for building Tripod pages, and it has all the tools you need!

Start by naming your page with a title. (Look for Section A in the top, left corner of the studio.) The page title appears in the bar at the top of your browser window. Click the Change button and a new window will appear. Type in your title and click OK. The window will disappear and you'll be back in the studio. Wait a moment for your change to show up in the studio window.

Remember to use a descriptive title. The title of the page is what appears in the bookmarks list when someone bookmarks your page. Try to avoid the default "My Tripod Page" as that only has meaning for you. Be specific and make sure the title describes the content of the page.

Choosing a Style

Section B in the studio enables you to choose a style for your page. Styles provide background images and horizontal rules by theme. Styles are cool because you can get a whole new look just by changing the style of your page. Browse through the style library, and try on a few styles until you find one that fits.

Click the Select button to open the Style Library. Use the More and Previous links at the bottom of the window to browse through the library. When you've found a style you like, just click it. QuickPage does the rest.

This is probably a good time to save your document. Click the Save button in the bar above your page's paste-up. You can preview your page after it's saved by clicking the Preview button. If you're done working with the file, click the Done button. You can leave the studio and go to an output page which shows you the URL for the page created and some other information. You can then quit your browser or continue surfing.

To edit a QuickPage, go the Filemanager at `http://servlets.tripod.com/servlets/FileManager`. Enter your member name and password if prompted for them. Click the checkbox to the left of the file you want to edit. Then select Edit With… from the Edit drop-down menu at the top of the file listing. A new window will open asking you if you want to edit the file with the Freeform editor or with QuickPage. Select QuickPage and click OK. Tripod will open your page in the Homepage Studio for you. If you need more information about working with the Filemanager, refer to Chapter 3.

Filling in the Blanks

Your page should now appear in Homepage Studio. The pasteup has numbered sections that correspond to the different areas of the page shown in the sample picture. Each section has a drop-down menu that lets you select the type of content you want. The visible option in the drop-down menu is Please Select…. When you click the menu, the following choices appear: Text Block, Links, Image/Linked Image, My Contact Info, Cool Links, Guest Book, and Page Counter.

Notice that all the sections have a status indicator as the first line. This line tells you if the section is empty or what type of content it contains. After you enter something into a section, a red checkmark will appear to the right of the section number. There will also be a Clear button, an Edit button, and a drop-down menu. The Clear button deletes the content of the section. The Edit button opens a new window that allows you to edit the information contained in the section. And the drop-down menu enables you to change the content of the section to a different type.

In general, building a page is simply a matter of filling out fields and clicking buttons. Every time you select a menu option, a window or palette is opened for you. Enter the appropriate information and click OK to update your page in the studio. This does not save the changes to your page. If you want to save your changes, you must click Save from the studio page. If you change your mind when entering information, clicking Cancel from the window or palette will return you to the studio without changing your page.

Make your selection by positioning the mouse over the option you want and clicking. QuickPage opens a new window with options appropriate to your choice. Let's review the options for each choice.

Text Block

If you want to enter one or more paragraphs of text, select Text Block from the drop-down menu. In the new window that appears, you can enter a headline and your text and change the appearance of the type (see Figure 7.4).

Enter the headline you want to appear at the top of your text. You may change the appearance (color, font family, and size) of the headline by choosing new settings for each option.

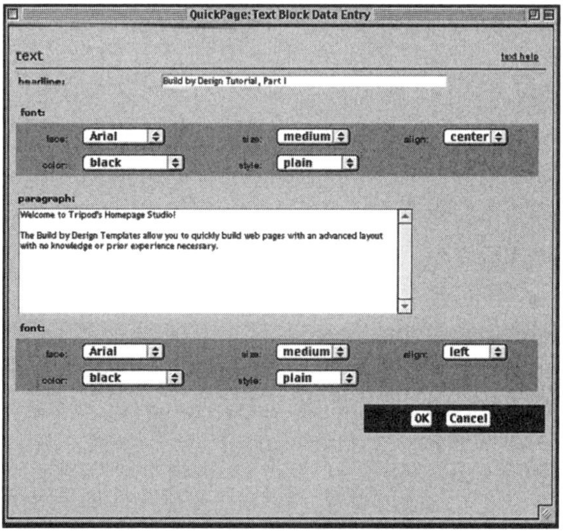

FIGURE 7.4
The Text Block Data Entry screen.

Position your cursor in the paragraph input box and enter text. If you have a word processing document that contains your text, you can "cut and paste" from the document into the input box. You lose any special formatting, but you don't have to retype your text!

If you're typing text into the input box, just hit Enter twice to start a new paragraph. You may change the appearance of the text by choosing new settings for the font. When you're done typing, click OK. The Text Block Data Entry screen closes, and you're returned to the Homepage Studio. Wait a moment for your changes to take effect.

TIP

If you do change the color of the text, a headline, or a link, make sure it contrasts well with your background color. If you make your headline white, and you've chosen a style with a white background, no one will be able to see your headline! Always use dark text on a light background, or vice versa.

Links

Links connect your page to your friends' pages and interesting pages at other sites. Links are the heart of the World Wide Web and what make it fun.

If you want to add links, select Links from the drop-down menu. Using the List of Links Palette (Figure 7.5), enter the URLs for pages you want to link to under URL heading. If the page to which you're linking has a descriptive title, enter that under the text heading. If the page's title isn't descriptive, give it a name.

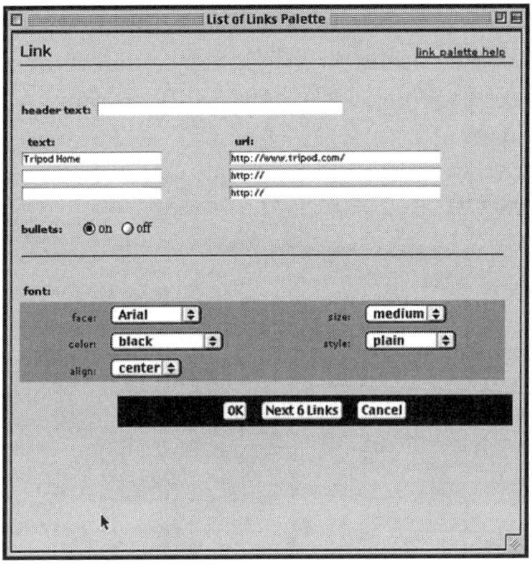

FIGURE 7.5
The List of Links Palette.

After entering your first three links, decide whether you'd like bullets to appear before each link. If you have more links to enter, click the Next 6 Links button and keep entering links. When you're done, click OK. The Link Palette closes, and you go back to the Homepage Studio. Wait a moment for your changes to take effect.

Image/Linked Image

Images spice up Web pages. Fortunately, you don't have to be a graphic artist to put graphics on your Web page. Other chapters in this book—Chapter 10, "Adding Graphics to Your Tripod Pages," in particular—deal with creating and editing graphics. If you're making your own graphics, you might want to pay special attention to them. Otherwise, you can find graphics in Tripod's Image

Library (see Figure 7.6) and Style Library or anywhere on the Web. Refer to the Content Collection section later in this chapter for more information on collecting graphics.

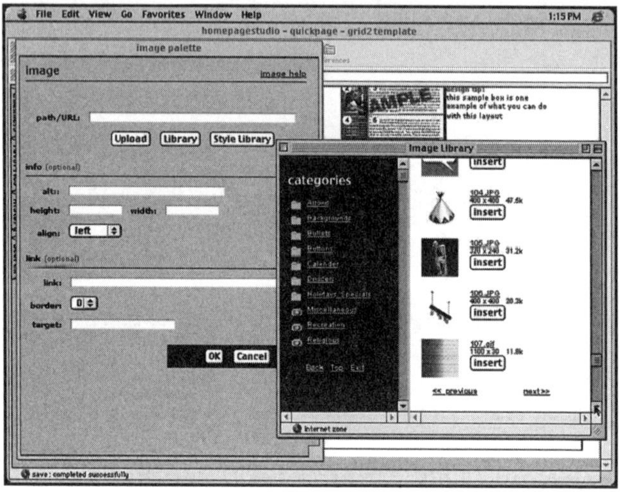

FIGURE 7.6
The Image Palette and Image Library screens.

First tell QuickPage where to find the image you want to use. If you've already uploaded the image to your directory, enter the whole URL of the image. The URL will look something like `http://members.tripod.com/membername/picture.gif` (or `picture.jpg`).

If you don't have your own image, you can pick a stock image from either the Image Library or the Style Library. Click the button for the library you want to use. Figure 7.7 shows a screen from the Image Library. The left frame displays the different categories of pictures available. Previews of each image appear in the right frame. After you find an image, click the Insert button and the

Image Library closes. QuickPage automatically inserts the path/URL, width, and height for you.

In the Info (optional) section, you should provide a phrase that describes the image in the alt field. The alt text appears in some browsers when you move the mouse over image. Otherwise, the alt text is displayed when image loading is turned off.

You only need to use the height and width measurements if you want to change the size of the image when it's displayed. If you chose an image from one of the libraries, these fields are already filled in with the exact measurements of the image. If you're going to change the size of the image, you should always make it smaller. If you try to make it bigger, the image will become jagged or pixellated.

Beware! If you change one measurement and not the other, or if you don't maintain the same proportions when resizing, you'll get some unexpected results! It's best not to change the width and height boxes or to leave them empty if you don't know the size of the image.

You can align the box to the right, left, or center of the section in which you are working by changing the align option.

You can make the image link to a new Web page by filling in the Link (optional) information. Enter the URL of the page to which you want to link in the link field. Enter **_self** in the target field if you want the page to load in the same window. If you want the link to open a new window, enter **_new** instead.

If you make the image a link, you can put a blue border around it so people know that it's a link. The default border is 0, which means that no border will appear. If you choose 1, 2, or 3 from the drop-down menu, a blue border will appear around the image. Keep in mind that some browsers display a thicker border if you set the border to a high number.

My Contact Info

The My Contact Info Palette has fields for you to enter your name, mailing address, and email address (see Figure 7.7). It's useful to add this information to your page if you want visitors to be able to contact you to report broken links or for more information.

Just fill in the fields you want to appear on the page. You can skip the ones you don't want displayed. You can change the appearance of the contact info by setting new options for the font. When you're finished entering information, click OK. The palette closes. Wait a moment for your changes to appear in the studio before continuing.

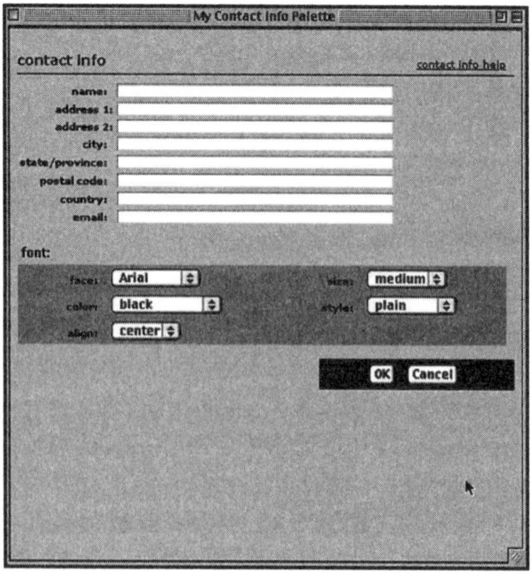

FIGURE 7.7
My Contact Info Palette.

Cool Links

Okay, you want to take your page a little further. Maybe hook up your visitors with some cool music CDs or books. You can use Homepages Cool Links to add that little extra something to your page. The following 10 Cool Links are available to you.

- CDnow Search Box
- Barnes & Noble Search Box
- Lycos Search Box
- GIF Girl Web Design Tips
- Chank's Free Rockstar Fonts
- Mad Crib for Teens
- Tripod's Internship Database
- Ask Evel Knievel
- Ask the Doctor
- Tripod's Cookbook Gallery

All 10 Cool Links are checked off when the Cool Links window opens. If you don't want to add the graphic and link to your page for one or more of the choices, just deselect them. When you're finished, click OK, and wait for your changes to appear in the studio.

Guest Book

Guest Books enable people to tell you and others what they think of your page. Their comments are automatically added to your page after they fill out the form. If you want to use a guest book on your page, you need to register at GuestWorld. Click the button to go to GuestWorld and fill out a form.

After you're registered with GuestWorld, the HTML code for a guest book will be emailed to you. If you already have a guest book, you can use it without having to register. Either way, after you have the code, cut and paste it into the text entry box on the GUESTBOOK HTML field. When finished, click OK, and wait for your changes to appear in the studio. (For more on guest books, see Chapter 9, "Adding Special Effects to Your Tripod Pages.")

Page Counters

Page counters record the number of visitors to your site. You count as a visitor to your own Web page! When you choose Page Counter from a section's drop-down menu, the Counter Configuration window opens (see Figure 7.8). You can change the appearance of the numbers by changing the font options.

You can also choose whether you want all the numbers in the counter to appear or only a fixed-length number by toggling between the No Fixed Length option and Fixed Length option. When you choose Fixed Length, you must specify the number of digits you want to appear.

Every once in a while, you might visit your page and see that a lot of people have visited your page. Don't worry about this. It just means that Tripod's servers are really busy at the moment. The correct number of hits your page has received should reappear within a couple of hours.

FINISHING UP

Let's review how to work with Build by Design templates. Starting at `http://servlets.tripod.com/hpstudio/quickpage/index.html`, you should choose a layout for your page. After naming your page and saving it in a directory, begin working on the page by giving it a name and choosing a style. Within each numbered section of the pasteup, there is a drop-down menu. Select the type of information you want for that section and enter your text or other data in the window or palette that opens. When finished, click OK to return to the studio. Remember to save your work often by clicking on the Save button in the studio.

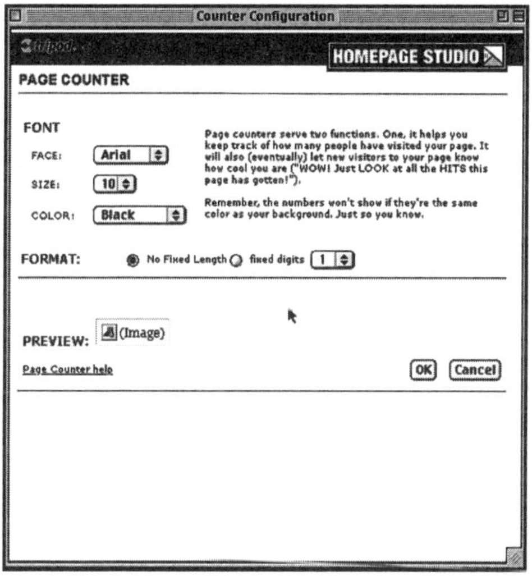

FIGURE 7.8
The Counter Configuration window.

DESIGN TIPS

If you don't know HTML—and what's more, you don't want to know HTML—the QuickPage templates are perfect for you. That doesn't mean that you shouldn't consider good design tips. Design is how well your page looks, and (thanks to Tripod's Homepage Studio) you don't have to worry about that. Design is also how well your page works, and that's up to you! Here are a couple of quick tips for making a well-designed page.

Being Specific

The more focused and organized your Web page is, the more people will like it. If you have one really long page that has information about your trip to Hawaii sandwiched between information about your kids' soccer leagues and information about your favorite television show, many visitors will be confused and just leave your page.

Instead, you should build three pages: one about your trip to Hawaii, one about the local soccer league, and one about your favorite television show. You can link the pages together using hyperlinks, but each page will be better off if it is separate from the others. For more information about organizing pages, see the Content Collection section in this chapter.

Using ALT Tags for Images

Design on the World Wide Web goes beyond the look of a page. Some visitors to your page might be visually impaired; others might have image loading turned off because of an unbearably slow Internet connection. You should use alternative text (or ALT tag) phrases to describe any images you use on your page. ALT tags also appear as little pop-up text boxes when the mouse is positioned over an image in certain browsers, so they can act as captions for pictures.

If you use a banner that says "Welcome!", then you can use the text phrase "Welcome!" (without quotes) as an

ALT tag. But if you use a picture of you and your spouse on your wedding day, a more appropriate tag might be "a picture of Bill and Lucy dancing on their wedding day." If a visitor with image loading sees that ALT tag, he or she might be more willing to load the image. Also, visitors using text-to-voice browsers (Web browsers that read Web pages) won't be left out of the fun.

When you select Image/Linked Image from the drop-down menu, you would enter your ALT tag in the alt field.

Including Contact Information

Of course you're building a Web page in which everyone is interested. Give people a way to contact you for more information or just to let them tell you what good a job you've done. Include your name, email address, and if you want, your mailing address at the bottom of the page. This is especially useful if you're building a Web page for a business or organization. Many potential customers or members might contact you off the Internet if they're concerned about security issues or don't have their own email address.

Content Collection

If you spend a little time planning your page before designing it, the end result will be fantastic! Use these five simple steps to move from thinking "I could build a Web page" to actually doing it.

- **Make a list** Make a list of what you want to put on your page. This list includes text, graphics, and multimedia. This checklist will help you keep track of each piece of crucial imagery, text, or other content.

- **Create a flowchart or outline** If you're going to have more than one page on your site, create a flow chart or outline showing what you're going to put where. For instance, your Web page could have links to a page about your summer vacation, a page about your children's school, and a page of links to other sites. You can use Homepage's Studio's Design by Topic templates for ideas for other pages.
- **Decide what you want** Decide exactly what you want on each page and, more importantly, where you're going to get it.

  Is the information you have up-to-date and accurate? Are you going to have a list of links or just text? You don't need to decide exactly what your graphics are going to look like yet, but you do need to decide whether you need them.
- **Start collecting the pieces** Start gathering the pieces one page at a time. Plenty of public domain art, music, information, and multimedia is on the Web. As you find each piece, check it off your list.
- **Sketch out your ideas** Do a quick sketch of each page or search through templates in the Homepage Studio (`http://servlets.tripod.com/hpstudio/quickpage/index.html`). Make sure you've got all the pieces for your page, and upload them to your disk space using Tripod's Filemanager (`http://servlets.tripod.com/servlets/FileManager`).

The rest of this chapter focuses on finding where to get the pieces you need.

Cruising the Information Superhighway

Yes, it's a clichè. But it's true. The Internet has all the information you need if only you can find it. You can find a lot of pages on the Internet by surfing, or following links from one page to the next. You'd probably never find the information you want, but you'd find a lot of information. It would be better if you could find a list of pages about the topic you're researching. The easiest way to do that is to use a search engine on the Web.

Get Personal

Your personal experiences are what make your page unique and interesting. Be sure to include information you've learned from other sources or your perspective. Don't just repeat what other people have to say.

As you probably already know, a *search engine* finds pages on the Web based on *keywords* that you provide. Appropriate keywords are the main topic words for what you're looking for. If you're looking for pages about a sports team, keywords might be the sport name (football) and the team name (Arizona Cardinals).

Let's try an example. From the top of the Tripod home page, you can search the Web or Tripod. Search for "football Arizona Cardinals" on the Web. The results are shown in Figure 7.9.

The search engine found a lot of pages. You can now read through the results and select the pages you want to read. But maybe you should narrow your search parameters. For instance, if you want to find out about specific information like Jake Plummer, you could add his name to the keywords and search again. If you don't get the results you are looking for, try a different search engine.

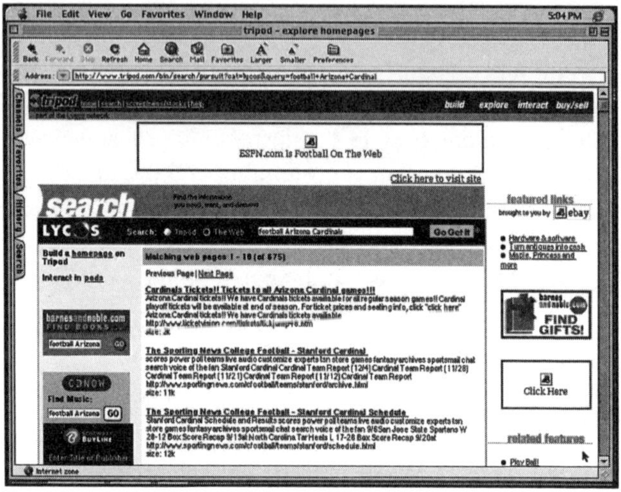

FIGURE 7.9
The results of your Tripod search.

Some of the most popular search engines are:

- Lycos: `www.lycos.com`
- AltaVista: `www.altavista.com`
- Excite: `www.excite.com`
- HotBot: `www.hotbot.com`
- Infoseek: `www.infoseek.com`
- Yahoo!: `www.yahoo.com`

Get Some Attention

All the exciting text you put on your page isn't enough. If visitors don't see something visual to hold their attention, they won't visit or recommend your page to their friends.

You can make pages attractive with graphics. Graphics are anything that isn't text, and sometimes even text can be a graphic.

Let's figure out where you can get graphics. You might already have them. If you're building a page about yourself, a hobby of yours, or your business, then you probably have pictures related to those topics laying around. You can get them scanned into your computer. If you really want to get fancy, you can use a digital camera to take new pictures and download them directly onto your hard drive.

Remember to include unique pictures and images. Visitors don't want to see yet another image they've seen on five other pages. Put up your personal pictures and creations.

But what do you do if you don't have the graphics you want? Well, it's time to turn to the Web. If you're building a page about lizards, you'll want to include at least one picture of a lizard. A quick look through Tripod's Image Library turned up the fellow shown in Figure 7.10.

If you can't find a picture you like, try looking through Tripod. CloudDreamer (a Tripod user) has put up a "Clip Art, Clip Art, and Tons of Clip Art Links" page at `http://members.tripod.com/CloudDreamer/index.html`. Or creep into the "Clip Cave" at `http://members.tripod.com/Rumley/PPBclipart.html`. If you still haven't found anything that catches your fancy, try The Web Developer's Personal Library (`www.stars.com/Vlib/Providers/Images_and_Icons.html`).

FIGURE 7.10
That's a lizard!

Thou Shall Not Steal (But Borrowing is Fine)

Before you snatch a graphic or photo and put it up on your site, you might have to get permission to do so. Many sites that offer graphics and clip art offer the terms and conditions for use before you can borrow the item. Some graphics are considered public domain as free for your usage. Others have been created through hard work and the creators don't want you to take advantage of all that effort without some reward. They might consider your use of their graphics stealing, and if they find out, they can ask you to remove the graphic from your site or complain to Tripod.

Celebrity photos are probably the most obvious issue here (unless it is a photo you have taken yourself or received from the celebrity's publicity office). In fact, using a photo of Jennifer Love Hewitt that appeared in Teen People, for example, might not bother the actress, but you could be headed for trouble with the photographer or the magazine. As you probably know, endless celebrity photos are on the Internet, many of which are used illegally. Most of the people who use these photos, as long as the photos are displayed in a way that is supportive of the subject, will never be sued or even asked to remove the photos. We just don't want to be the ones to encourage you to do so!

If you do find a photo on the Web that you'd like to use, contact the site builder and ask permission to use it.

Many clip art collections also contain separators and bullets that you can use on your pages. If you built your pages using QuickPage and picked them, then the separators, or horizontal rules, have already been added for you. If you know a little HTML, you can add the HTML coding necessary to add the graphics to your page.

Remember, just like the content of your page, graphics should be centered on a theme. If your page is about lizards, include images of reptiles, but avoid images of footballs or unrelated topics.

Your page's background can be a plain color, a texture, or even an image. If you chose a style for your page, the background is already included. If you know HTML, then you can change your background to a color or image. The most important thing to remember is that there should be lots of contrast between the color(s) of your background and your text. Keep your background from being too colorful or too busy, either of which can make it difficult to read.

Some Final Words on Graphics

Borrowing public domain clip art might be enough for you, but you can also create your own graphics. What!? Honestly, it's not as difficult as it might seem. You'll have to spend a bit of money on graphics software, so creating your own graphics depends largely on your budget and your desire to do so.

You can also buy graphics, which is the easiest option if you have a bunch of extra cash burning a hole in your pocket. For a personal home page, this is usually not worth the money. But, if you are trying to build a business site with a degree of professionalism, you might think about it.

For more on graphics, check out Chapter 10.

Listen Up

A Web page about your garage band that does covers of classic rock songs begs for sound clips so that everyone can hear how great you are. If you're serious about getting that executive position, then your sound track probably shouldn't be included with your online résumé.

You should be very selective about adding sound to your Web page. Sound files are large so they can take a long time to download. Also, you don't want to embarrass anybody who might be surfing the Web instead of working, do you? (Not that we're speaking from experience!)

To add music and other audio for your site, you can create it yourself or find it on the Web. You can also buy it, but at this point, this might not be worth it. As with posting copyrighted photos or graphics, offering things such as commercially released recordings in RealAudio or MP3 format on your site is asking for trouble. The recording industry is rightfully becoming very touchy about this issue, so be smart.

MIDI

MIDI is a popular sound format on the Web. It's created with a synthesizer and strictly instrumental. Popular songs and seasonal songs, like Christmas songs, are easy to find in the public domain done in MIDI format. MIDI files are easy to add to your page (see Chapter 11, "Adding Multimedia to Your Tripod Pages," for more information). They are small files in size, so they download quickly.

Check out the MIDI site at `http://members.tripod.com/DrgnStudio/Drgn4/Midi.html` for lots of ideas. Also visit MIDI Heaven at `http://members.tripod.com/midiheaven7/sites.htm`, which might be the most complete MIDI site on the Web.

WAV

Another type of audio file is WAV (pronounced "wave"). WAV files are usually sound effects, like the sounds you hear on your computer when you open or close Windows. They're usually short and small, which makes them fairly usable for Web pages. They're perfect for adding a small accent to your Web page. You might add the Communicator hailing sound to your Star Trek fan page to welcome visitors and get their attention.

Small, simple sound files like WAV and MIDI are for adding music or simple sounds to your page. What about music with vocals—or even somebody talking? Other sound formats, like AU, also exist. You can find AU files on the Web or make your own by recording sounds into your computer with a microphone. Remember to get permission from the owner if you're "borrowing" any sound files.

We're Getting There

Now that you know how to use Homepage Studio's QuickPage and know the basics about finding information on the Web and collecting graphics and sound files, you might want to move on to bigger challenges, such as creating your own original graphics or learning HTML. Learning to do HTML code or design graphics is fun and customizes your Web page.

So how do you do all this stuff? Keep reading.

PART III

Get Noticed in Your Pod

CHAPTER 8

Developing Forms on Tripod

Tripod includes full support for Web forms. Support consists of a specific forms handler that processes the contents of a Web form and then presents the contents to you via email.

Creating interesting, useful forms with HTML is certainly not easy. It takes some specific understanding of the HTML tags that create forms, some design tips, and the ability to link the form to the forms handler so that the form can be processed. That said, forms aren't impossible to master and can be a great addition to your site due to their interactive nature. Forms enable people to share information with you in a fun and organized manner.

The first step to understanding forms is deciding what they will be used for. A form is often used to collect names and email addresses of your site's visitors. You can then create a mailing list from those responses that can be used to send newsletters or site update alerts. Forms can also be used to gather much more information. For example, you can take a survey about any number of topics, depending on your site's topic.

A Simple Form

Forms are designed with a specific set of HTML tags. Forms are defined in your HTML page with the <FORM> tag as follows:

```
<FORM>
What's Your Name<INPUT TYPE=TEXT SIZE=20 NAME=
➥"USERNAME">    <INPUT TYPE="SUBMIT"
ACTION="mailto:user@tripod.com">
</FORM>
```

This simple form will ask the visitor to enter his or her name and will mail the results to `user@tripod.com`. The opening and closing <FORM> tags define the beginning and end of a form. This enables a Web page to have multiple forms.

This is a very simple form that doesn't even use the built-in forms handler that Tripod provides. As you'll learn, you can create more advanced and user-friendly forms.

The Form Tags

When you design your form, you should know all the ins and outs of HTML form design. Although there are visual page editors that help design forms, designing them directly with your HTML code provides the most control.

All forms must begin with an opening <FORM> tag and end with the closing </FORM> tag, as follows:

```
<FORM>...</FORM>
```

You can add two attributes to the opening form tag: METHOD and ACTION. The METHOD attribute tells the form which method of submission is being used: GET or POST. Don't worry about the GET method; on Tripod, all your forms will use the METHOD="POST"

was set to 15. You can use any number for your page design, but avoid excessively large numbers, which will adversely affect your design. Numbers between 10 and 60 work well.

The MAXLENGTH attribute actually limits the number of characters a person can type into a form. This prevents users from typing essays into your forms when all you want is the name of their favorite singer.

The VALUE attribute is used to place a start-up value in the text box. This will be the default value that is loaded into the box when the form is displayed. Keep it blank if you don't want an initial value. It can be useful to preinput through value tags the most common answer (e.g. Value="USA"). Or you can provide an example for a special type of input (e.g. Value="youremail@yourdomain.com") that you want someone to replace with their specific information.

Radio Buttons

A radio button is a form element that forces users to pick just one choice from a group of options (refer to Figure 8.1). When a user chooses one of the options, the other options in the group are cleared. Radio buttons can be great when asking your visitors to rate something. For example, if you had a site about skiing and wanted people to rate various ski resorts, you could offer a radio button on a scale of 1–5 or from "Awesome to Awful." Visitors could then choose one rating per resort, making for idiot-proof responses. Example:

```
<INPUT TYPE="radio" NAME="Resort Rating" VALUE="Best"
CHECKED>
```

A radio button, like a text box, is an offshoot of the <INPUT> tag. However, the TYPE attribute is now set to "radio" instead of "text."

All radio buttons in a single form that share the same NAME attribute will be considered as a single group. The grouping is what makes the "one and only one" factor of a radio button work.

The VALUE attribute refers to what information will be sent through email when the user makes a specific selection. In the example, if the user selected that specific rating for the ski resort, a line in the resulting email would read:

```
Resort Rating="Best"
```

If you include the CHECKED attribute in a radio button tag, that item in the group will be preset to selected when the form loads. Use it to select only what will be the most common answer for the group. If you want to avoid any bias in your surveys, don't use the CHECKED feature.

Check Boxes

Check boxes are a cousin of radio buttons that enable the user to check off a selection in a form (refer to Figure 8.1). The primary difference between a check box and a radio button is that a user can make multiple selections to a group of check boxes. For example, if you wanted to ask what people did when visiting their favorite ski resort, you could use a series of check boxes that ask if they skied moguls, expert trails, intermediate trails, beginner trails, or if they went snowboarding. A radio button would ask which of the choices they enjoyed most.

A typical checkbox <INPUT> tag looks as follows:

```
<INPUT TYPE="CHECKBOX" VALUE="Moguls">Moguls
```

Like radio buttons, the <INPUT> is back using TYPE= "CHECKBOX" to define the input element that will be displayed as a check box. As in all cases, the VALUE attribute will be passed through email to the user. As with radio buttons, you can preset the check box to appear as checked when the form initially displays by including the CHECKED attribute in the tag.

Text Areas

What do you do if you want to accept multiple lines of text via a form? Text boxes are limited to one line. However, the text area element addresses this issue (refer to Figure 8.1). This element lets users enter multiple lines of text into a single form element. Typically used for areas such as "comments," text areas offer a clean area in which users can submit as much text as they want.

Unlike other form elements, this tag has an open tag/close tag structure. Begin your text area with <TEXTAREA> and end it with </TEXTAREA> as follows:

```
<TEXTAREA NAME="Site Comments" ROWS="10" COLS="35"
WRAP=PHYSICAL>Please post your comments about my site
and how I can make it better. </TEXTAREA>
```

The text between the tags appears as editable text inside the text area element. The NAME attribute is used so that the results in your email are properly labeled. The ROWS and COLS attributes let you set the dimensions of the text area for the form. COLS is similar to the SIZE attribute used in the <INPUT> tag, and ROWS sets the number of lines for your text area.

Adding "wrap=physical" to the <TEXTAREA> tag forces the text area to word wrap long sentences. It is recommended that you include this attribute.

Menus

The menu element lets people choose from a list of choices on a form (refer to Figure 8.1). Menus are defined using two tags. The <SELECT>...</SELECT> tags are used to set the start and finish of a specific list of options; the <OPTION> tag defines each individual selection in a single menu.

For example, if you wanted to let people choose their level of skiing ability, you could set up a menu in which they would pick from a list of possible answers.

```
<SELECT NAME="Ski Level" SIZE="1">
<OPTION VALUE="Extreme" CHECKED>Extreme
<OPTION VALUE="Pro">Pro
<OPTION VALUE="Expert">Expert
<OPTION VALUE="Intermediate">Intermediate
<OPTION VALUE="Beginner">Beginner
<OPTION VALUE="Bunny Slope">Bunny Slope
</SELECT>
```

The NAME attribute in the <SELECT> tag sets the overall name of the menu that will then correspond to the choice selected in the email you receive. If the user picked "Extreme," there would be a line in your email reading:

```
Ski Level=Extreme
```

As in other form elements, SIZE sets the number of visible elements for the menu. Set this to one if you want a simple "drop-down list" or more if you want more than one menu element to be visible at a time.

The <OPTION> tag has one main attribute—the VALUE setting that is passed through if the user makes that selection. As with radio buttons and checkboxes, CHECKED can be optionally used to define an initial value for the menu.

Image Inputs

Images can also be used to receive input from a user (see Figure 8.2). Based on the way an image input is received (as an x,y coordinate), it will be difficult to determine what the user's answer was. In the end, it really only works for a few select situations where the image used to take input is very simple with easy boundaries to determine where the user clicked. Thus, you will want to think carefully before using an image input as a form element.

FIGURE 8.2
Images can be used as input elements.

Start by creating an image and saving it as a GIF or JPEG.

Using our old friend the <INPUT> tag, you can display the image as an input element on the form:

```
<INPUT TYPE="image" SRC="theworld.gif" NAME="Where I
Live">
```

The TYPE attribute is now used to define the input type as an image. As with the <IMG> tag used to display a picture, the SRC attribute sets the URL within your Tripod site where the picture is located. Finally, as with every other form element, the NAME tag is used to identify the answer in your email.

Where image inputs is slightly different is in the values they return. The values produced by an image input will be the x,y coordinate of the area on the image that was clicked. This is why it is difficult to find uses for image inputs. Most people won't want to examine repeatedly the returned values to see where exactly on their image the user clicked.

When an image input is clicked, the form data will be immediately submitted. Thus, an image input should be placed at the end of the form, or it should be the only element contained on a form.

Submit Buttons

At the end of nearly every form is the "submit" button. This button lets the visitor tell the Web server that he or she is finished filling out the information and would like to submit the form.

You can also include a "reset" button that will let someone clear a form and fill it out from scratch if they want to make numerous changes.

Add a submit button by using the <INPUT> tag as follows:

```
<INPUT TYPE="SUBMIT" NAME=" My Answers   ">
```

The NAME attribute determines the wording on the button. Inserting a few extra spaces before and after the words makes the button larger than it would be otherwise.

To add a reset button, use the <INPUT> tag and set the TYPE attribute to reset:

```
<INPUT TYPE="RESET" NAME="   Reset!    ">
```

FORMS VIA EMAIL

Instead of using the forms remailer, which is a program that remails the form back to you, you can use "mailto:" in the ACTION attribute of the <FORM> tag to send the contents of a form via a user's email account. This is useful if you want to offer a form that is then sent to an email address other than the one attached to your Tripod account.

```
<INPUT TYPE="Submit" Value=" EMail This
Form" ACTION="mailto:person@domain.com">
```

When the user clicks the Submit button, a dialog box appears to indicate that the form is going to be sent out using the user's email program. The user is offered the choice of sending the form using this method.

This is useful when it comes to gathering responses and mailing them to other entities—for example, if you wanted people to fill out a form to protest the actions of a government.

Hidden Tags

To pass values from a form without the user's input, use the <INPUT TYPE="HIDDEN"> tag. This can be used to send special information to a script such as a forms handler that instructs it to do various tasks.

Tripod's form remailer script doesn't support any special hidden tags, but in the future it or other scripts that Tripod might produce could require them. An example of a HIDDEN tag might look like this:

```
<INPUT TYPE="HIDDEN" VALUE="SPECIAL INFO">
```

You can still use hidden tags even though they won't trigger anything in the forms processing process to pass information to you. One use might be to include a hidden subject code to make it easy to see which form someone used if you have multiple forms on your site asking for the same information. To do that, just create a HIDDEN tag that has a VALUE attribute that contains information like “REQUEST FOR RECIPE INFORMATION” in it and that info will be passed through on every email you get as a result of that form.

Listing all the hidden input tags at the beginning or end of your form makes it easier to read.

Building A Complete Form

With all the elements described, you should be able to assemble an entire form for your site. Here is a form that asks for information and opinions about various ski resorts. The information could be easily compiled and shared on your Tripod homepage.

```
<HTML>
<BODY BGCOLOR="GRAY">
<H1>Share Your Ski Resort Ratings...<BR></H1>
<FORM METHOD="POST" ACTION="/cgi-bin/mailto">

<B>What resort did you visit?</B><INPUT TYPE="TEXT"
NAME="Resort Name" SIZE="30"><BR><BR>

<B>When did you go?</B><INPUT TYPE="TEXT" NAME="Visit
Date" VALUE="D/M/Y" SIZE="10"><BR><BR>

<B>Did You…</B>

<INPUT TYPE="CHECKBOX" NAME="I " VALUE="Skied">Ski?
<INPUT TYPE="CHECKBOX" NAME="I "
VALUE="Snowboarded">Snowboard?<BR><BR>

<B>What Level of Skier/Snowboarder Are You</B>
```

```
    <SELECT NAME="Level">
        <OPTION VALUE="Extreme" CHECKED>Extreme
    <OPTION VALUE="Pro">Pro
        <OPTION VALUE="Expert">Expert
    <OPTION VALUE="Intermediate">Intermediate
        <OPTION VALUE="Beginner">Beginner
    <OPTION VALUE="Bunny Slope">Bunny Slope
    </SELECT><BR><BR>

<B>How Many Different Trails Did You Hit?</B><INPUT
TYPE="TEXT" NAME="Trails" SIZE="5"><BR><BR>

    <B>Rate This Resort:</B><BR>

<INPUT TYPE="radio" NAME="Resort Rating" VALUE="Best
Ever">Best   Ever<BR>
<INPUT TYPE="radio" NAME="Resort Rating" VALUE="It
Ripped!">It Ripped!<BR>
<INPUT TYPE="radio" NAME="Resort Rating" VALUE="Very
Good">Very Good<BR>
<INPUT TYPE="radio" NAME="Resort Rating"
VALUE="OK">OK<BR>
<INPUT TYPE="radio" NAME="Resort Rating" VALUE="A
Joke!">A Joke!<BR><BR>


    <B>Any tips or comments about the resort?</B><BR>
    <TEXTAREA NAME="Why Go" ROWS="10"
COLS="50">Comments...</TEXTAREA>
    <BR><BR>
    <INPUT TYPE="Submit" Name="  Submit! ">
    <INPUT TYPE="Reset" Name=" Start Over ">
</FORM>
</BODY>
</HTML>
```

There is an example of an entire form that utilizes the lessons we taught earlier in the chapter. Figure 8.3 shows the form.

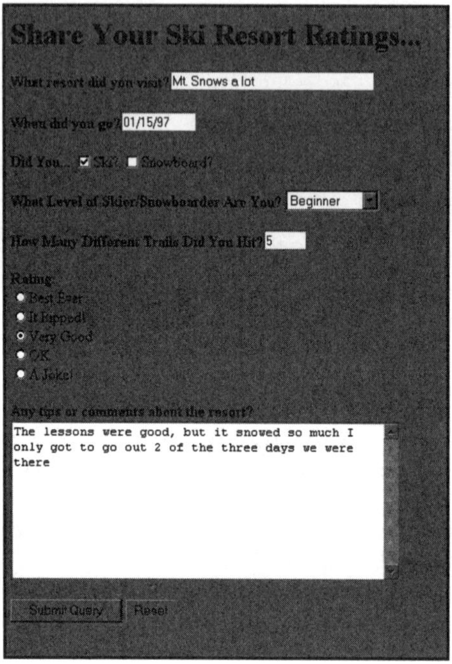

FIGURE 8.3
The complete ski resort form.

HELP YOUR FORMS

The goal of a form is to get someone to fill it out. A form that no one ever completes is useless. Use the following tips to add some spice to your forms:

- **Make the questions funny or have a snappy field heading.** In our sample form, when people were asked to rate the resorts, choices were "It Ripped!" rather than "Excellent" and "A Joke" rather than "Below Average."

- **Keep forms short.** No one wants to spend 20 minutes filling out a form that looks like it came from the IRS.
- **Share the results.** What's the point of asking people for their opinions if you don't share those opinions with your site's visitors?
- **Don't make people type out answers repeatedly.** People hate essay exams. Use checkboxes, radio buttons, and menus to offer choices and rankings.
- **Send confirmation notes.** If you request people to share their emails when signing them up to a mailing list, send them a confirmation note that you received their registration. For the most part, unless you set up an autoreply filter on with your favorite email package, you'll have to reply to incoming forms by hand. Unless you've created the most popular site in existence, this shouldn't be too difficult.
- **Use JavaScript to validate your forms first.** The fact that a field is required won't stop someone from entering, for example, a letter when you want a number. Although the process is too extensive to cover here, JavaScript can be used to precheck forms for valid answers before a user submits the form. Any good JavaScript book will have a section devoted to checking forms for correct entries.
- **Use tables to format your forms.** The entire example form was done without tables and looks like a long list of questions. That same form formatted in a table offers more control of the layout. The great thing about tables is that by using multiple columns and the extra positioning capabilities of tables you can create much more complex forms. If you want

the best-looking forms, learn more about using the host of table-related HTML tags.

- **Use images in place of the standard submit button.** Some people dress up their submit and reset buttons by substituting a graphic for the default button style that the browser would normally use. To do this, use the image input tag discussed above and make the graphic read Submit. Note: you can't use this method to create a graphical reset button.

YOUR OWN EMAIL NEWSLETTER

Using an automated filter and the simple form code listed below, you can make it easy for someone to provide his or her email address and automatically subscribe to or unsubscribe from a list of people with whom you will communicate on a regular basis.

```
    <FORM METHOD="POST" ACTION="/cgi-
bin/mailto">
Site Newsletter.  Subscribe/Unsubscribe:
<INPUT TYPE="TEXT" NAME="Reply To" SIZE=30
VALUE="myemail@mydomain.com">
    <SELECT NAME="Subject" SIZE="15">
        <OPTION VALUE="Subscribe
Newsletter" CHECKED>
    <OPTION VALUE="Unsubscribe Newsletter">
</SELECT>
<INPUT TYPE="Submit" Value=" Submit ">
</FORM>
```

Use your email program's filtering system to check for the various subject lines of "Subscribe Newsletter" or "Unsubscribe Newsletter." Most major email packages let you create autoreplies and scripts that automate the addition or deletion of mailing list members.

Use mailto: in the ACTION attribute of the <FORM> tag to have the contents of a form automatically sent to an email address other than that specified in your user profile.

Instead of using <FORM METHOD="POST" ACTION="/CGI-BIN/formail?[your membername]"> to submit a form just to you, you can point a form's contents toward any desired email address by using the Mailto: option in the ACTION attribute of a <INPUT TYPE="Submit"> tag and supplying a valid email address. For example:

```
<INPUT TYPE="Submit" Value=" EMail This
Form" ACTION="mailto:myname@mydomain.com">
```

When the user clicks on the Submit button in most browsers, a box will pop up saying that the form wants to send its contents out using the user's email program (Figure 8.4). If the user chooses "yes," then his or her email program is automatically launched and the form's contents are attached and mailed out as noted. This is a good method if you want people to mail you their forms using your Tripod email account. It's also good if you want to have the contents of the form emailed to someone other than the owner of the site.

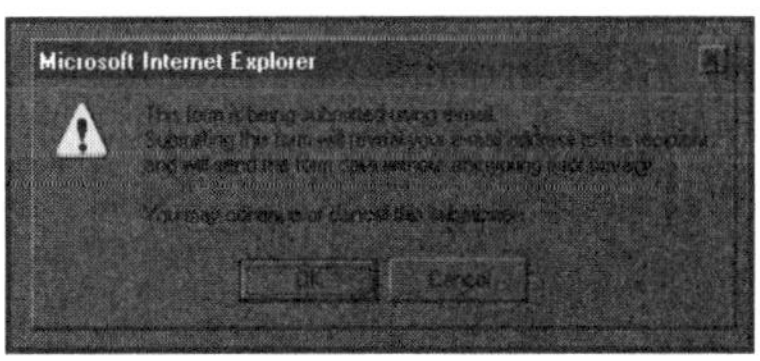

FIGURE 8.4
A user will be presented with a warning before submitting a form that uses the mailto: option instead of the Tripod forms processor.

Forms Are Powerful

Forms on Tripod are one of the best methods you can use to create interaction between you and the people who visit your site. With a little experimentation and understanding of the form elements and some of the tricks explained here, you should be able to add some very powerful and fun forms to your site.

Make the forms meaningful, fun, and interesting. Your form should be relevant to your site's subject matter, able to be filled out in minutes, and include content that can be shared in a meaningful way with visitors.

CHAPTER 9

Adding Special Effects to Your Tripod Pages

You can make your site more interesting and attractive to visitors in a number of ways—all of which are discussed in this book. Some of these are the special effects—such as hit counters and guest books—offered by Tripod. This chapter covers all of these effects, which can be added from the Build Homepages page. We will also cover some additional Java effects and show you how to earn money with an associate Web site.

Tripod Hit Counters

We've all seen hit counters. They're those online odometers that show how many hits a page has received. Although these hit counters can be tampered with (just like odometers!), if used honestly they can indicate the popularity of your site to its visitors.

Adding a counter to your site is easy. Simply perform the following steps:

1. Log in and go to the Filemanager (`http://servlets.tripod.com/servlets/FileManager`).

2. Click the check box to the left of the filename to which you want to add the counter (in our case, the homepage, which is called index.html).
3. If the file was created using QuickPage, edit using QuickPage by using the Edit drop-down list. Choose Edit With…
4. In the resulting dialog box, select QuickPage and click OK.
5. If you are building a new page, you will be asked to choose a layout. For this example, select Layout 2, which enables you to place the counter in one of five sections.

TIP

For the counter to appear at the bottom of the page you must have placed other objects before it. If the other sections are left empty, the page counter will appear at the top of the page.

6. Go to the section where you want your counter to be and click A Page Hit Counter. The Add a Counter page will appear, enabling you to personalize your counter (see Figure 9.1).
7. To personalize your counter, type the words you want to include. In Figure 9.1, "This page has been visited (14) times," was entered into the fields.
8. You can then choose color and positioning. When you have completed your selections, click Make This Counter. (A number of tips are under the button.)

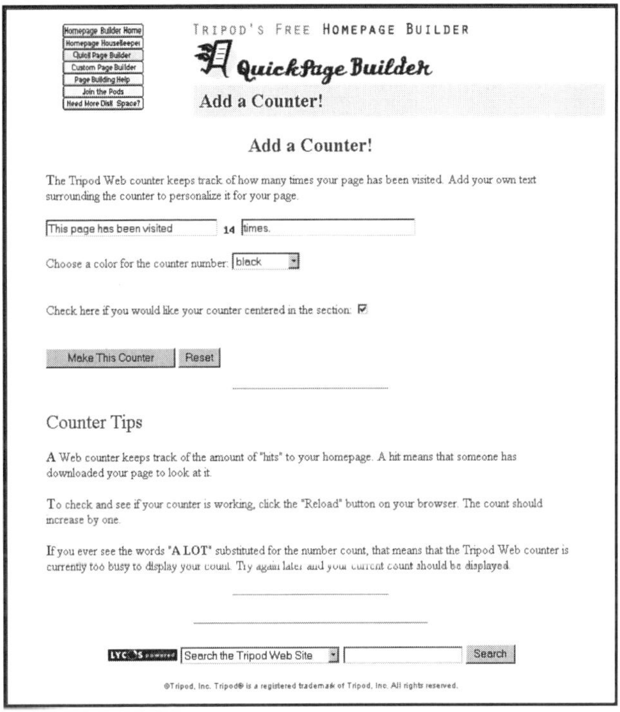

FIGURE 9.1
Personalizing your counter.

9. The Add a Counter page gives you a preview of your counter and the HTML code. Clicking OK brings you back to the layout page, allowing you to see what the counter will look like on the page before you save it.
10. To add the counter, click Save Page.

Using HTML to Add Hit Counters

If you choose a different page builder that uses HTML, the code for the counter is:

```
<IMG SRC="/bin/counter/[page name]">
```

This code can be placed on any page and in any location on that page. You can also place your own text around the counter. This code only provides the counter. If you know RGB hexadecimal colors, you can change the color of the counter by placing the number after the page name and before the end quotes. The code will then look something like this:

```
<IMG SRC="/bin/counter/index.htmlff0000">
```

This code creates a counter with red numbers.

Tripod Stats

If you have ever wondered who visits your site, where they come from, or how often they visit, you can find out with Tripod Stats. This program, powered by Nedstat, provides all of this information and more, such as page views per week, day, or hour.

Follow the links from the Tripod homepage to Build Homepages to Tools to Tripod Stats. To sign up, choose the page on your site for which you want to receive statistics. We wanted to see statistics for our homepage, so we chose index.html from the drop-down menu and clicked Submit.

Next you will be given the HTML code to place on your page so that the button and the link will appear on the desired page. (Make sure you place this code on the page you indicated.) This page will also show you what your button will look like.

Guestbooks

Placing a guestbook on your page is a popular effect. A guestbook enables visitors to leave their names and their comments—all good, we hope—about your site. Some of your visitors will likely have sites of similar interest and a guestbook is a good place for people to leave messages like, "I love your Sammy Sosa page. Come check out my Mark McGwire page when you get a minute!" They might even leave an email address and, before long you might be as friendly as Sosa and McGwire were during their historic home run chase.

Guestbooks can provide valuable information for you as well. You can get an idea of what types of people are visiting your site and what they think. You never know when a valuable tip that can help you improve your site might come from a guest who signed in to your guestbook. If guests leave their email addresses, you can always contact them when you update your site or have a special event happening.

Any visitor can read the guestbook. Tripod allows you to add a guestbook free of charge by using the GuestWorld Guestbook program. This comes with the ability to customize the background and field locations of your guestbook. You can even download all of this information to your computer and generate guestbook statistics.

GuestWorld Guestbooks can be used by anyone and require no programming experience. When you register your guestbook with GuestWorld, you agree to comply with their rules and regulations. Failure to do so can lead to the removal of your guestbook.

Registering your GuestWorld Guestbook

To register your guestbook with GuestWorld, perform the following steps:

1. Go to the Build Homepages area of Tripod (`www.tripod.com/build/`) and click Tools.
2. Click GuestWorld Guestbooks.
3. Complete the information and click the Register button below the Terms of Agreement.
4. Assuming you have completed the form correctly, you will be presented with a Congratulations page that includes the information needed to set up your guestbook. The use of the HTML code is explained, and you can view your guestbook by clicking Sign My Guestbook or View My Guestbook. The page also includes the information you sent to GuestWorld. Keep this page handy in case you need it in the future.

TIP

Be sure to fill out all of the fields; if you don't, your registration will be rejected.

5. To place the guestbook on any of your site's pages, copy the contents of the box starting with <!---start of code--->. After the code is copied, go to one of the page builder tools.
6. You can put your guestbook on any or all of your pages. Paste or type the code into the existing code on the page where you would like it to show up.

7. After the guestbook code is entered, you can preview it or simply click Save Page.

Voilà, you have a guestbook!

Answering Machines

Tripod also offers an optional answering machine. The answering machine is similar to the guestbook in that it enables visitors to leave messages. However, only you can read the messages left on the answering machine.

To set up your Answering Machine go to `http://members.tripod.com/service/answering_machine`.

Going here automatically sets up your answering machine. For others to access your answering machine or to link the answering machine to your Web site, the URL is

```
http://members.tripod.com/bin/answering_machine?
➥member_name=[your Tripod member name]
```

For example, if your member name is "zip," the link will look like this:

```
<A HREF="http://members.tripod.com/bin/
➥answering_machine?member_name=zip">the clickable
➥area</A>
```

This link enables "the clickable area" on the screen to link directly to your answering machine, where visitors to your site can leave a message.

Leaving a message on the answering machine is easy. Tripod prompts you through the steps. Click Submit when the message is complete. A confirmation page tells you that the message has been sent. To exit, just use the Back button on your browser.

To read your messages, go to `http://members.tripod.com/service/answering_machine`.

If you are not logged in to the Tripod system, you will be asked to do so. The answering machine will appear and you can click Read to view your messages. Included in each message is the date and time that the message was sent. The messages appear in the text window, and you can look at previous messages or continue to the next message by clicking the Back and Next arrows.

The Begin and End arrows take you to the first or last messages on the machine. The Delete button deletes the message you are currently viewing.

To personalize the message on your answering machine, log on to the machine and click the Outgoing Message button. You can then change the message in the text box. Click the Change button to replace the old message with the new one.

TIP

You can also go to the Build Homepages section, click Tools, and then click the Online Answering Machine link. Tripod will step you through the above process and offer help if you need it.

Personal Chat Rooms

Only Premium Members can create personal chat rooms. The chat program is browser independent and is totally customizable. You can decide who can enter your chat room, its appearance, and when it is open. If you are interested in adding a chat room to your site, a Premium Membership costs about $3 a month.

For more on personal chat rooms and Premium Membership, see Appendix A, "Premium Membership: Tripod's First Class Services."

Creating and Adding Special Effects with DHTML, Java, and JavaScript

You can also look to Java Applets, Dynamic HTML effects, and JavaScript effects to enhance your pages.

Java is a programming language created by Sun Microsystems that enables people to create specialized programs that run safely on numerous types of computers and Web browsers. You can upload and use hundreds of small Java programs—called applets—on your Tripod site. This can be used to add things such as spinning logos or scrolling tickers to your site.

When putting applets on your site, be sure of five things:

1. Make sure you have all the files to run the applet. Even a small applet can require several files to work.
2. The applet can't require the ability to write back to the Web site. Tripod won't let you have server-hosted applets that write data back to their systems. Most applets don't require this.
3. You must have permission from the applet's owner to use the applet on your site. Many applets are shareware or free for noncommercial use.
4. The applet can't contain any advertising. Although it is fine for an applet to contain a link to the author's site, some applets host banners and other advertising, which is a violation of Tripod rules.

5. Get the instructions on installing the applet. Most applets come with readme files containing sample code and parameters used to tell the Web page how to display and configure the applet. Some applets reference small text files in the same directory as the Java code.

Where to Get Java Applets

You could write your own Java applet. However, you can save a lot of effort by visiting one of the following sites. These sites point you to the best available Java applets.

- **Gamelan (`http://www.gamelan.com/javaprogramming/applets/`)** Gamelan is well known in the Web community for being one of the best—if not the best—place to find Java applets for your Web site (see Figure 9.2).
- **JARS (`http://www.jars.com/`)** JARS (Java Review Service) organizes, reviews, and links to hundreds of useful Java applets created by developers from around the world.

DHTML

Dynamic HTML, or DHTML, is a new type of Web page language that enables you to create interesting effects for your pages including animation and drop-down menus. The biggest problem with Dynamic HTML is the slight difference between the way it works with Internet Explorer and Netscape Navigator. DHTML also requires your site's users to be visiting with a version 4.0 or better browser. However, DHTML can be used to create some neat special effects.

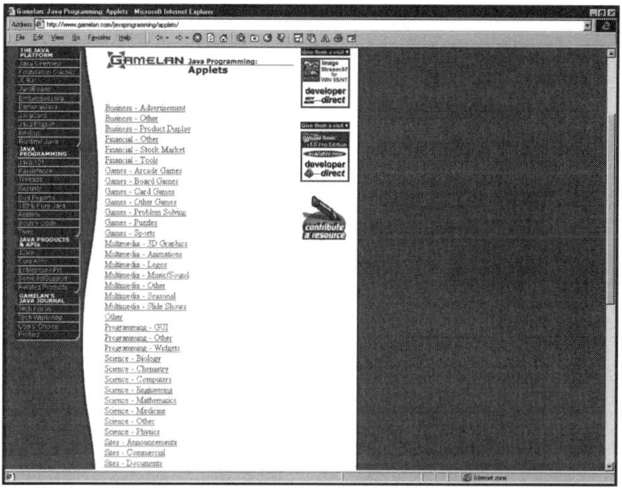

FIGURE 9.2
The Gamelan site has links to many fun Java applets.

For example, Internet Explorer viewers can add a transition between pages on their sites (see Figure 9.3). This provides a slideshow-style presentation between pages.

To create the transition, drop some HTML code into the <HEAD>…</HEAD> section of your Web page source code. In this code, you must specify three things:

- When the transition happens (on page entry, page exit, site entry, or site exit)
- The duration of the transition (in seconds)
- The transition effect to use (see Table 9.1)

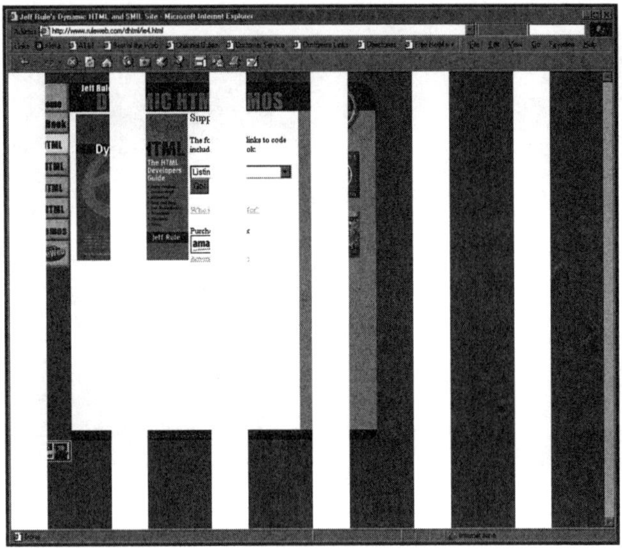

FIGURE 9.3
DHTML offers page transitions for Internet Explorer users. This page is shown in transition.

Table 9.1 IE 4, Dynamic HTML Transition Effect Codes

Transition name	Value
Box in	0
Box out	1
Circle in	2
Circle out	3
Wipe up	4
Wipe down	5
Wipe right	6
Wipe left	7

Transition name	Value
Vertical blinds	8
Horizontal blinds	9
Checkerboard across	10
Checkerboard down	11
Random dissolve	12
Split vertical in	13
Split vertical out	14
Split horizontal in	15
Split horizontal out	16
Strips left down	17
Strips left up	18
Strips right down	19
Strips right up	20
Random bars horizontal	21
Random bars vertical	22
Random	23

The code to insert is a simple <META> tag. You can have up to four specific tags—to set the transition on page entry, page exit, site entry, and site exit. Here are examples of the code:

```
<META http-equiv="Page-Enter" CONTENT="RevealTrans
➥(Duration=3,Transition=4)>
```

```
<META http-equiv="Page-Exit" CONTENT="RevealTrans
➥(Duration=3.500,Transition=10)>
```

In the first <META> tag, the fourth transition type is played when the user enters the page. It lasts three seconds. In the second <META> tag, the 10th transition is played when the user leaves the page. It lasts 3.5 seconds.

DHTML Resources

Several great Web sites exist that can teach you Dynamic HTML in far more detail than can be provided here. Some include sample code that you can copy and modify for your Tripod site.

- **Webmonkey's DHTML Tutorials (`http://www.hotwired.com/webmonkey/dynamic_html/`)** The folks at Webmonkey are always creating great tutorials on the latest browser technologies. Their DHTML tutorials are no exception.
- **Jeff Rule's Dynamic HTML Demos (`http://www.ruleweb.com/dhtml/`)** This is one of the best sites for learning DHTML. This site provides plenty of examples that work in both Internet Explorer and Navigator, as well as some that are browser-specific.
- **Inside DHTML (`http://www.insidedhtml.com/`)** Inside DHTML has more examples, tutorials, and articles than anyone could read in a week, much less a day.

JavaScript

Unlike Dynamic HTML, JavaScript has been around since versions 3.0 of both Internet Explorer and Netscape Navigator. Unfortunately, like DHTML, JavaScripts work differently, depending upon the browser. However, the differences are not as dramatic as those encountered with DHTML.

JavaScript enables you to create a number of special effects, such as rollover buttons (which change characteristics when the mouse rolls over them), links, or the opening of a new window when someone clicks a link. However, because rollovers and other JavaScript effects are somewhat dependent upon your specific pages, it is hard to deal with specifics here. Instead, you should visit the following sites:

- **JavaScript World** (`www.jsworld.com`) JavaScript World features a number of modifiable scripts that create special effects like calculators, pop-up menus, and scrolling tickers.
- **The JavaScript Resource** (`http://www.serve.com/hotsyte/`) The JavaScript Resource is one of the best all-purpose sites for information and sample code concerning JavaScript.
- **JavaScripts at Webmonkey** (`http://www.hotwired.com/webmonkey/javascript/`) Not unlike its DHTML site, Webmonkey has developed an excellent resourcc on using JavaScript.

The Ultimate Special Effect: Earning Money from Tripod Affiliate Store Programs

Want to earn somc cxtra cash with your Tripod site? Tripod offers this possibility through its Approved Affiliation Program. For example, the Cosmic Credit program, a CDnow affiliate program, enables you to earn money by linking your site to CDnow. You can save money on your CDnow purchases, attract visitors, and make money for doing practically nothing. Tripod also has a similar affiliate program with `Barnesandnoble.com`.

CDnow Cosmic Credit

The Cosmic Credit Program enables you to set up links to CDnow. When people click from your site to CDnow and make a purchase, you earn credit. You can use your credit to save money on CDnow purchases and, after your credit reaches $100, CDnow will send you a check for the amount earned.

To sign up for Cosmic Credit, perform the following steps:

1. Go to Build Homepages and click Tools.
2. Click Earn Money On Tripod and then the corresponding CDnow Click Here link.
3. Click Sign Me Up! on the left side of the page to do just that.
4. On the Cosmic Credit Registration page, fill out the form (including the URL to your site).
5. After completing the form, click Submit. You will be told how to link to CDnow site and begin earning credit.

CDnow will tell you how your site is featured on its site, how to post banner messages, and the special benefits Cosmic Credit members receive.

You can also choose Click Here to Build a Music Store with Our Easy to Use Template. No HTML required! You will be stepped through the process of creating a music page.

Signing up with *BarnesandNoble.com*

The Barnes & Noble Affiliate program is for book fanatics who want to promote their favorite books, authors, or genre on their Web site. Like the Cosmic Credit program, when someone buys a book at Barnesandnoble.com through a link from your site, you earn money or credit.

To sign up with Barnesandnoble.com, do the following:

1. Go to Build Homepages and click Tools.
2. Click Earn Money On Tripod.
3. Choose the Click Here link that corresponds with the Barnes & Noble program.

   At the Barnes & Noble affiliate page, you can join the affiliate program, create a site with Barnes & Noble, or check out more information on the program. By joining this program, you can earn up to 7 percent commission on book sales and 3 percent commission on software sales.
4. At the application page, complete all areas with asterisks (*) next to them. The rest of the information is optional.
5. Before clicking Yes to submit the information, read the Affiliate Network Agreement.

The application takes about a week to process, at which point you will receive a confirmation email that explains how to link to Barnesandnoble.com to start your bookstore.

TIP

Tripod says that there will probably be more affiliate programs on the way, so keep checking the Affiliate Programs page for updates.

HeadHunter.net

HeadHunter.net is a job placement service that helps you make money by driving traffic from your site to HeadHunter.net's site. HeadHunter supplies banners and monitors traffic, and you get $5 for every 1,000 pages viewed by users who link from your site to HeadHunter's.

To register with HeadHunter.net, do the following:

1. Go to Build Homepages and click Tools.
2. Click Earn Money On Tripod.
3. Click the corresponding HeadHunter.net link.
4. If an affiliate site with HeadHunter.net fits your site's theme, choose Click Here to Get Started.
5. Choose Click Here to Get Registered.
6. Complete the form and click Register.
7. Resubmit your email address for confirmation. You will receive an email with your password.

Chip Shot

Chip Shot is a must for any golf-related site. The Chip Shot Partners Program will pay up to 20 percent on sales. You will receive weekly email updates and a monthly check for referrals.

To sign up with Chip Shot, do the following:

1. Go to Build Homepages and click Tools.
2. Click Earn Money On Tripod.
3. Click the corresponding Chip Shot link.
4. Click Become a Part of our Program Today!
5. Read the Operating Agreement and fill out the application.

Cool Links

Tripod's Cool Links (found at Build Homepages) can help you get links to sites that are affiliated with Tripod. These help you build a better site, not make money.

At the Cool Links page (`http://build.tripod.com/hpstudio/cool_links/index.html`), you can copy any of the links from the drop-down boxes and paste the code directly into your site's code (see Figure 9.4). Some of the links are to sections of Tripod and others are to Tripod affiliate pages. You can place a Lycos/Tripod search box on any of your pages to help your visitors search the Web, or you can add a Barnes & Noble or CDnow search box to enable visitors to find books, music, or other products at either of these sites.

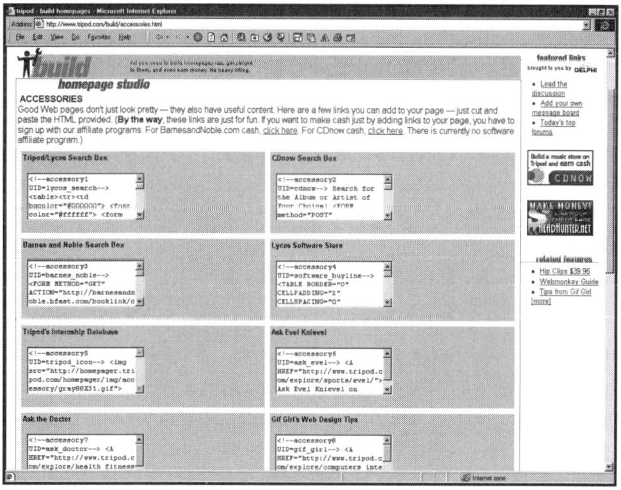

FIGURE 9.4
Some of the Tripod Accessories.

TIP

Be sure to place the code where you want it to appear on your page. In other words, if you want the links at the bottom of the page, don't paste it at the top of your code.

FrontPage Enabling Your Site

FrontPage is a program designed and produced by Microsoft that is used to help create and maintain your site. With this program you can design and create your site on your local computer and then publish it to your Tripod site. You do not need to log on to the Internet to edit or create your site; you can do it all from your computer, and then log on to the Internet to transport the information to your Tripod site. Some components that FrontPage possesses are the ability to add text searches, personal conferences, and more.

To FrontPage enable your site, go to Build Homepages, click Tools, and then select Microsoft FrontPage Enabler.

NOTE

Before signing up for FrontPage, you must read the FAQ for a complete understanding of the program. Trust us, you don't want to read the FAQ after you sign up. This program isn't for everyone, and the FAQ allows you to make an educated decision.

After reading the FAQ and deciding that the program is worth joining, click the Yes, Do It! button to make your site FrontPage enabled. If you are not logged on to your site, Tripod will ask you to enter your username and password and click OK.

Your new URL will be `http://members.tripod.com/`*`username`*, the same as it was before, but without the "~". Don't forget to tell everyone your new URL!

Don't delete any files after enabling FrontPage. This changes the file extensions, and you don't want to undo something that is necessary to run FrontPage. You can still use Tripod's Homepage Builder and Custom Page Editor to edit your site. You will notice that enabling FrontPage extensions adds five directories to your site:

- private
- vti_bin
- vti_cnf
- vti_pvt
- vti_txt

Do not delete or alter these files, which will disable the FrontPage extensions. To help you avoid this problem, Tripod makes it very difficult to delete these files.

FrontPage Enabler is a free service that can be cancelled at any time by going to `http://members.tripod.com/service/frontpage/resetFrontpage`. If you are logged in to your site, the service will be disabled immediately.

CHAPTER 10

ADDING GRAPHICS TO YOUR TRIPOD PAGES

A few short years ago, working on the Internet meant exchanging text and reading glowing green words on small, dark green computer screens. Most of the information was technical and targeted toward researchers. For a while, it was the government types, academicians, and hard-core computer geeks who were having all the fun. Then, the World Wide Web burst onto the scene with a flourish, and the Internet began to draw standing-room-only crowds on an international level. (As you've probably noticed, almost everyone has a Web page these days, from grandma to the President.)

Suddenly, the Internet enabled people to use pictures, images, animations, and other eye-appealing Web page accouterments to communicate on the Net. If you think about it, the arrival of the Web can be likened to the invention of the television during a radio-centric era. Although radios are still in use today, televisions play a much larger role in information dissemination and couch sales. Likewise, even though people continue to swap textual information on the Internet, the graphics are the unifying force of the Internet's popularity.

Now, as you venture to join the Web fray, the power of graphics is passed to you. Carrying that responsibility might seem like a lot of pressure at first, but, as you'll see, adding graphics to your Web page is easy. Further, adding graphics is the quickest way to communicate your ideas and add pizzazz to any page. Adding graphics is what this chapter is all about.

Adding Basic Graphics—The HTML

Before we get to the fun part about how to gather graphics, let's get the nitty-gritty HTML part of our discussion out of the way. It's kind of like eating the peas before enjoying the mashed potatoes. As you work through this section and the next, you might want to open your favorite HTML editor to practice some of the code. (Remember, Tripod provides a couple of handy HTML editors, and there's always Microsoft FrontPage.) For now, you can practice adding a graphic to an HTML document by using any graphic file you have stored on your hard disk, floppy, or CD—just make sure you know the file's path.

The <IMG> Tag

In the HTML world, you add an image to an HTML document by adding a reference within a document that points to an image file. To create an image reference, you use the <IMG> tag. To indicate which image file to which you want the <IMG> tag to point, you use the SRC attribute, like this:

```
<IMG SRC="images/snack_master.gif">
```

The preceding HTML code indicates that you want to include the snack_master image on your Web page.

Further, the code specifies that the snack_master image can be found in a folder named *images*. So, you see, adding an image to an HTML page is basically a matter of telling browsers where to find the image.

Of course, you probably want to control how a graphic appears on your Web page. Well, you're in luck. As with most HTML tags, you can add a number of attributes to modify the <IMG> tag's default settings. For example, you can control where your image aligns by using the ALIGN attribute within the <IMG> tag. To center align the snack_master image, the code would appear like this:

```
<IMG SRC="images/snack_master.gif" ALIGN=CENTER>
```

There are a number of other image attributes, including HEIGHT, WIDTH, ALT, and BORDER to name a few. If you want to play around with image attributes, pick up a good HTML handbook or simply surf the Net and look at other people's Web pages' source code. Additionally, there are a number of tutorials available on the Web. For example, visit Webmonkey at `www.hotwired.com/webmonkey`. Also, always remember to check Tripod's Help pages or Appendix A of this book for quick answers to your HTML questions.

Besides adding standard graphics to your Web pages, you can add a number of other types of graphics that are typically found on Web pages.

Adding Other Graphics—More HTML

As you've most likely noticed, images aren't the only graphics that appear on Web pages. Just like print media, Web pages have graphical elements aside from pretty pictures. For example, you can use images to create lines and backgrounds on your pages. Furthermore, Web pages can include nontraditional graphics, such as buttons and image maps. In this section, we look at some of the tricks and tactics for using graphics as Web page elements.

Rule Lines

The easiest graphical elements that you can add to Web pages are lines, called *rule lines*, or just *rules* for short. Rule lines help you to divide your Web pages into logical sections.

There are two ways you can add rules to your Web pages: You can insert a graphic as the rule line, or you can use standard HTML coding.

To use a graphic as a rule line (there are lots of rule line graphics available on free clip art Web sites, and you can create your own in paint programs as we discuss in a moment), you simply use the <IMG> tag to insert a reference to the rule line graphic on your page. Be sure to follow the <IMG> tag with a
 (link break) tag or enclose the image tag between paragraph tags (<P><IMG SRC+"..."></P>) to ensure that your rule line image appears on its own line. (Otherwise, you might have text wrapping around your rule line, which usually looks really bad.)

To create rule lines using HTML, use the <HR> tag. You can use the <HR> tag's ALIGN and WIDTH attributes to modify the default rule line settings. For example,

```
<HR WIDTH="50" ALIGN="CENTER">
```

creates a 50-pixel-long rule line that appears horizontally centered within the browser window. You can also create rule lines sized as a percentage of the browser screen by using a percent sign in the WIDTH attribute. For example, if you want to center a rule line that takes up 80 percent of the width of a browser window, you would enter:

```
<HR WIDTH="80%" ALIGN="CENTER">
```

There are other attributes available for the <HR> tag. But, the basics are presented here. Again, turn to HTML references, the Web, and Tripod's help files for more in-depth HTML information. You can find many free rules on the Internet. Of course, you can also create your own graphic rules in paint programs. Some key concepts to keep in mind when you create rules for your Web pages include:

- Rule lines should be narrow and roughly 400 to 600 pixels long.
- When you make one rule line, make a set of rule lines of varying length. Then, you can use the rule lines throughout your pages to help create a consistent look and feel.
- Rules that fade from a dark color to white (called gradients) are a stylish alternative to monotone rule lines.
- You should try to use rules that reinforce your page's theme. For example, a string of martinis might make a good divider line on a Web page about nightclubs.

Backgrounds

As you learned earlier in this book, you can apply a background color to your Web pages. As an alternative to supplying a background color, you can use a graphic as a background. You can use graphics in a number of ways. For example, you can tile a small graphic, fill your background with a large graphic, or create a sidebar graphic.

The next few sections describe each of these background techniques.

Tiling Small Graphics

Background graphics can be recognizable graphics or they can be textures. Using an image for a background is similar to using the <IMG> tag; the main idea is to direct browsers to the image file that you want to use on your Web page.

To add an image as a background, use the BACKGROUND attribute in the <BODY> tag, like this:

```
<BODY BACKGROUND="starry_sky.gif">
```

By default, a background image *tiles*, or repeats, both vertically and horizontally until the browser window is filled. (When an image tiles, it repeats from top to bottom and left to right across the Web page—similar to kitchen floor tiles.) Normally, background images are small, somewhat dim graphics (so any text placed over the graphic will show up). You can find lots of samples of background graphics on the Web. Figure 10.1 shows the Nava Art Gallery's good use of tiling a GIF image to create an interesting background. Visit the Nava Art Gallery to see online versions of featured artists.

SMOOTHING BACKGROUNDS

If you're thinking of creating custom backgrounds for your page, make sure you find a resource that explains how to create a seamless background, such as `www.pixelfoundry.com/Toms/Makeback/index.html`. When you use a tiled image for a Web page background, you want to ensure that the edges of the repeated images blend cleanly. Clean edges rarely happen automatically, so learning how to smooth your edges is a worthwhile skill. You might also look at your favorite graphics program; many of the more popular ones include wizards and single-click features to help create seamless tiled images.

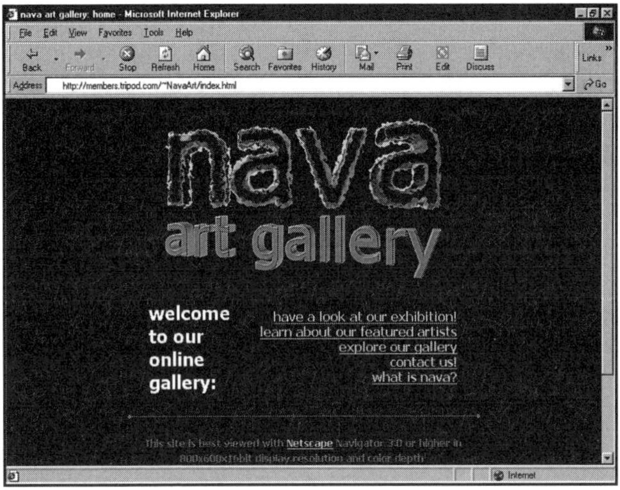

FIGURE 10.1
This site takes advantage of using a tiling GIF image to create an attractive background for the Web page.

Filling Your Background

In addition to using a small graphic that tiles to fill the background of your Web page, you can use a large image to serve as a complete background for your page. To use this approach, simply insert a large picture as the background. Basically, this approach avoids the appearance of tiling by filling the entire background of a page. When you use a background that you don't want to tile, you must be sure that the graphic is large enough. Otherwise, higher resolution systems whose browsers are running in a maximized state might cause the graphic to tile, and the results can be disappointing. If you use a large graphic as a single-image background, make sure you preview your page using a variety of desktop settings and browser window sizes.

NOTE

You can easily create your own backgrounds in paint programs, but before you go through all the trouble, look around on the Web for a variety of free backgrounds. Free backgrounds are available on many clipart sites and on a variety of sites all over the Web. You might start by typing **backgrounds** into the search engine within the Tripod community. Many Tripod members offer backgrounds and links to background sites, thereby speeding up the background search process considerably.

Creating Sidebar Graphics

A *sidebar background* is a background image that is so long that it ends up tiling in a stacked manner. The result is that the background creates a pattern that runs down a page. Most commonly, sidebar backgrounds are used to create a stationary-type of look, with a color or textured band displaying down the left side of the page. Figure 10.2 shows some sidebar backgrounds provided on the Kozmik Pearl page at `http://members.tripod.com/~KozmikPearl/sidebars.html`. Figure 10.3 shows a simple sidebar that adds to the attractiveness of the Angler's Guide (`http://members.tripod.com/bassmster/`).

Buttons

After you're comfortable adding backgrounds to your Web pages, you are ready to graduate to using buttons as graphics. As you know from surfing the Web, virtual buttons come in more styles than any notions shop could possibly stock. You can create Web page buttons as individual images, or you can group them together in a single image to create an image map. You can find a number of tutorials on the Web describing how to make buttons and image maps.

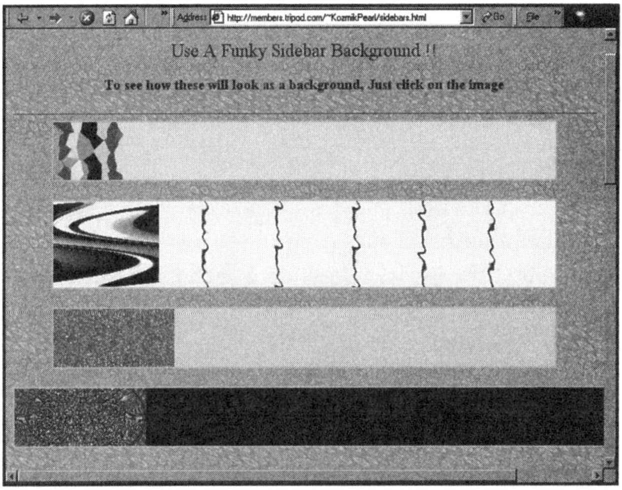

FIGURE 10.2
The Kozmik Pearl page features some sample sidebar backgrounds.

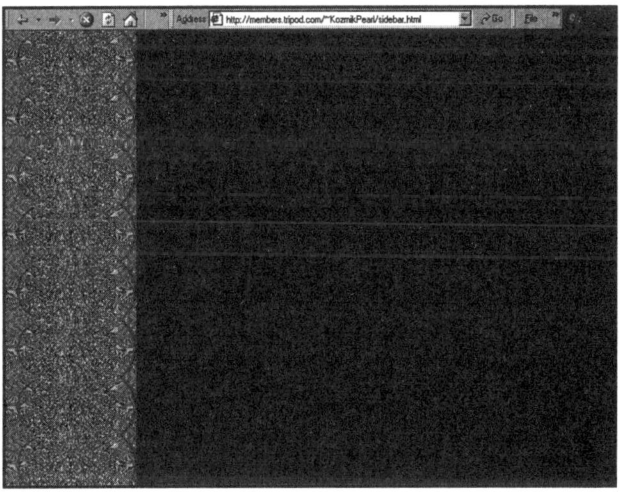

FIGURE 10.3
The Angler's Guide uses a sidebar to add to the site's clean design.

One of the most common uses of buttons is to replace a hyperlink with a button. Basically, to use a button as a hyperlink, you simply replace the hyperlink text in an HTML document with an <IMG> reference, like this:

```
<A HREF="target_file.html"> <IMG
SRC="cool_button_graphic.gif"> </A>
```

In the preceding code, you can see that the anchor tags surround the image reference. When users click the cool_button_graphic.gif image, they are taken to the target_file.html page.

Usually, buttons are small rectangular, oval, or circular graphics that contain text that describes the type of page to which the button is linked. For example, a button labeled HOME usually means that the button will take you to the site's home page. Sometimes, in place of button text, Web page designers use a simple picture or icon (such as a picture of a house). Before you decide what type of buttons you want to use on your site, take a look at some buttons on the Web. See what styles, color combinations, fonts, and graphics work for you, and then blend what you like best into custom buttons that suit your needs and represent your site's motif.

Image Maps

If you are really motivated, you can create an *image map* on your page. An image map is a graphic that is formatted to contain clickable areas. Each clickable area links users to a different Internet resource. For example, you could have a picture of the Scooby Doo gang on your Web page, and then you could make each one of the "meddling kids" a clickable resource. Users could click Thelma to visit the Clues page or click Scooby Doo to see popular Scooby Snack recipes.

Creating an image map is a two-part process. First, you have to obtain an image. Then, you have to mark off parts of the image to serve as hyperlinks. You can create the links by using an image map editor. Image map editors automatically create the HTML code that makes an image map work.

Some image map editor programs that you can use to create image maps are LiveImage (`www.mediatec.com`) and MapMaker (`tns-www.lcs.mit.edu/cgi-bin/mapmaker`). Using MapMaker, you can create image maps online. You can also create image maps by hand, in conjunction with a paint program, some patience, and a piece of paper and pencil (for keeping notes regarding where on the image each clickable area occurs). Again, refer to online Web tutorials, HTML reference guides, and design books for instructions on creating image maps.

Congratulations! You've made it through the technical side of adding graphics to your Web page. The remainder of this chapter deals with the more leisurely issues of graphic file formats and graphic acquisitions. At this point, you should have an inkling of what it takes to add a graphic to your Web page. To summarize:

- You need an HTML document.
- You need an <IMG> tag within your HTML document.
- You need a graphic file that the <IMG> tag can reference.

We've covered the first two bulleted items. Let's move on to the third.

Looking At Web Graphics

Before you can find something, you have to know what you're looking for. Therefore, before hunting down the perfect graphics, we need to clarify the finer points of Web graphics in general.

As you probably know, graphics (whether on the Web or not) have always served multiple purposes. For example, all those portraits hanging in the Louvre can be considered works of art, wall decor (depending on the subject), or historical documentation. Similarly (and closer to home), snapshots can serve as remembrances of an especially enjoyable vacation, embarrassing driver's license mug shots, or even evidence in court. Clearly, classifying graphics is tricky business. But, placing the general multifaceted nature of graphics aside, Web graphics can be loosely classified into two categories: illustrative items and interface elements.

Illustrative graphics include photographs, charts, drawings, and artwork. These graphics represent the picture-says-a-thousand-words contributions to your page. In contrast, *interface graphics* include buttons, rule lines, banners, backgrounds, and image maps (you should be familiar with those concepts from earlier in this chapter). Interface graphics are the workhorse complements to your Web page's illustrative graphics and text. Of course, returning to the nature of graphics, illustrative and interface roles often overlap. In other words, illustrative graphics often serve interface purposes (such as a photograph that is also a hyperlink), and vice versa. Figure 10.4 shows both illustrative and interface graphics. If you'd like to visit this page, point your browser to `http://members.tripod.com/MrSuave`.

The key to choosing Web page graphics can be summarized in two words: *appeal* and *size*. Obviously, you want to keep your graphics appealing, but they should also be no larger than 20K, if you can help it. This makes sense, because, as you know, large, complex graphics (the one's that take minutes to download) are clearly unappealing to Web surfers, no matter how awesome the graphic looks after (or if) it makes it to a user's desktop. Fortunately, the Web helps out somewhat on this issue by only accepting certain graphic file formats.

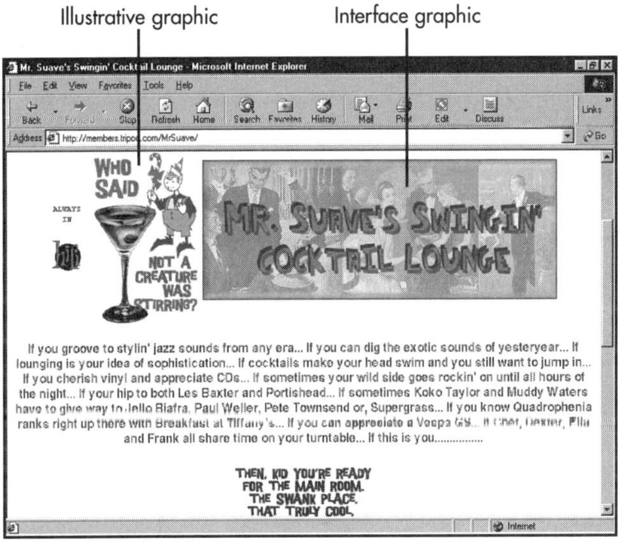

FIGURE 10.4
Mr. Suave's Web site uses graphics for illustrative as well as interface roles. You can click the main graphic to enter Mr. Suave's Web site.

WEB-FRIENDLY GRAPHIC FILE FORMATS

In a nutshell, the popular browsers recognize three basic graphic file formats: GIF, JPEG, and PNG. In other words, graphic files that have those extensions (picture.gif, picture.jpeg, and picture.png) are recognized by most popular Web browsers. These file formats are all compressed (saved as efficiently as possible) to help speed up transmission time. Of course, an image stored in these formats won't download fast automatically—it'll just download faster than it would if it was stored in another graphic file format (if that format was supported on the Web).

GIF (Graphics Interchange Format)

GIFs are the most widely used graphics on the Web. They load fast and take up small amounts of space. The GIF format supports 8-bit graphics, which means the graphics are limited to 256 colors. GIFs are great for graphics that don't require many colors (for example, many icons and buttons are GIF files).

A widely used feature supported by GIFs is transparency. This means that GIFs enable you to assign one color in the image as a transparent color. Then, when a browser shows the GIF, the transparent color enables the Web page background to show through. That's how Web pages create the illusion of nonrectangular figures.

Finally, an animated GIF is a special version of the GIF file format that enables you to create animations by layering graphic files. Each graphic file is slightly changed from the previous file, and then they are cycled through to create an animation—just like those old-fashioned flip books. Moving icons are prime examples of animated GIFs.

Many sites provide animated GIFs that you can download and use on your Web page. In addition, you can try to create your own by

- Obtaining an animated GIF program. Turn to the Web to find some good animated GIF programs. For example, visit Dierk's download page at `www.anicursor.com/download.html#creag` for some animated GIF editors (see Figure 10.5).

- There are newer graphic editors specifically for the Web, like Macromedia's Fireworks and Adobe Image Ready which include support for animated GIFs. Paint Shop Pro 5 also includes an Animated GIF editor known as Animation Shop.
- Drawing the frames of your animation.

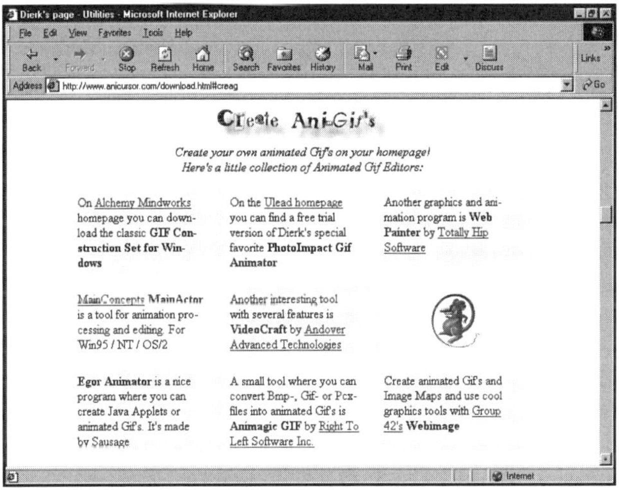

FIGURE 10.5
You can find a number of animated GIF editors on the Web.

Perform a quick search for the term *GIF* using Tripod's search bar, and you'll get almost 240,000 links to GIF-related resources (animated, transparent, and plain GIFs). For example, visit Johnny's GIF Gallery at `http://members.tripod.com/~Johnny05/gallery.htm`. You can also search Tripod's media library at `http://build.tripod.com/hpstudio/medialibrary/index.html`. Finally, you can use Lycos to find GIFs on the Web by searching for: *GIF AND collection*. Lycos rewards you with a long list of GIF collections on the Web.

JPEG (Joint Photographic Experts Group)

JPEG stands for *Joint Photographic Experts Group*, which is the name of the group that created this file format. JPEGs support millions of colors, so photographs that you see on the Web are usually JPEGs. JPEGs compress well and can be encoded as Standard or Progressive. Standard Encoding means that the JPEG image loads line by line—from top to bottom. Progressive Encoding means that the image slowly loads into focus. In other words, progressing encoded images appear blurry at first, but they slowly become more focused as the data is downloaded.

Figure 10.6 shows a JPEG image of the Big Buddha in Kamakura, Japan (`http://members.tripod.com/GlennH/wa_japan.htm`). This site is filled with JPEG images from Japan, Hawaii, Singapore, Malaysia, and many other countries. Click the Wanderings link to see a listing of adventures Glenn shares on his Web pages—the JPEGs he shares on his site are often astounding.

PNG (Portable Network Graphics)

PNG stands for *Portable Network Graphics*. The PNG format is a new format, which means only the newer versions—4.0 or better—of Microsoft Internet Explorer and Netscape Navigator support them (currently, this is a drawback that only time can diminish). PNG was created in response to the news that the makers of GIF's compression algorithm decided to start to enforce the algorithm's patent. You really don't need to know what that means (it's like the government—you try not to look too closely to see what's going on), just know that PNG is a newer alternative to GIF.

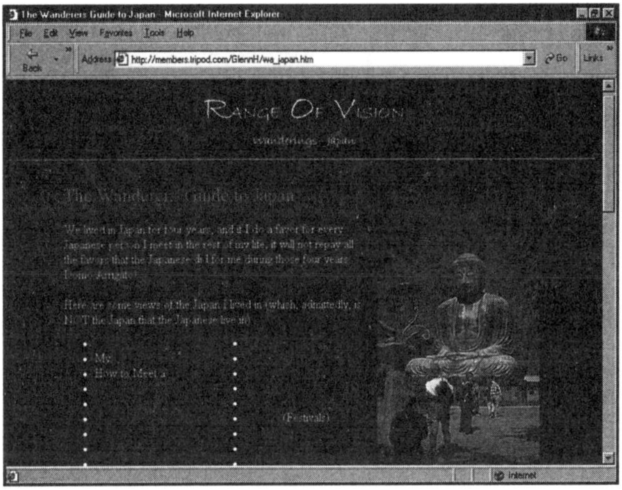

FIGURE 10.6
Visit Glenn Hughes' Tripod page to enjoy Glenn's wanderings and wonderings around and about the world.

PNGs support the same types of graphics as GIFs, but PNGs have a more powerful compression scheme. If you'd like to learn more about PNGs, you can visit the official PNG Groups home page at `www.group42.com`. Figure 10.7 shows the PNG Group's home page. You'll find lots of information and tools, and even some free "Psycho Clip Art" on the products page.

So those are the acceptable graphic files formats—GIF, JPEG, and PNG. All the graphics you use on your Web page should be saved in one of those formats. That's all well and good you say, but, there you are—still sitting and ready to create a Web page, with nary a graphic at hand. Or so you think. As you'll see in the next section, the reality is that you have lots of graphics on hand and many more within reach.

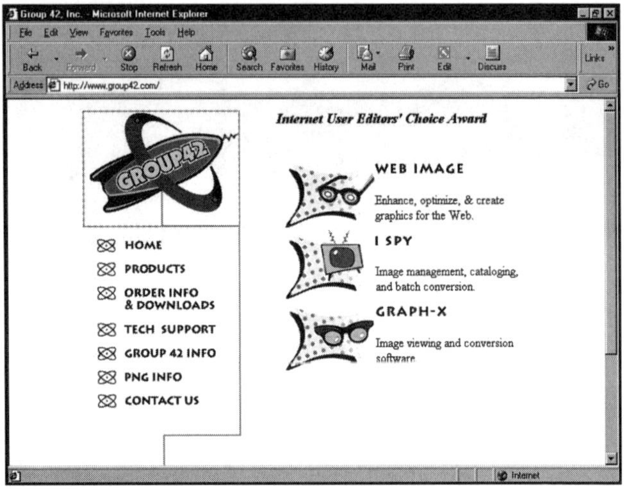

FIGURE 10.7
Visit the PNG Group's Web site for the latest PNG information and tools.

ACQUIRING GRAPHICS

Finally, you're ready to acquire graphics for your Web page. Lucky for you, Web graphics are plentiful—you just need to know where to find them. You can obtain graphics in a number of ways. For example, you can

- Buy clip art CD-ROMs, available at your nearest computer store retailer (as well as any other place that sells computer software).
- Use clip art that comes with applications you already have on your computer.
- Download images from Web collections.

The last option—downloading images from Web collections—presents a wealth of opportunity. You can download freeware or you can purchase clipart from major vendors. To download an image from a free Web collection (or to download almost any other Web graphic)

1. Display the image you want to download.
2. Right-click the image, and save the image to your computer.

This short process saves the image to your computer and makes a local copy of the image available for you to use and modify as you wish.

As previously mentioned, you can also buy graphics online. Some recommended vendors include

- **Artville** `www.artville.com`
- **Corbis** `www.corbis.com`
- **Cyberphoto** `www.cyberphoto.com`
- **DiAMAR Interactive** `www.diamar.com`
- **EyeWire** `www.eyewire.com`
- **Goodshoot** `www.goodshoot.com`
- **John Foxx Images** `www.johnfoxx.com`
- **Photodisc** `www.photodisc.com`
- **PhotoEssentials** `www.photoessentials.com`
- **Rubberball** `www.rubberball.com`

In addition to finding and purchasing graphics, you can create graphics for your Web page. If you own a scanner or if you know how to use a digital camera, you're well on your way to creating Web graphics.

Creating Web Graphics

First things first—if you'll be creating your own graphics, get some resources. You might want to pick up some Web graphic handbooks that explain how to keep file sizes small (such as by limiting the number of colors in your images by using color palettes). And, check out popular graphics sites on the Internet. For example, visit the Creating Killer Web Sites page (`www.killersites.com`) for graphics tips and other Web page creation information.

Another good site packed with Web graphics information and a generous supply of tutorials is the Media Builder site at `www.mediabuilder.com/graphicstutor.html`. And, for a long list of graphic design links on the Web, visit Ellen's Place at `www.ionet.net/~jellenc/graphic.html`. Finally, visit Candie's Peppermint Graphics site at `http://members.tripod.com/~MintGraphics/links.htm` (see Figure 10.8). The Candie's site has links to a number of popular graphic tutorial sites on the Web, including HandsOn With Dr. Ozone and Andy's Art Attack sites.

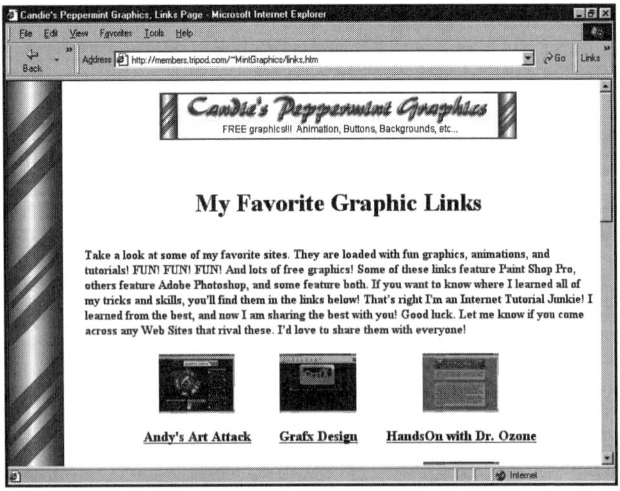

FIGURE 10.8

Candie's Peppermint Graphics site is one of Tripod's many sites dedicated to helping others design graphics and Web pages.

All right—we've talked; we've tossed around some HTML; you've surfed; now, it's time to get down to the business of creating your own graphics. You can create graphics in a number of ways. Specifically, you can scan pictures, use a digital camera, use your computer's video camera, and work with a graphics program.

Scanning For Quick Results

If you have photographs lying around, you're on your way to having Web page graphics. One of the easiest ways to acquire a Web graphic is to scan a photograph by using a traditional flatbed scanner, such as Hewlett-Packard's ScanJet. Basically, a scanner takes a picture of your photograph and saves it as a file on your computer. After you have scanned a picture, you can manipulate the file just as you manipulate any other graphic files. When you scan photographs, you usually have to clean them up a little before you use the picture on your Web page. You can use graphics programs, such as Paint Shop Pro, to clean up your pictures. Most Web graphic books describe techniques for cleaning up scanned images.

There are a number of popular scanners around, including:

- Agfa (a favorite among graphic artists)
- Microtek (popular among production types)
- Umax (good quality for relatively low price)

If you don't have a scanner, you can purchase one for $99 and up. If you're a casual user, you can probably get by with using a low-to-medium-level scanner (priced around the $200 to $500 range). Before you buy a scanner, check out major computer magazines, such as *PC Magazine*, and their Web sites to read up on the latest scanner deals. (Turning to magazines and Web sites before buying any new hardware is always a good idea.)

NOTE

Once again, the Web proves to be one of your most valuable resources for Web page design. If you're looking for scanning tips—from how to buy a scanner to cleaning up your scanned images—visit the A Few Scanning Tips Web page at `www.scantips.com`.

Newer breeds of scanners include slide/film and photoscanners. Slide/film scanners scan film strips or high-quality slides directly. These scanners cost from $800 to $2,000, so this type of scanner represents a major investment. Photoscanners represent the opposite end of the spectrum. Photoscanners scan snapshots—basic 3.5" × 5" and 4" × 6" photographs. Photoscanners are inexpensive—you should be able to get one for $150 to $200—and some computers even have them built in. For casual users, photoscanners present a good, inexpensive way to create scanned images.

Finally, you can use PhotoNet. Basically, PhotoNet provides an option by which you can pay other people to scan your photographs. With Kodak's PhotoNet service (see Figure 10.9), you drop off your film at one of 40,000 participating retailers and request PhotoNet online. When you pick up your prints and negatives, you will receive a claim card with an Access Code and a secure Owner's Key so you can view your photos online.

To view your photos, go to `http://kodak78.photonet.com/account.htm` and create a free account (or log in to your existing account). Click Pick Up Photos, and enter the Access Code and Owner's Key.

You can share the Web address information with friends, family, and coworkers so that they can view and download the images or even order prints, if they desire.

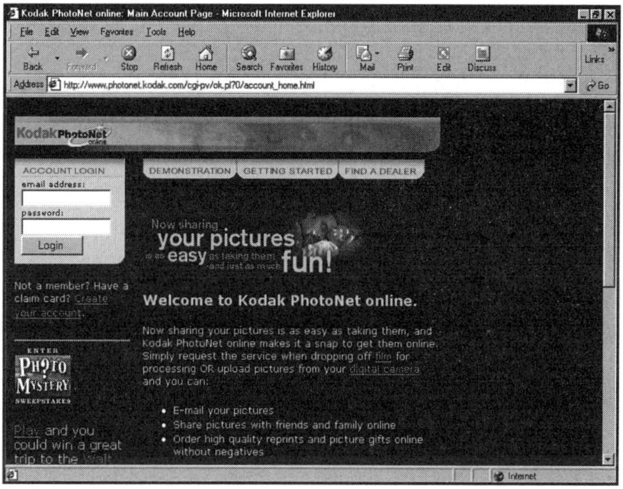

FIGURE 10.9
Consider using PhotoNet services to develop your film as scanned images instead of prints.

Finally, other companies provide scanning services aside from the PhotoNet service. For example, Seattle Filmworks (`www.filmworks.com`), one of the older Web-based photo developers around, scans your film and emails the files to you. All you do is send them your film and indicate that you'd like a scanned picture. Within a few days, they'll email scanned versions of your pictures, ready for you to use on your Web page. Along those same lines, Seattle Filmworks also saves your images to disk or CD, if you request that option on the order form.

Along the similar lines as scanning, you can also take pictures with special cameras—called digital cameras—for the express purpose of creating digital files.

USING DIGITAL CAMERAS

Now that digital cameras are becoming more reasonably priced, they are quickly becoming popular among computer professionals as well as computer hobbyists. A digital camera enables you to snap a picture and then instantly download the picture into your computer. Digital cameras create a quick-and-easy way to convert pictures into a digital format. The main drawback is that, while digital camera prices are coming down, most affordable digital cameras do not operate with fancy lenses and other features included with most 35mm cameras. The few digital cameras that offer 35mm capabilities cost well into the thousands of dollars, which makes them impractical for most people creating Web pages.

You might be interested in purchasing a digital camera for your own use. There are a number of digital cameras on the market, and most people know very little about digital camera basics. Here, as usual, a little homework helps you to purchase the best tool for your needs. Following are some hints and tips you can use when looking to purchase a digital camera:

- **Determine your needs** Can you get by with low-resolution (640 × 480) images? If so, you can probably purchase a digital camera for under $400. If you need higher resolutions (1024 × 768 and greater), a camera will probably run you from $600 to $1,000.
- **Go online** Visit C|Net's Computers.com Web site (`www.computers.com`) and Ziff-Davis's Computer Shopper.com site (`www.zdnet.com/computershopper`) to find reviews, prices, and other information about the latest digital cameras.

- **Go window shopping** Wander around camera shops and other consumer electronic outlets to get a feel for what types of cameras people are selling, buying, and recommending.
- **Pick up a magazine or two** Read the reviews in major computing magazines and on computing magazines' Web sites. Most computing magazines thrive on presenting comparison lists for hardware products.
- **Look under the hood** Remember, instead of using film, you'll be using a lot of batteries. Many cameras offer power packs that you can use when using the camera near an electrical source. You might also look into buying a battery charger and rechargeable batteries.
- **Count the pictures** The number of photos digital cameras can hold in memory varies depending upon whether the camera offers removable memory cards, and whether the camera offers a preview screen.
- **Visit Tripod member sites** A number of Tripod sites discuss how to buy digital cameras. For example, visit `http://members.tripod.com/~redhawk2007/dcool.htm` and `http://members.tripod.com/~Images_On_Line/cameras/cameras0.htm` for checklist and feature considerations when you are buying a digital camera.

Capturing Video

Another quick way to get snapshots onto your computer is to use a computer video camera, such as a QuickCam. These types of video cameras are becoming increasingly popular for online conferencing purposes. You can purchase a video camera starting around $70 and moving on up into the hundreds-of-dollars range. Most video cameras come with software that enables you to take a "snapshot" of your video—basically, a still shot obtained from the video. Using your computer's video camera to take a snapshot is a good way to create pictures directly on your computer. This tactic is especially handy if you're gathering pictures of people and pets. For more on capturing video, see Chapter 11, "Adding Multimedia to Your Tripod Pages."

Using Graphics Programs

Finally, if you're feeling creative, you can create your own graphics for your Web pages. You can use any paint program, such as Paint Shop Pro, Adobe Image Ready, and Photoshop to name a few. As mentioned earlier in the chapter, you can use paint programs to create your own background images, buttons, rule lines, animated GIFs, and other Web page graphics. In addition, you can use paint programs to clean up scanned photographs and to modify existing graphics.

Many Web design books are packed with information describing how to use paint programs, and the Web is home to lots of graphics tutorials. You can also visit many graphic programs' product Web sites for downloadable programs, tips, hints, and links to valuable resources. Here's a small sampling of just a few of the helpful graphics program Web sites:

- **Paint Shop Pro 5** `www.jasc.com` (shareware)
- **Adobe Image Ready** `www.adobe.com`
- **Adobe Photoshop** `www.adobe.com`
- **Lemke Software's Graphic Converter 3.3.1** (for the Mac) `www.lemkesoft.de/us_gcdownload.html`

You can use a graphics program to

- Modify existing images
- Create your own images
- Recolor images
- Resize graphics
- Crop pictures

Whenever you work with a Web graphic in a graphics program, remember to save the file as GIF, JPEG (JPG), or PNG.

Compressing JPEGs

If you save your graphic as a JPEG, you should try various compression levels to achieve optimal results. Keep in mind that the more you compress a JPEG image the smaller the file size is. However, a highly compressed JPEG image does not appear as sharp as it does when it is less compressed. Save your JPEGs with various compression levels to see what level works best for your needs.

Drawing Tablets

If you're pretty good with freehand drawing, consider purchasing a drawing tablet. Drawing tablets are special pressure-sensitive tablets that you can use to create pictures on your computer. Most graphics packages support drawing tablets (including Paint Shop Pro). Wacom, Inc. (`www.wacom.com`) offers a number of popular drawing tablets that range from $150 to $700.

By now, you should know how to place graphics into HTML documents and what tactics you can use to acquire graphics for your Web page. You know the basics. Now, the final section of this chapter introduces some fine tuning issues that you should keep in mind when working with Web page imagery.

Fine Tuning Graphics—Colors and Size

After you've gathered and created your Web graphics, there are a couple of key ways to make your Web graphics conform to the "appeal and size" requirements discussed at the beginning of this chapter. Specifically, you can reduce the number of colors in an image and limit an image's size.

Reducing Colors

You are more likely to keep your graphics' file sizes small if you use fewer colors and larger areas of solid color. When creating or choosing graphics for your site, try to keep the number of colors in an image to a minimum. Most graphics programs offer a variety of color reduction tools. At times, you might need to use as many colors as possible, but in general, fewer colors means smaller files—and smaller files means faster loading pages.

NOTE

A *browser-safe palette* is a specialized palette consisting of 216 colors that are shared by all the major browsers for both Windows and Macintosh. Using this palette ensures that your images appear the same in all browsers. This brings up an important point—you should always test your images by viewing them in the major browsers with your computer set at the 256-color mode. If you are not happy with the quality, optimize the image and reapply the palette.

Reducing Image Dimensions

Last but not least, you should consider the size of your graphics. Smaller graphics mean smaller file sizes. As long as an image seems to maintain its detail and sharpness, keep resizing it smaller.

One tactic used on some Web pages is to create thumbnails (smaller versions of larger photographs). In this presentation format, designers often provide a set of thumbnails (miniature versions of images), and users click the thumbnails to see a larger, more detailed picture. You can display a gallery of the thumbnails, which loads more quickly than a gallery of full-sized graphics. After the thumbnails are loaded, users can click to see larger versions of selected images.

To create a thumbnail, simply use your graphics package to shoot the image in question down to a smaller size and save the new image under a different name. Place the new image on your page, and link it to the larger image so that when someone clicks the thumbnail, the larger image loads.

Looking Good

As you can see, finding graphics for your Web pages isn't hard—graphics are everywhere, if you know where to look. Furthermore, including images on your Web pages is simply a matter of revisiting your favorite HTML editor. Hopefully at this point, you feel that obtaining graphics isn't the challenge. Instead, the challenge lies in deciding which graphics to use and where to place them on your page. Above all, remember to experiment as you work with graphics. One of the most creatively freeing aspects of the Web is that nothing is set in stone—if you don't like it, change it!

Graphics are great, but there's no need to stop there. How about some multimedia! Let's move on to Chapter 11.

CHAPTER 11

ADDING MULTIMEDIA TO YOUR TRIPOD PAGES

When it comes to adding a little pizzazz to your site, nothing does the trick like a little multimedia. Whether it is animation, sound, a video file, or some combination of all three, a multimedia element on your page can make it come alive like nothing else. The problem is that all that glory comes with a cost—multimedia files can be big and bandwidth-heavy. Although streaming technologies like RealAudio and RealVideo have helped, multimedia is still among the most costly of items to add to a page in terms of the time needed to experience it and the amount of your available home page space it can take up.

Despite the drawbacks, many site builders are learning to effectively add multimedia elements to their sites. By minimizing bandwidth issues and using multimedia in clever and strategic ways, smart designers are having their cake and eating it too when it comes to the benefits of multimedia.

And Tripod doesn't turn its back on people who want pages full of multimedia, sounds, and animation either. By giving you 11MB of space, you have more than enough room to support larger multimedia files. Tripod also offers media libraries of sounds and video clips to add to your site. In partnership with `Thingsworld.com`, Tripod also offers you the ability to place multimedia Things on your page.

Forms of Multimedia

Three classic forms of multimedia are found on the Web: vanilla audio, plain video files, and multimedia applets (single files that can contain video, graphics, text, sound, and music). As the Web has grown from its early days, and as new file formats and technologies have arrived, many derivatives of these three areas have been developed. Today we can identify close to fifteen different types of multimedia files one might post on a site. Only a few formats, however, have become widely used and supported on the Web.

Audio

Dozens of different audio file types are in existence today. The most popular on the Web can be broken into three categories: digitized audio, streaming digitized audio, and synthesized audio.

Digitized audio includes the two most popular formats supported by the Netscape and Microsoft browsers—.wav and .au. A .wav file is the major file format for digitized audio clips on the Windows platform. .au is the .wav file format equivalent for the Unix operating system. Both formats are widely used, although .wav seems to be the most often posted. AIFF files can sometimes be encountered, especially among Mac-oriented sites.

A relatively new format known as MP3 has come to the forefront recently. Featuring a 12:1 compression ratio and excellent fidelity, it has become the new favorite standard for distributing CD-quality music tracks. MP3 files have been receiving a lot of attention because many people are using this format to offer CD-Quality tracks of their favorite songs to others. This is fine so long as those tracks are legal to redistribute. If you have a band of your own, using your Tripod site to redistribute one or two of your band's songs can be a great way to promote yourself using your free Tripod home page.

What they give back in quality in comparison to well-done .wav or .au files, the two major streaming audio formats—RealAudio and ASF (Active Streaming Format)—make up for in immediate availability. By streaming the file down to the user, your visitors will begin hearing the audio as soon as the first few seconds are accessed by the media player they've installed. RealAudio is the dominant streaming audio format and ASF is a Microsoft alternative.

Finally there is synthesized audio. By using the synthesizer chips that are built into most computers and sound cards, Midi files (.mid) and Beatnik Files (A Midi derivative created by Thomas Dolby) are incredibly small in comparison with their length. That is because little actual sound data has to be stored in the file. Midi files are the most popular and can be found throughout the Web. Beatnik files are also known as .rmf files (Rich Music Format) and are created by a special editor from HeadSpace, the company behind the format. Although MIDI files don't require a special plug-in for most browsers, Beatnik files do.

VIDEO

Even though dozens of specialized video formats (known as *codecs*) exist, only a few key file types dominate the world of online video. In all cases, the file types break into two key categories: digitized video clips, and streaming video clips.

The most popular major video clip formats are .avi files, QuickTime files, and MPEG files. An .avi file is primarily a Windows-based format and files of this sort can be widely found on the Web even though QuickTime files are supported by both Mac and PCs. This is because, until recently, Windows users had to install a special QuickTime player to view QuickTime movies. Today the newest version of the Windows Media Player enables you to replay QuickTime files. MPEG (Motion Pictures Experts Group) is an industry standard format that isn't used as much, despite its very high quality for video playback.

Three major formats of streaming video exist. RealVideo is perhaps the most widely supported format, as it is supported by the millions of RealMedia players people have downloaded from RealNetworks in the past few years. Vivo Movies are another popular streaming format. Now a part of RealNetworks, the Vivo movie format has a good following because the movies don't require much special server power to stream to end users. Finally, as with streaming audio, Microsoft has developed an alternative format from RealVideo known as ASF (Active Streaming Format supports video as well as audio). Despite Microsoft's backing, it still isn't used nearly as much as RealVideo or even Vivo.

Animation/Multimedia Applets

In the early days of the Web, Macromedia took its multimedia development tool (Director) and, in a bold move, changed the playback system for Director files. Instead of only being able to be played back from a hard drive or CD, they could be played back directly from the Web in a Web browser. They called the new system Shockwave, and it positioned Director as the development tool of choice for creating single file multimedia applets for the Web.

Macromedia later purchased another tool, known then as Futuresplash, which enabled people to create vector graphic-based animations and renamed the product Macromedia Flash! (see Figure 11.1). Because they use mathematical formulas to create smooth vector graphics, Flash! files are very small in comparison to other forms of multimedia files. Over time Macromedia has added more features to Flash! to support bit-mapped graphics, streaming playback for faster loading, and sound. It has become a highly used multimedia format on the Web.

Provided you can create the files, your Tripod site supports both Flash! and Shockwave/Director multimedia files. In both cases you develop the files using Macromedia's development tools, Director, or the Flash! editor. You then post the finished file to your site. Users then can surf to the site and, if they have the right plug-in or Java capability installed in their browsers, can view the file. Most of the major Web browsers install support for Shockwave and Flash files automatically.

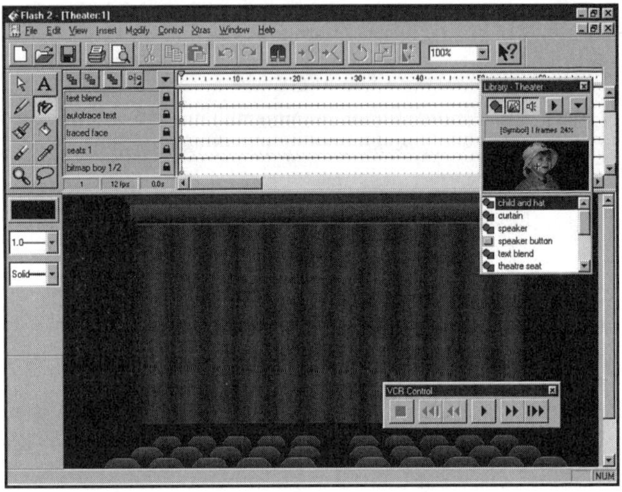

FIGURE 11.1
Macromedia's Flash Editor.

Flash! and Shockwave aren't the only forms of multimedia you can use on your site. A popular additional multimedia technology called, well, Things from ThingWorld (`www.thingworld.com`) is available to Tripod members (see Figure 11.2). Things are small multimedia applets that you can add to your page. A Thing is a story that is told in three states. It has a natural or default state in which the Thing is introduced. In this state, the Thing might blink, wiggle, or play an animation. When you place your mouse over a Thing, it begins to tell its tale. When you click the Thing, the end of the story unfolds. As you interact with them, Things change color, make sounds, and come to life. These Things can be used to spice up your home page almost like decorations on a Christmas tree. ThingWorld makes available a number of Things on its site including the characters of Comedy Central's South Park, Curious George, and Hasbro's Monopoly game.

FIGURE 11.2
Tripod gives you access to ThingWorld.com's Multimedia Things collection. Choose one and put it on your site.

A Pause to Talk about Copyright Issues

When it comes to copyright issues and the Web, some of the biggest problems involve multimedia elements. So much of the best content one might use as multimedia on a site is in fact copyrighted material. We've all seen the archives of sound clips from people's favorite movies, or the video snippets of interviews of famous celebrities or athletes. Entire songs are now being distributed illegally via the MP3 music format. The Internet contains a virtual flood of multimedia that is technically illegal to post.

So why does this happen so much? Why don't companies enforce their copyrights? Why do people still build pages to their favorite show, star, movie, or singer and load them up with sounds, movies, photos, and music that is essentially not of their own creation? These are questions worth understanding because, depending on the site you're building, it pays to understand the specific laws concerning multimedia copyright and how they are playing out on the Web.

What Does Copyright Mean and What is Copyrighted?

A copyright protects the original creator of a work from others who would use the work without providing compensation or credit. Most copyright law deals with what is known as "intellectual property," which is any property that, because of how it is developed, can be reproduced from the original. This can include photos, music recordings, video, software, and writing.

Just because something can be copied doesn't mean it can be copyrighted. For example, an idea or thought can't be copyrighted, but the presentation of that idea or thought can be. Items that aren't original in a satisfactory form can't be copyrighted by another person. And, based on U.S. law, works that are said to be in the "public domain" are not able to be copyrighted, and thus are free to use. This includes all works published before January 1, 1992, and works produced by the government (for example, photos provided by NASA) among others.

In short, consider anything of any creative value to be copyrighted unless you can definitively prove otherwise or there is a verified disclaimer that states you can use that work under specific rules (for example, clip art companies might let you use their art after you pay a fee.)

THE FAIR USE RULE

Many a Web page creator can get tripped up by the concept of "fair use" as it pertains to copyright. The concept of "fair use" is to allow people to copy a specific copyrighted work without consequence, as long as the use of that copy is for a fair purpose. An example often given is a reviewer quoting from a book as part of a critique or a teacher using a reproduction of a painting for classroom purposes.

Where many people get caught is when they assume that their copying falls within fair use. Most often this is rooted in using a copyrighted work on a personal home page that isn't "commercial" by nature. This is because people feel a copyright isn't violated because they're not making money off of it. However, that's not entirely true, and it is such a gray area that you risk being caught in violation of copyright law even if you're not trying to sell the work.

Another fair use that has been cited often is what is known as a derivative work. This is the process of taking a copyrighted work and then twisting it and changing it so much that it becomes something new. Courts have upheld these rights, especially for things like parodies and musical sampling, but not all the time. In many musical cases, if the sample that was used wasn't changed enough and was obviously too close to the original, artists have successfully sued.

In short, consider carefully whether you are using fair use properly or are using fair use to make an excuse for copyright violation. When in doubt about fair use, you're probably in danger.

THE "CATCH ME IF YOU CAN" METHOD

Many personal home page users put up video and audio clips of a copyrightable nature because they're not worried about being caught. The thinking usually falls along the lines of "I'm doing this television show (or movie, actor, musician, and so on) a favor by promoting it and its work." The thinking is that, if all of this work is in good taste and is doing some good for fans of the subject and the subject itself, what's a little copyright violation between friends? Many site operators also figure that companies won't spend the time it takes to track them down and prosecute them.

All this is true to some extent—until someone gets stung. On the first note, many multimedia clips produced about certain subjects are not copyrighted by the subjects themselves. For example, an interview from Entertainment Tonight of your favorite actor is copyrighted by Paramount, the producer of Entertainment Tonight, not the actor. The actor might love that you're playing their interviews for all his or her fans to see, but Paramount might think differently. On a second note, more and more companies that hold copyrights on articles, interviews, videos, music, and so on are going after people who copy their work. Don't assume that you won't at least get a letter from an attorney or from Tripod asking you to remove the content immediately.

In short, people get away with things all the time, but even with the best of intentions you might find yourself on the opposite end of people who don't care about all the good cheer you're spreading.

The "Turn a Blind Eye" Paradox

There is a saying that all publicity is good publicity. It is probably what causes some companies to sit somewhat idly by while people violate their copyrights. For example, Comedy Central, the creators of South Park certainly turned a blind eye for a bit while huge South Park sound and video archives proliferated throughout the Internet. It helped make South Park the hit that it is.

Many times, TV shows and movie producers love the attention the "fan sites" give them. The same can be said for musicians and other performance-oriented mediums. However, as stated above, don't let this give you an air of comfort, because a key rule of copyright law says protect it or lose it. Essentially, the laws concerning copyrights force a company to go after people violating its copyright, or they risk losing the copyright. So even if Comedy Central loves all the South Park fan sites, they might have to be strict about copyright issues despite the PR boost.

The Future: Embrace and Supply

How does a company like Comedy Central rectify the issues concerning copyright, its fan sites, and its own need to keep everyone happy and enthusiastic about South Park? The solution many companies like Comedy Central are finding is to create "fan kits" and authorized downloadable files. Essentially, they embrace the free sharing and fan site ethics of places like the home pages you can build on Tripod and extend to people multimedia they can use with permission. In many cases, this multimedia might be superior to the illegally copied versions of multimedia found elsewhere. Who better to create quality .wav files and multimedia animations of South Park than Comedy Central itself?

In short, creative companies are finding ways to allow fans to build home pages without violating copyright laws. If you're building a fan site of any kind, it can be very worthwhile to look for authorized multimedia to put on your page rather than take a chance all your work will be wasted if someone forces you to pull it down.

NOTE

If copyright issues really interest you, a great book to read is *Electronic Highway Robbery* by Mary E. Carter (Peachpit Press, 1997, ISBN 0-201-88393-7) or the Copyright Resource Page (`http://www.aimnet.com/~carroll/copyright/faq-home.html`).

Using Multimedia

The trick to using any form of multimedia on your Tripod site, as stated earlier, is to use it strategically. Unless the purpose of your site is to distribute large multimedia files (which it might be if you're a band, poet, or animator) this means using it sparingly and with good effect.

Using Sounds

Sound effects can be a fun addition to your site. One way to use them is to load them into the background of a page using JavaScript. Code Listing 11.1 provides a cross-browser method to loop a background sound effect when your page loads. The code checks to see which kind of browser the user has before choosing the appropriate method that works. Change the bolded section to the filename of the sound you want to load into your page.

You can also use this code to loop MIDI files. If you want to just play the sound a certain number of times, replace the values for the two LOOP attributes from infinite and true to any number you want.

> **NOTE**
>
> Make sure that the sound works well when looped (played over and over again). You can do this by designing the sound correctly in your sound effect editor.

Code Listing 11.1

```
<script language="JavaScript">
<!--
if(navigator.appName.indexOf("Microsoft",0)>=0)
     {
     document.write("<bgsound src=crickets.wav
➥loop=infinite>")
     }
     else
     {
     if(navigator.appName.indexOf("Netscape",0)>=0)
     document.write("<embed src=crickets.wav align=
➥bottom border=0 width=128 height=128 hidden=true
➥autostart=true loop=true autoplay=true>")
     }
//-->
</SCRIPT>
```

MIDI and Music Tracks

Many people like to load a MIDI track to play upon the loading of their pages. Unfortunately, this can be really annoying. This is primarily because MIDI tracks don't sound great on many machines because the MIDI tracks either were designed poorly or because the computer's built-in synthesizer isn't very good. MIDI music quality varies greatly from machine to machine; so what sounds good to you might sound awful to the next person. MIDI files can also tend to be a bit louder on playback than a normal sound file. A way around this is to use digitized audio like a .wav or .au file. However, the size of the file might be too large.

The great draw of MIDI, of course, is that a MIDI file is small enough to squeeze even a large song in under 60KB. The derivative Rich Media Format of Beatnick (`www.headspace.com`) tends to produce slightly larger files, but the sound quality is much higher because the Beatnick player ensures that the sounds won't vary as much from platform to platform.

Creating Audio Files for Your Tripod Site

When it comes to creating audio files, you need two basic items—a sound card that accepts either a microphone or line-in, and a sound recording and editing program. In many cases you can also use a CD-ROM that is connected through your audio card. This lets you record any sounds coming directly from a CD in your computer's CD-Drive. If your machine can't do this, refer to the manuals that come with your CD-ROM drive and your sound card for help in setting up that feature.

If you want to record from your stereo or microphone, you need to plug the audio source into the audio-in of your sound card. Most sound cards have this port clearly labeled on the back of the card. If sound capabilities are included with the machine (as is the case with many Macintosh machines), look somewhere along the back of your computer for an audio/microphone in-port. If you plan on using a microphone, remember that the simple microphones included with many computers are just that—simple, unsophisticated microphones. If you're semi-serious about quality, go to a local music store and purchase a basic recording microphone for under $100.

With the sound source plugged into your computer (or with a CD in the CD-ROM drive) you simply run your favorite digital audio recording and editing package (see Appendix B, "Web Page Building Resources," for a good list of tools) and begin recording and saving the audio.

About Audio Quality: Frequency and Sampling Rates

Audio quality is determined by a number of things, but chief among them is the size of the frequency spectrum under which you capture and save the file. This is also known as the *sampling rate*. Replaying the individual sound waves that make up the original sound can reproduce all types of known sound. The higher the frequency you capture, the better the sound will be to the human ear. Human ears can't really distinguish sounds beyond the +/-44100KHz range, which is why CD technology is based on 44100KHz. Of course, the higher the frequency, the larger the file and bandwidth needed to support it. In many cases, such as voice narration and simple sound effects, the need to have CD-quality sound is low. That is why audio engineers on the Web often use a lower quality sampling rate for sounds. Although the level of quality drops, so does the size of the file.

Table 11.1 shows the four major sampling rates in which audio is recorded and what type of sound that rate is suitable for capturing.

Table 11.1 Sound Quality Settings in Hz

8000	Telephone quality.
11025	Low-end radio quality. Good for voice.
22050	FM Radio quality. Good for music and voice.
44100	CD quality. Excellent for all sounds.

NOTE

Sometimes pops and hiccups can be introduced into the sound digitization process by slow machines and hardware that can't keep up with recording the incoming sound. To ensure the best quality recording, optimize your hard drive and machine to run as fast as possible.

You should always try to make the best possible quality of the sound files for your site. However, to balance the speed and size of the file with quality, you have to learn to make tradeoffs. When you decide to record audio for your site, try to capture it initially at the highest quality rate (44100Khz or better). Then, using the built-in tools of your favorite sound editor, "resample" it down to the lowest acceptable rate that matches the purpose of the file to the rates shown in Table 11.1. Every good sound editor offers a resampling feature. By capturing at the highest rate first and then letting the computer resample the sound, you ensure getting the best quality sound capable at the final files sampling rate.

Creating MP3 Files

If you want to create your own MP3 files you need a product known as an *encoder*. The encoder takes a normal

.wav or other audio file type and compresses it into the special MP3 format.

A number of encoders are available as freeware, as demoware, and commercially. A listing with links can be found on MP3.com (`www.mp3.com/software/windows/encoders.html`). Xing's Audio Catalyst is an excellent commercial package, although many MP3 users also like Fraunhofer's MP3enc 3.1 package.

Producing an MP3 file takes a lot of horsepower; make sure you have a large amount of hard drive space (an original CD-quality .wav file will run 40–50 megabytes) and a machine with a good processor. The purpose of MP3 is to compress very high quality sound into a small file size. Start by capturing a vanilla .wav file (or other format if your particular MP3 encoder supports other formats) at the highest quality possible. After you have that, merely tell the encoder the name of the .wav file to encode and the name of the MP3 file to spit out and you're done. The resulting MP3 file depending on the file characteristics will be 3–5MB in size.

Producing Midi Music Files for Your Tripod Site

Midi files exist in large numbers on the Web. Places like the MIDI Farm (`www.midifarm.com`) provide you with a huge archive of MIDI-styled music to make use of on your site.

To make your own MIDI tunes, you need a program called a *sequencer*. This is a tool that lets you score music or record it from a synthesizer attached to your computer. Most computers require you to get a MIDI connection card for your system to do this. If you're the musical type, chances are you already know how to accomplish this. The Midi Farm has the necessary info in its Library section.

In some cases, even if you aren't a musician you might want to make changes to a MIDI file you intend to use. This could be to change the instruments used, change the tempo or any other characteristic of a MIDI file. The best way to do this is to use a shareware MIDI file sequencer/editor. Try WinJammer (`www.winjammer.com`) and, for the Mac, you might download the trial version of Metro 4 from Cakewalk (`www.cakewalk.com`).

Using Video

When it comes to taking up space and time to download, nothing comes close to digital video. The sheer amount of information needed to create a suitable video clip is high. Even a small, 20–30-second clip can take up 400—500KB of space and take roughly one to two minutes to download. Even though streaming the video can help with the download time, you give up some quality and you don't save much on space. These issues, plus the requirements to create the video in the first place, have made video something few sites have chosen to add. Just like other forms of multimedia though, video can be a good addition to your site, if it's used correctly.

Video on the Web works best if the content contained within the video file is focused on the site's purpose and brings to the site's content something not possible through other means. For example, if you wanted to do a site on baseball, you might be best off showing the rules of the game using text and photos because a video version would take far too long to load. However, if you wanted to show someone how to swing a bat or field a ground ball, a 30-second video clip could be more informative than any text or illustration.

What You Need To Produce Video

Tripod offers a video clip gallery for sites that are not interested in creating their own video. You might also find useful clips available on other sites. However, it's not too hard to create your own video clips. In fact, there are many ways to go about creating your own video content.

The first place to start is to determine exactly what your computer's video capabilities are. Many newer computers and graphics cards are shipping with the ability to digitize video directly. These machines or cards usually feature a direct video in port on the back of the machine. They also usually come with a simple, free package you can use to create video files. If your machine doesn't offer a video in plug, you'll need a video capture device or video card. The following are a few major products worth considering, including Play's Snappy device and Iomega's Buz. Both products sell for under $200 and provide good quality video capture for the casual user. Higher-end broadcast quality boards exist, but they're much more expensive.

Snappy
Play Incorporated
2890 Kilgore Road
Rancho Cordova CA 95670-6133
916-851-0800
`www.play.com`

Play's Snappy can be found in many major computer stores, catalogs and Web sites. It is a PC-only product.

Buz
Iomega, Inc.
1821 West Iomega Way
Roy, UT 84067
801-778-1000
`www.iomega.com`

Buz is available for both the Macintosh and Windows platforms.

Smart Video Recorder III
Intel
2200 Mission College Blvd.
Santa Clara, CA 95052-8119
408-765-8080
`www.intel.com`

Smart Video Recorder III is a well-liked but PC-only video capture card.

After you acquire the hardware for your computer, you need to acquire the hardware for video capture. Because the computer hardware can accept any standard video source, this can be anything that outputs a standardized video signal, including a VCR, Camcorder, DVD player, video game console, laser disc, or satellite box.

NOTE

One thing you might want to capture is your computer screen. This is useful when you create tutorials. Windows users can use Flickerfree's WinStructor (`www.flickerfree.com`) program (Figure 11.3). WinStructor is a screen-capture application that enables you to take captures of sections of the computer screen at regular intervals and save the picture sequence in the .avi format. It can also record your spoken instructions from a microphone while capturing the actions on screen, which makes it ideal for producing instructional videos.

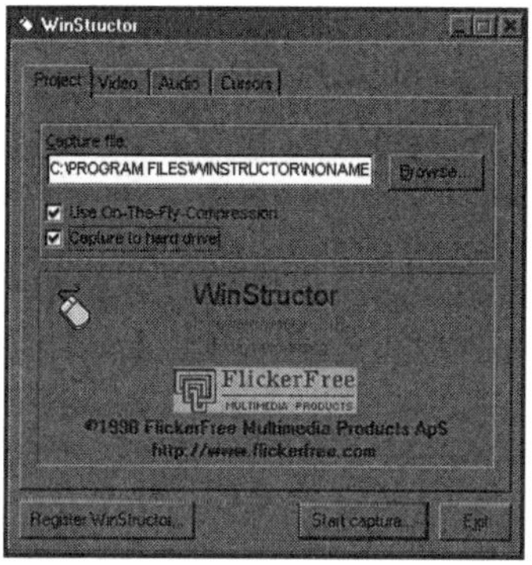

FIGURE 11.3
WinStructor is a program you can use to create movies of your Windows desktop, which is great for creating tutorials on how to use different programs.

To capture the video, you need a program that enables you to record the video stream to your hard disk and then optionally edit the results. The top video-editing package used by many desktop video developers is Adobe's Premiere. However, this top-notch program doesn't come cheap ($700), although you can download a trial version from Adobe's Web site. Instead, for most casual Web developers a host of lower-end video editing programs can work—one of which might have been included with whatever capture hardware you purchased. If you're not satisfied with the free product included in with your capture device, consider the following two alternative shareware and lower cost programs.

Personal AVI Editor
Flickerfree Multimedia
Vesterbro 57, Box 7115
DK-9200 Aalborg SV
Denmark
+45 70 224 555
`www.flickerfree.com`

Personal AVI Editor is a Windows capture and AVI editor. It can create .avi files from existing .avi- and .bmp-files and can capture video from any Windows supported video capture card and record audio from any Windows supported sound card.

Ulead MediaStudio Pro
Ulead Systems, Inc.
970 West 190th Street, Suite 520
Torrance, CA 90502
310-523-9393
www.ulead.com

Ulead MediaStudio Pro is a lower cost commercial Windows video editor available in trial demo form.

Codecs and Quality

After you've captured the raw video, you need to edit it and save it. When you save video to a file, the two most important decisions are the file format and the compression method, also known as codec. For the most part, there are two major codecs from which you can choose—Cinepak and Intel Indeo. Most video editing software will include these codecs, or you can download them from the Web.

Some codecs provide better quality output, and others compress the video more. Essentially, every codec has some tradeoff. When in doubt about a specific codec, Cinepak is the best bet because it is so widely supported. If you want to match up the codec you want to use with the features you need, you might want to check out Terran Interactive's www.codecs.com site. There you will find a wealth of information about each major digital video format and links from which to download them.

The codec you use, however, isn't the only thing that affects quality. When you create a digital video file, you want to do everything to produce the highest quality video, including the following:

- **Optimize your system** Increase memory so you can smoothly capture larger clips and edit them in memory. Defragment your hard drive so the file capture is as smooth as possible, and stop running any programs that are running in the background that might slow down the system.
- **Experiment with frame rates** The frame rate determines how much data is compressed as the video is captured; the lower the frame rate, the lower the video quality. Most multimedia users push to get 15 frames per second (fps) as the minimum acceptable frame rate for digital video. However, some videos (for instance, videos with limited motion) can go as low as 10 or 12 fps with no apparent loss in smoothness. Try capturing at different frame rates to see which one works best for you.
- **When capturing video you intend to turn into streaming video, look for video that doesn't change a lot or have lots of motion** The more motion and change there is from frame to frame, the harder it is for compression to take place and for the streaming to be as smooth as possible.
- **Avoid dropping frames** If possible, don't drop any frames during capture. Video files with dropped frames appear to stutter during playback because some of the original video frames are missing from the file. If your capture utility reports dropped frames during capture, try capturing and editing together several shorter clips.

- **Calibrate audio levels** Use the software that controls recording levels to calibrate the input of audio to all of the audio sources. Set the audio level for your PC so that the majority of sound is close to 0 decibels. Going past 0 decibels is likely to result in distorted audio.
- **Consider capturing the audio at a lower rate than 44Khz** Depending on the need for the accompanying audio track, you can reduce file size by saving the audio as 22KHz, 11KHz, or lower.

PRODUCING STREAMING VIDEO FILES

To produce a streaming video for your site, you needn't do much differently than you would for a normal .avi or QuickTime file. The catch is whether you have the proper tool or driver with your video editor to save your video in one of the three major streaming formats (RealVideo, Vivo, or Active Streaming Format). Adobe's Premiere product supports most of these formats, or you can purchase or download plug-ins for them. For casual video producers, freeware or low cost tools that you can use with your similarly lower cost video editor software are the better option.

For RealVideo you can use the RealEncoder (Figure 11.4) program found on RealNetworks' site (`www.real.com/products/tools/index.html`), which is free. Real offers a deluxe version of the encoder called RealPlayer Plus for $89.95 on its Web site. For Microsoft's ASF files, the company offers a free encoder on its NT Media Services site (`www.microsoft.com/ntserver/nts/downloads/recommended/mediaserv/default.asp`). Even though the NetShow server requires NT, you can download just the encoding and content tools and run them on either

Windows 95 or 98. For Vivo files, purchase the Video Now product ($149.95) from Vivo's Web site (`www.vivo.com`).

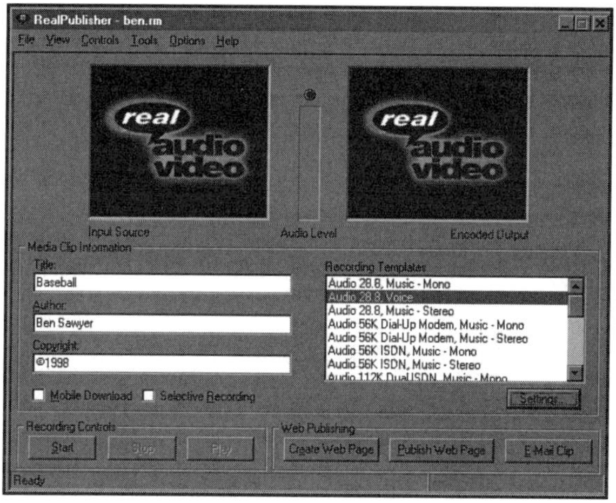

FIGURE 11.4
Real Networks gives away a basic version of the Encoder program from its site; a feature-rich version can be purchased for $89.95.

With all of these programs, you must first create a valid video file (.avi, QuickTime, and so on) and then load that into the encoder, which then compresses it and rearranges the data to change it into the streaming format.

Macromedia Shockwave & Flash

For a typical Tripod user, creating Shockwave files using Director might be a bit of a stretch. The cost of Director and its learning curve are not for the incidental or casual page builder. However, you might find a Shockwave applet to download and put on your site. Flash is a much easier product to use and costs less than $150. You can download a 30-day trial version from Macromedia at (`http://www.macromedia.com/software/flash/trial/`).

As mentioned earlier, Tripod supports ThingWorld's Multimedia Things, small dynamic multimedia applets. To put a Thing on your site simply go the ThingSearch area (Figure 11.5) of the Tripod Web site (`http://thingworld.tripod.com/tripod_search.asp`). There you can pick out and search for the multitude of Things available. Users visiting a site with a Thing on it will have to download a simple plug-in to view the things you put on your site. After this program is quickly downloaded, the multimedia Thing will load. Things can also be taken by the user and placed on her or his desktop, used as a screen saver, or added to the user's Web page.

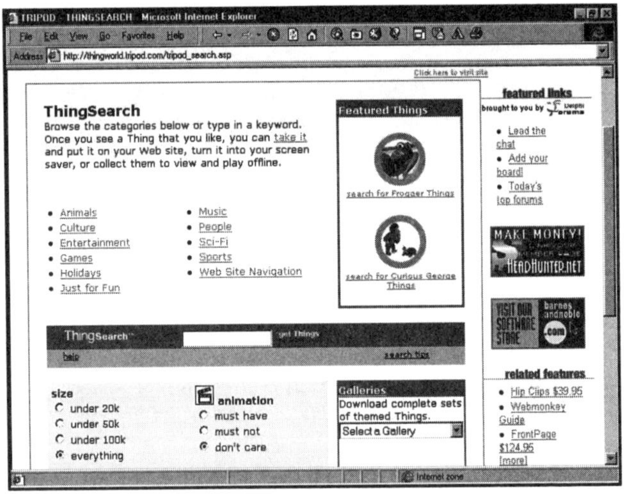

FIGURE 11.5
The ThingSearch area on Tripod.

Java, Dynamic HTML, and SMIL

You can also create multimedia programs using some of the newer Web languages like Java, Dynamic HTML, and SMIL. To create multimedia Java applets, you might want to use either Jamba from Interleaf (`www.jamba.com`), or Liquid Motion from Microsoft (`www.microsoft.com/liquidmotion/`). Both of these applications enable you to create in a visual method high-quality Java-based multimedia applets for your site.

Dynamic HTML is a tag-based extension to HTML that, among other things, enables you to create multimedia programs and effects for your pages. If you want to use Dynamic HTML you should consult a good book on the language, such as *Dynamic HTML Visual Quickstart* by Jason Teague (Peachpit Press, ISBN 0201353415).

Finally, there is SMIL (pronounced "smile"), a new multimedia language that works, like HTML, using simple <tags> to define elements like movies to play, pictures to load, or sound files to play back. It is a relatively new language and is mostly supported by Real Networks, the makers of the Real Player (which over 20 million Web users have downloaded). SMIL is a very powerful way to create multimedia for your site. If you want to learn more about SMIL, visit Just SMIL (`www.justsmil.com`), which has tutorials and links to all the major SMIL resources on the Web.

Multifaceted Multimedia

To make your site as comprehensive as possible, a little multimedia can go a long way. By using it effectively, the richness of sound, music, and video can bring life to a site and make it one that people can deeply experience and from which they can even learn.

Thanks to clip libraries provided by Tripod, and the information provided here, you shouldn't have a problem acquiring, or creating, your own multimedia elements for your site. The first level of page builders can master text and imagery without much difficulty. The investment in understanding when and how to use sound clips, MIDI files, and video is what can separate the multitalented home page builder from the rest of the pack.

CHAPTER 12

Attracting Visitors to Your Tripod Pages

What if you threw a party and nobody came? If you forgot to send invitations, it would be your own fault. The same is true of your Web site. You can't expect people to know about your site unless you tell them about it.

By building in Tripod, you immediately have a good start—kind of like taping an invitation to a neighborhood telephone pole. Even if you don't promote your site, your presence in Tripod will probably still lead to a few visitors. On the other hand, if you want a really hopping party, send those invitations! (Of course, you'd better have something to keep your new friends interested after they get there, but we've already covered that.)

Links

Links, assuming they are placed in the right spots, can be like handing an invitation to a friend and asking the friend to make copies and send them to his or her friends. Of course, you should pick a friend who has a lot of other friends who would be interested in your party. In other words, getting a link from a site that has little traffic and no relation to your site is hardly worth the effort. Don't bother asking someone whose only friend is a classical music freak to spread the word about your listening party for the new Metallica album.

Surfing with Potential Links in Mind

You can start looking for potential links before you even begin to build your site. For example, if your site is dedicated to fly fishing, you will almost certainly have visited a number of other fly fishing sites. If you haven't, you should. Not only will this provide ideas, but after your site is complete, you can approach these sites about linking to yours. Whatever you do, don't ask for a link before your site is up and looking good. Would you link your site to a half-finished, poorly organized site? Not unless you want to irritate your visitors.

Making Convincing Contact

Send the site creator an email describing your site and include the URL so the creator can check it out. Assuming he or she wants to link to your site, he or she will likely ask for a link in return. Keep this in mind, because you don't want to approach someone about a link, then refuse to link back to his or her lousy site.

People might ask why they should bother linking to your site. If they do, stress the benefit to both sites of swapping links. If they decide to pass, you might still consider linking to their site.

Marking Links Clearly

Whenever you link to an outside site, be sure that your visitors realize they are being transported to a different site, not to another part of yours. Trying to pass off somebody else's work as your own is frowned upon.

Adding Links to Your Site

Adding a link on your page via plain HTML code is fairly simple. After the owner of another site has sent you a Web page address, simply open up the HTML file for the page on which you want to place it, and use the HREF tag as follows:

```
<A HREF="PLACE HTTP://www.wherever.com">Place the text
➥for the link here</A>
```

If you want, you can also put the HREF tag around an image. This could be useful if the site to which you are linking has a graphical logo you want to highlight instead of text.

```
<A HREF="PLACE HTTP://www.wherever.com"><IMG SRC="Logo
➥of site.gif here"
BORDER=0></A>
```

When using an image, note that most people set the border attribute to 0 because otherwise you get a thick blue line around the image (which is caused by the link tag).

Many times when linking to another site, people like to force open another window and load the linked-to page or site into that new browser window. This ensures to some degree that the visitor still has a browser window open to your page even though they might branch off to another site.

To do this, simply add the attribute of target="_blank" to your HREF tag as follows:

```
<A HREF="PLACE HTTP://www.wherever.com"
➥target="_blank">Place the text for the link here</A>
```

Cross linking with another site is an excellent way to build traffic. By using the HREF tag, graphics, and spawning new windows you can cross promote your site like a pro.

Web Rings

A Web ring is just what it sounds like it would be—a group of related sites that are linked together so that visitors can hop from one to the next, eventually returning to the first site in the ring. Visitors usually don't have to go from one to the next, but can visit members of a ring randomly, skip around, or browse through a list of ring members, almost like selecting sites from a search engine. The best thing about Web rings is that they generate visitors who are interested in the topic of your site. A ring is managed from one site.

One Web ring service especially worth checking into is WebRing (`www.webring.com`). WebRing allows you to create a new ring or join an existing ring. If you want to join an existing ring at WebRing, visit that ring's homepage. The process changes from ring to ring.

If you want to join a Web ring, go to the ring's host site and follow its instructions. The ring's host site can usually be found by visiting `www.webring.com`, searching for the subject, or browsing the index and, after you have chosen the desired ring listing, clicking Home. If you can't find the ring's host site, contact a ring member via email and ask how to get involved. From there you will be pointed in the right direction.

Search Engines

It takes some effort to make search engines work for you. The technology is not yet perfect and the results depend on how precise you are when submitting your site and how intelligently people use the engine. The next few sections provide you with some insight on how to maximize your ranking, as well as a bit on the various search engines.

What Are They Looking For?

Different search engines look for different things. Some use the number of external links to a site as a determining factor in its popularity. Some search engines use spiders (artificial intelligence) that dig through your site and index every page automatically; others require that you submit every page yourself. Some read META tags, which are included in your site's code and describe its contents, and some don't. For more on the specific engines, read on. Remember that search engines are always apt to change their submission requirements, so we advise you to visit the various search engines to learn more.

Speaking of META tags...

META Tags

It is possible for you to control how your page is indexed by search engines by using the META tag to specify keywords (the words that people searching for a site will likely type into a search engine) and a short description of the site's content. Information within the META tag is not displayed when the document is loaded into a browser. However, it can be extracted by servers and search engines for use in identifying, indexing, and cataloging your page. Selecting keywords is discussed later in this chapter.

META tags, including the page title, keywords, and description, are included between the <HEAD>...</HEAD> tags at the top of the page.

Here is an example of a META tag:

```
<HTML>
<HEAD>\<TITLE>The Web Developer's Virtual
➥Library</TITLE>
<META NAME = "Keywords" CONTENT = "HTML, CGI, Java,
➥VRML, browsers, plugins, graphics, HTTP servers,
JavaScript, Perl,\ActiveX, Shockwave"<

<META NAME = "Description"
CONTNT="Locate Web authoring & software Internet
resources at The WDVL, a well-organized
goldmine with over 500 pages and thousands
of links about HTML, CGI, Java, VRML,
browsers, plug-ins, graphics, HTTP servers,
JavaScript, Perl, ActiveX, Shockwave, etc."> </HEAD>
```

The Web Developer's Virtual Library is a good place to go for more information on META tags. The Meta Tagging for Search Engines page is `www.stars.com/Search/Meta/Tag.html`.

...And More

Quality META tagging is a good start. However, search engines take a number of factors into account. Again, keep in mind that different engines work differently (more on that later).

- **Does their spider dig?** Some spiders go through an entire site. Others do no digging at all. If a particular engine's spider doesn't dig, submit each desired page individually. Most search engines provide information on how they operate at their homepages.
- **That's why they're called "key"words** As you probably know, keywords are what people type into search engines when seeking information on a topic. For example, if you wanted to find sites about Seattle musicians, you might use words like "Seattle," "music," "grunge," "Hendrix," "Pearl Jam," "Nirvana," and so on. The key to keywords? Get feedback. The keywords you want to use in your META tags might not be the same as those that are likely to be used by the general public. Have friends help generate a list of keywords for your site or provide feedback on the keywords you have selected. Use the top keywords in your title, headings, text, and of course, META tags.
- **Judging a site by its title** It is important to have an accurate, descriptive title. Resist the urge for self promotion that leads to so many title's like Jim's Kickin' Home Page. Unless the page is about the new techno mixmaster, the title Jim's Kickin' (we made that up), is useless. Instead, choose a title that clearly defines the page's content. An example of a solid, descriptive title might be "Joe's Grateful Dead Concert Chronology" for a site that lists all the Grateful Dead's concert dates, locations, and set lists.
- **Repetition** Good or bad, good or bad, good or bad?: Back in the "old days"—which in the Web world is a couple of years ago—word repetition was a common way to improve a search engine ranking. If a

page said "NBA" 150 times, it must be the best pro basketball site out there, right? Well, obviously not. Some search engines now penalize sites for unnecessary word repetition. Others still use word repetition as a criteria for high-ranking. Know how each handles this irritating, irritating, irritating, irritating practice before you submit.

- **It's about what?** Many search engines place a greater emphasis on words located near the beginning of the page, which makes sense, because a page about Dawson's Creek that doesn't mention "Dawson's Creek" until the bottom of the first page, probably isn't such a great site.
- **Help spiders learn to read** Even though Web spiders can read, they don't like to if the text is embedded in a graphic. Others don't recognize META tags, but instead use the first text on the page as the summary. For these cases, be sure your page starts with text that can serve as an enlightening description.
- **Get linked** Some search engines determine a site's popularity—and thus the site's ranking—by the number of external links to the site. Because of this, obtaining links is doubly important when it comes to attracting visitors.

Automatic or Individual Submission

Whether you decide to submit your site individually to all of the search engines in which you are interested or have a submittal service do the work for you depends on a couple of things. Do you have the time, and is it important enough to tailor your submission for each search engine? Possibly not. However, not tailoring your submission to the quirks of particular search engines can lead to poor rankings. If you have some time, but not a lot, you might want to submit your site directly to a couple of the more important engines and let an automatic submission service handle the rest.

Not surprisingly, Yahoo! (`www.yahoo.com`), which is technically a Web index rather than a search engine, has a list of automatic submission sites you should check. The biggest, most popular submission service is Submit-It (`www.submit-it.com`). Submit-It offers a number of services, but the one you will most likely be interested in is Submit-It Free Classic (`http://siteowner.linkexchange.com/Free.cfm`), which is, of course, free. Submit-It Free Classic does include Infoseek, WebCrawler, and AltaVista; however, it doesn't submit your site to Lycos, Yahoo!, or HotBot.

The best advice is to learn as much as you can about the particular engine to which you are submitting. Most search engine home pages will tell you what they look for and how to maximize your ranking.

From AltaVista to Yahoo!

You've probably heard of and used many of the top search engines. Most of them have an icon for adding URLs and will guide you through the submission process. Here are some of the top search engines. Because search engines sometimes change their processes for submitting a site, we suggest you visit them and follow the directions.

AltaVista

To submit your site to AltaVista (`www.altavista.com`), click the Add a Page link at the bottom of the homepage.

AltaVista asks that you only submit your main page and says its spider (or crawler) will follow links throughout the entire site. Do not submit keywords or a description with the URL. Use META tags to control the description that is returned with your site's name. AltaVista offers an example of a META tag and how it will appear in your listing at `http://www.altavista.com/av/content/addurl_meta.htm`.

EXCITE

Excite (`www.excite.com`) doesn't recognize META tags. Click the Add URL link at the bottom of the homepage to submit your site and to get more information about Excite's indexing process. Excite suggests you use descriptive phrases near the top of your pages to help your ranking. Submit just your homepage URL; and Excite says its spider will access your site every two weeks, crawl through each page, and note any content changes.

HOTBOT

HotBot (`www.hotbot.com`) asks you to submit each page but limit your submissions to 50 URLs in a 24-hour period. That ought to do it for you. To begin submitting pages, click the Add URL link at the bottom of the homepage and follow the simple instructions. HotBot suggests you use META tags and descriptive keywords in the title. You will receive a confirmation email after your page(s) have been submitted.

INFOSEEK

InfoSeek (`www.infoseek.com`) does not accept automatic submissions. Sites from large domains (such as Tripod) should submit each page through email. Send one URL per line to `www.request@infoseek.com`. Infoseek suggests that you "use a highly descriptive title, include a META tag description, and create META tag keywords that contain comma-separated phrases." Unnecessary repetition might lower your ranking. For more on submitting to Infoseek, click the Add URL link on the home page.

Lycos

Hey, we've heard of this one! Lycos (`www.lycos.com`) allows you to submit more than one URL from your site as long as the URLs represent distinct pages (see Figure 12.1). Multiple pages that contain the same content will not be added. The Lycos spider will try to travel through links contained on the pages you submit. Lycos says you can count on its spider to travel down one level from the submitted page.

Your site will be entered into the Lycos catalog within two or three weeks. Keep your site live. The Lycos spider revisits all sites on a periodic basis. If the spider can't connect to your site over a period of approximately four weeks, it will be deleted from the Lycos rolling catalog.

WebCrawler

WebCrawler (`www.webcrawler.com`) indexes every word on your site up to 1 megabyte of text. The keywords are the text on a page. More weight is given to titles than to text or META tags. To submit your URL, click the Add Your URL link at the bottom of the homepage. WebCrawler asks that you submit only the main URL to your page. For more information on WebCrawler's submission policies, go to `http://webcrawler.com/Help/GetListed/HelpAddURL.html`.

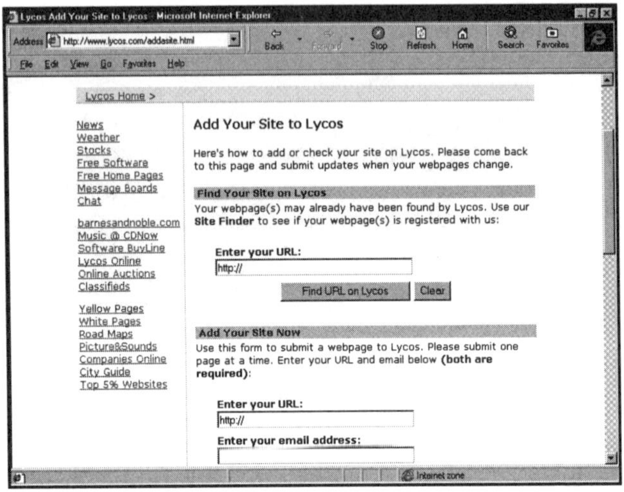

FIGURE 12.1
Add Your Site to Lycos (`www.lycos.com/addasite.html`).

YAHOO!

Yahoo! (`www.yahoo.com`) is an index, not a search engine. It is also the most visited site on the Internet. Submissions to the catalog are handled by people. To submit your site, click How To Suggest A Site at the bottom of the Yahoo! home page and follow the step-by-step instructions. When submitting, you will be asked to select a category (and subcategories) under which you want your site to be listed. Yahoo! does not accept all submissions. Don't submit your site to Yahoo! until your site is in good shape.

AWARD AND ANNOUNCE SITES

You should also try to get your site listed on award and announce sites. This is a bit trickier than a simple search engine listing: award sites only list outstanding sites and announce sites that are temporary.

Top Award Sites

Award sites are exactly what you think. On a regular basis they honor some of the best sites on the Web. Getting listed by an award site is extremely difficult; your site must be truly outstanding. However, even if you don't get listed, award sites are worth checking out to see examples of excellent work and also to scout out potential sites with which to swap links. Visit the following:

Lycos Top 5% of the Web (`http://point.lycos.com/categories/index.html`)

Cool Site of the Day (`http://cool.infi.net`)

TooCool (`http://toocool.com`)

ProjectCool (`www.projectcool.com`)

Top Announcement Sites

Announcement sites are for new sites. After you have completed your site, submit it to an announcement site to get a bit of short-term exposure. Visit the following sites and follow their procedures for submittal.

Netscape's What's New (`http://netscape.yahoo.com/guide/whats_new.html`)

What's New Too (`http://newtoo.manifest.com`)

Nerd World What's New (`www.nerdworld.com/whatsnew.html`)

Promoting Within Tripod

Now that you have an idea how to promote your site outside the Tripod community, let's return home—think globally, act locally, and all that. Tripod offers a number of opportunities to attract visitors. As previously mentioned, simply existing on Tripod and being an active member of the community will draw in your fair share of visitors. But you can do more, thanks to Tripod.

SmartAds Banner Exchange Program

SmartAds—Tripod's banner exchange program—is a great place to start. SmartAds, powered by Smart Age, helps you promote your Web site on a network of personal home pages and commercial sites.

The promotional banner you create is shown on targeted sites across the network; in exchange, you display banners for other network members on your site. By joining this program, you become part of one of the largest banner exchanges on the Web, making your site known to thousands of potential new visitors. You can choose the types of sites on which your ad will be displayed or let SmartClicks' Smart Targeting technology place them on the sites that work best for you.

By telling you where your ad is most visited, Tripod Clicks can let you know where your ad is most successful, helping you to make decisions about your ad's placement.

Tripod's Banner Builder

One of the great things about Tripod's banner exchange program is that, with the Tripod Banner Builder, you can build banners in a matter of minutes. Tripod's Banner

Builder enables you to choose from six different banner templates, ranging in complexity from static text to triple-animation. Before Banner Builder existed, banner exchange partners had to have their own graphic design software to make a banner. Tripod's Banner Builder enables you to build a banner through your browser—no other software is necessary.

To start building banners, perform the following steps. Different banners have different instructions, all of which are very easy to follow. Here is one example:

1. Go to `http://homepager.tripod.com/build/banner_builder/options.html`, where you will find the banner templates (see Figure 12.2).

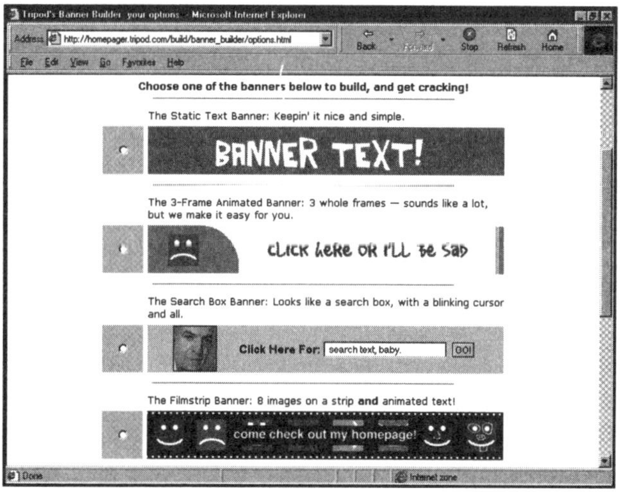

FIGURE 12.2
Some of the choices provided with Banner Builder.

2. Select a template by clicking the check box to its left.
3. Click the Now Build It button at the bottom of the page.

4. Log in and follow the directions. (We chose the static text banner).
5. In our case, we chose a background color, entered the desired text, and then chose a font and a text color.
6. Save the banner by clicking Build Me. There's the banner (see Figure 12.3).

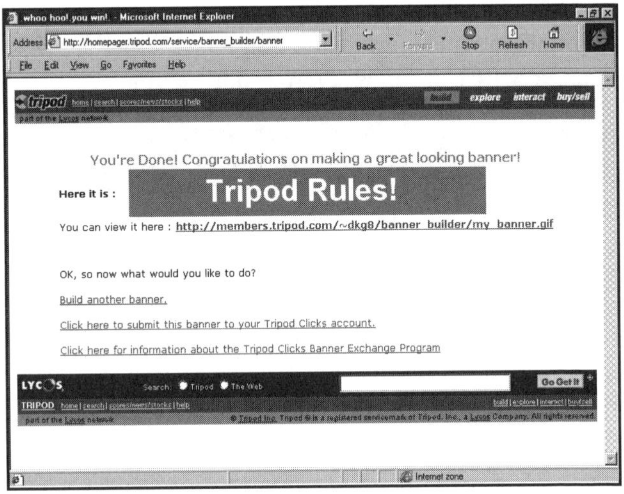

FIGURE 12.3
Simple. There's the banner.

From here you can view your banner, build another banner, submit your banner to your Tripod Clicks account, or get more information about the Tripod Clicks Banner Exchange Program.

A Bit More About Banner Networks

We mentioned banner networks in the Tripod Clicks section. Tripod page builders can join a banner network and, in exchange for allowing banners to be placed on your site, get your banner placed on other member sites. The more people who click the banners on your site, the more your banner is displayed elsewhere.

Tripod is a partner of SmartAge (`www.smartage.com`), a company that offers advertising opportunities for Web page builders. SmartAge provides the SmartClicks program mentioned above. Banner networks provide an opportunity for Tripod members to advertise their sites without spending a penny.

Get Involved

Or, as Tripod says, interact with people. In the real world, people become well known by being active in their communities. The same is true with Tripod, which has nearly endless opportunities for you to meet people with similar interests. Pods, Chats, Message Boards, and Contests, all of which are fun, give your site added visibility, and are discussed in more detail in Chapter 2, "Getting Started with Tripod."

Our suggestion is to go to `www.tripod.com/interact` and start interacting.

PART IV

Appendixes

APPENDIX A

Premium Membership: Tripod's First Class Services

As a Tripod member, you are entitled to build your own Web sites, join Pods, create banners, participate in message boards, and a lot more. If you want even more benefits and can manage $3 a month (after a one-month free trial period), however, you should consider upgrading to Premium Membership.

This chapter outlines the benefits, costs, and terms of Premium Membership and walks you through the signup process.

Premium Membership Services

For just $3 per month, Premium Members receive 22 megabytes of extra disk space (twice as much as standard members), a personal chat room, email forwarding, and access to the Premium Membership Image Library. For an additional $3 per month, Premium Members can choose to have ads removed from their site. To learn more about the benefits of Premium Membership, go to `http://tripod.com/planet/membership/premium/`. See Figure A.1.

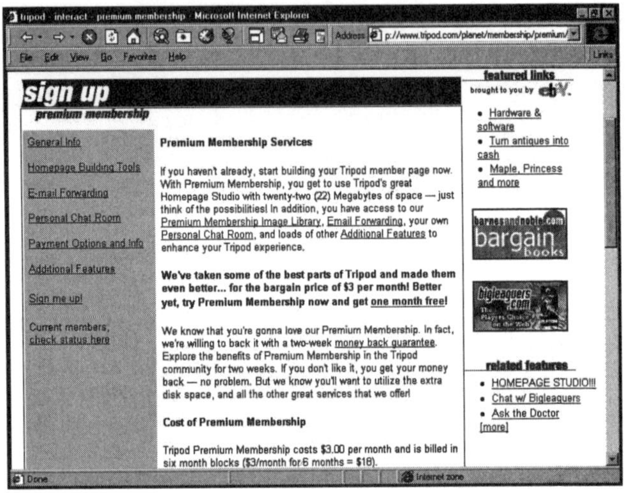

FIGURE A.1
Tripod's Premium Membership page.

Extra Disk Space

Tripod Membership offers you 11 megabytes of free disk space—the upgrade to Premium Membership doubles your space and doubles your fun. Even though 11 megabytes is a lot (and who can argue with the price!), if you find your Web site growing and becoming more space-consuming with added images, sounds, etc., the Premium Membership is worth the price.

Personal Chat Room

As a Premium Member of Tripod, you can design and maintain your own personal chat room. You enjoy a customized, browser-independent service and can interact with people anytime you choose. Your personal chat room is open 24 hours a day, seven days a week. As the owner of a chat room, you design its appearance and decide who can participate. You can also link to your chat room from anywhere on the Web. For more information on chats and personal chat rooms, check out Tripod's Help page, at `http://help.tripod.com/bin/help/C-H_With_Chat/A-Questions_About_Tripod_Chat`. For more on chats, see Chapter 2, "Getting Started with Tripod."

Email Forwarding

If you are tired of losing friends and contacts because you change your email address every three months, Tripod Premium Membership offers a great service: email forwarding. You receive an address in the form of `membername@tripod.net`, in which *membername* is your name. Hand out your Tripod address, and all of your mail is automatically forwarded to the address with which you registered to become a Tripod member. If you change your job or finish school, inform Tripod of your new email address, and your mail is forwarded. To activate email forwarding, log on as a Premium Member and click email forwarding. Your Tripod email address and forwarding service is activated instantly.

If you need to inform Tripod of a change in your email address, go to `http://www.tripod.com/service/change_email/get_new_email` and submit your new address (see Figure A.2). Tripod sends a message to your new email address to verify the change. This message includes a verification code and instructions on how to verify your new address. Tripod will not update your email address until you have followed the instructions and verified the change.

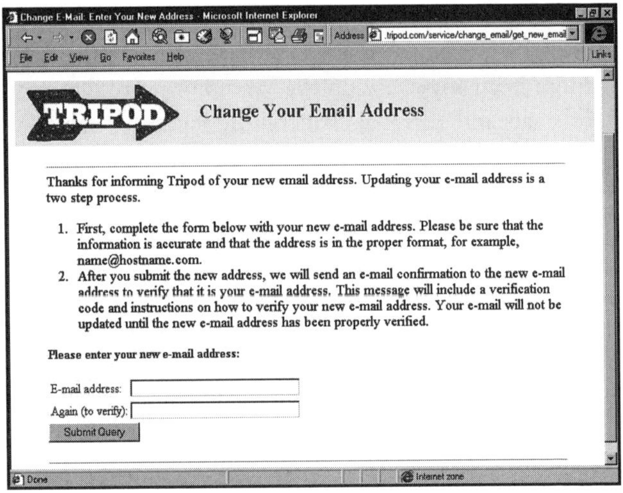

FIGURE A.2
Tripod's email forwarding service.

Premium Membership Image Library

Premium Members have access to Tripod's exclusive Image Library. The Premium Membership Image Library is a directory of fun and interesting graphics and illustrations. This image bank features illustrations by the Arts Parts Collection, a professional clip art and illustration company. The images are in black and white; you select the appropriate color scheme for each illustration. Tripod's Colorizer Technology enables you to customize the illustrations to make your pages original and exciting. To access Tripod's Premium Membership Image Library, go to `http://homepager.tripod.com/tools/imagelibrary/premium` (see Figure A.3).

To demo Tripod's Colorizer, click Demo Colorizer Here or go to `http://homepager.tripod.com/service/demo/imagelibrary/spectrum_paint.pl` (see Figure A.4). Select colors from the two color palettes on the right side of the screen to create an original illustration. Each palette contains over 200 browser-safe colors. If the image or illustration is one color, the image appears all black and you have one palette to design the image. If it is a two-color graphic, the image appears in black and white and there are two palettes from which you can choose to create a customized illustration.

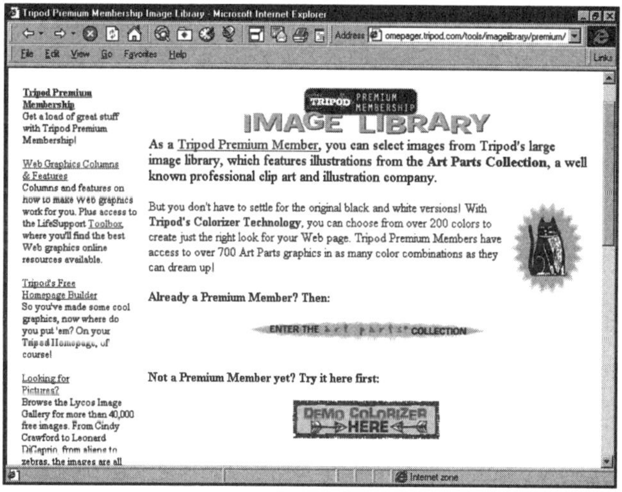

FIGURE A.3
The Premium Membership Image Library page.

The Arts Parts Collection is a library of illustrations organized by category. To select an illustration subject category, go to `http://homepager.tripod.com/tools/imagelibrary/premium/artparts` (see Figure A.5). Click the subject of your choice and select from a variety of images. After you have chosen an illustration, click the image and the Colorizer is activated. Choose colors from the color palette, and your image is complete.

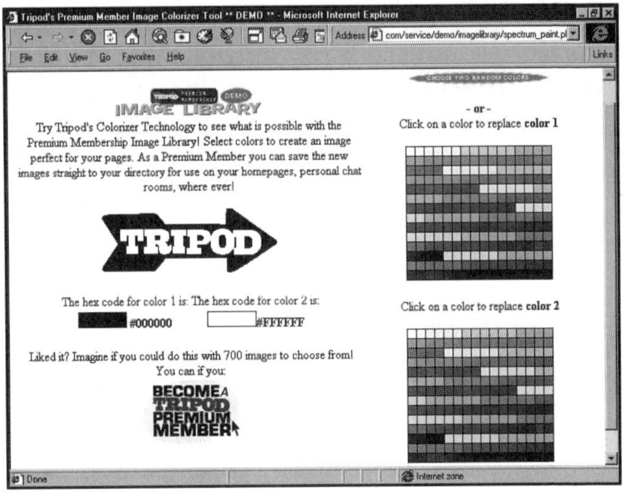

FIGURE A.4
Tripod's Demo Colorizer.

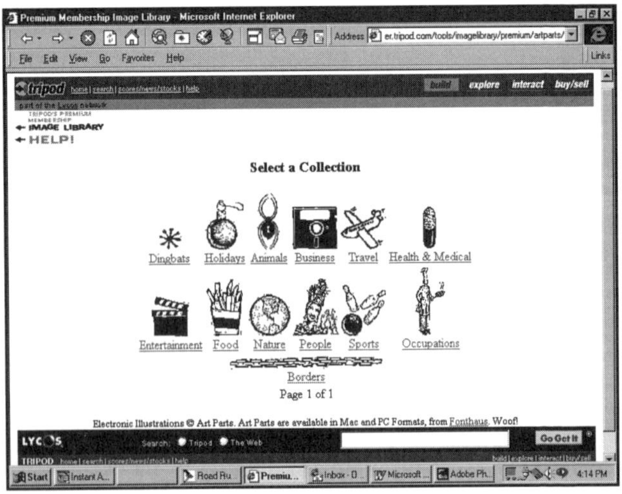

FIGURE A.5
The Arts Parts Collection category page.

Ad Removal

Tripod's Premium Members have the option to remove any ads that appear on their pages and personal chat rooms. Tripod offers the advertisement removal service for $3 on top of the Premium Membership price of $3. So, for $6 a month, you receive all the benefits of Premium Membership and an add-free site and chat room.

Additional Features

As a PremiumMember, you also receive a 20% discount on all Tripod apparel, as well as a free subscription to the exclusive newsletter "The Premium Membership Review." This newsletter features reports on Tripod services, promotions, and contests. There is also a Premium Membership Status Page to inform you of remaining disk space and email forwarding status.

Cost of Premium Membership

Your Premium Membership cost of $3 per month is paid biannually. Premium Members prepay for a six-month block—$18 (or $36 for the removal of advertising). Tripod offers a one-month free membership to new members and a two-week money back guarantee. If you want to terminate your membership within the first two weeks of signing up, Tripod gives you your money back as long as the cancellation is submitted within the two-week period and your membership was not canceled due to a Terms of Service violation.

Payment

Payment for Premium Membership must be made in U.S. currency. Tripod accepts three methods of payment: credit card submitted through their secure server; credit card submitted by fax; and check. For more information on payment options, go to `http://www.tripod.com/planet/membership/premium/paymentfaq.html`.

Payment Online: Credit Card

To pay via credit card over the secured server, you must use a Secure Socket Layer (SSL) compatible browser such as Netscape Navigator or Microsoft Internet Explorer. All contact information must be accurate and current. If the billing address of the credit card does not match the address submitted, the credit card cannot be accepted.

When your credit card is accepted, you are informed by email that your Premium Membership has been activated. Your credit card is billed every six months for the corresponding amount until and unless you decide to cancel your premium membership.

Payment via Fax or Postal Mail: Credit Card

To pay via credit card by fax or snail mail, print out the Premium Membership form and fill out all the contact and credit card information. You must provide your signature on the form. The same credit card stipulations for online payments apply to credit card payments via fax and mail. You are informed by email that your Premium Membership has been activated. Tripod bills your credit card every six months to renew your membership.

Payment by Mail: Check or Money Order

Checks should be made payable to Tripod, Inc. and should include your current address and telephone number. Print out the Premium Membership form and fill out all the contact and credit card information. You must provide your signature on the form. Orders are processed the day that payment is received. You are informed by email that your Premium Membership has been activated. Every six months, you receive an email reminder to send payment to renew your membership.

Keep Contact Information Current

It is important that you keep Tripod informed of your current contact information. If at some point your billing address or home address changes, be sure to inform Tripod of the change. To change your contact information, go to `http://www.tripod.com/service/change_userdata`, update your information, and click Submit.

Cancellation of Premium Membership

You can cancel your Premium Membership whenever you please. Just send a message via email to `pm_unsub@tripod.com`.

Terms of Service Agreement

The Terms of Service Agreement is the same for Premium Membership as it is for the Basic Tripod Membership. To become a Premium Member, you must go to `http://www.tripod.com/planet/membership/premium/tos.html`, read the Terms of Service, and click the Accept or the Not Accept icon. You are not eligible for Premium Membership unless you accept the Service Conditions.

Sign-up

To become a Tripod Premium Member, click Sign-up on the Premium Member page or go to `https://`

`secure.tripod.com/service/premium_membership/signup/PM_signup` and log onto the Tripod site as a member before upgrading your membership. Tripod prompts you to submit your username and password if you have not already signed up.

Now you are ready to upgrade your membership and complete the sign-up process. Select the membership plan that you prefer (Premium Membership for $18, paid biannually or Premium Membership for $36 with advertising removal, paid biannually). After choosing your level of Premium Membership, read the Terms of Service agreement. Tripod requires that you submit an acceptance of the agreement before upgrading to Premium Membership.

On the following page, submit your personal information including name, address, telephone number, and email address. If you are paying by credit card, submit the name of the cardholder, the card number, and the expiration date. Be certain to write the name of the cardholder as it is written on the card. Do not omit middle initials or submit shortened names. Finally, select your payment method (online credit card transaction, mail fax credit card transaction, or mail check or money order payment).

Tripod confirms your payment selection and your contact information. Now you are officially a Tripod Premium Member!

APPENDIX B

Web Page Building Resources

We have tried to provide as much information as possible within these pages. There's more out there—a lot more. As someone who is building a Web page, you are certainly aware of the overwhelming amount of information available on the Web. We've tried to collect some of our favorite spots in a number of categories to help you make your page even better. Also included here are some of the spots we've previously mentioned, giving you the major page-building resources in a single spot.

Basic Web Design Help

One of the most important things about building a site is how the information is organized—your information is useless if your users have to dig to find it. The following sites cover Web design in a way that will show you how to make your pages a joy to navigate.

Yale Web Style Guide

`http://info.med.yale.edu/caim/manual/`

This outstanding site reflects some of the lessons learned by the designers during their 12 years of multimedia software design, graphic interface design, and book design that have now been applied to Web design. This site approaches Web design as a "challenge that combines traditional editorial approaches to documents with graphic design, user interface design, information design, and the technical authoring skills required to optimize the HTML code, graphics, and text within Web pages."

Design in Motion

www.itp.tsoa.nyu.edu/~review/current/focus/Roxby1.intro.html

This beautiful site covers the dynamic design of the World Wide Web and helps you make sense of the rapidly changing technologies.

Web Design Tips

www.colin.mackenzie.org/webdesign/

This site is geared toward new Web developers and has a number of tips—including How to Avoid Cliches, Getting to the Point, and Layout/Design—and much more.

HTML References

Although Tripod offers the ability to create a Web page without knowing a stitch of HTML, learning this language enables you to take your pages to the next level. Check out the following sites, and you'll realize that HTML isn't as difficult to learn as you might think.

The HTML Stylehouse

www.htmlstylehouse.com

The tutorials here can be used by beginners and experienced developers. Tutorials start with the basic (HTML—What Is It? and How To Get Started in HTML) and continue from there. There is also a monthly quiz—no cheating!

Webmonkey's Tutorial

`www.hotwired.com/webmonkey/teachingtool`

Webmonkey has endless information on everything from E-Business to DHTML to Stylesheets. The HTML area includes looks at HTML specs, and tutorials on mastering tables, frames, tags, and so on.

How'd They Do that With HTML?

`www.nashvill.net/~carl/htmlguide.index.html`

This site includes tutorials on background and colors, transparent and interlaced GIFs, dynamic menus, background sounds, and more.

Microsoft's Beginner Guide to HTML

`www.microsoft.com/workshop/author/html/beghtml.asp`

The title says it all. This site is very well illustrated and comprehensive.

Microsoft's HTML Reference Guide

`www.microsoft.com/workshop/author/html/reference/elements.asp#ie_40_htmlref`

This is a chart of HTML tags. Click the tag for a description of its use and an example.

Microsoft's HTML Coding Tips

www.microsoft.com/workshop/author/html/mytips.asp

HTML tips, tricks, and secrets from Robert Hess.

Forms Reference

Do you want to add forms to your site? The following site provides you with plenty of help.

NCSA Forms Tutorial

http://www.ncsa.uiuc.edu/SDG/Software/Mosaic/Docs/fill-out-forms/overview.html

Includes information on the Form Tag, the Input Tag, and more.

DHTML References

Want to go further? Check out these Dynamic HTML (DHTML) sites.

Webmonkey's DHTML Tutorials

http://www.hotwired.com/webmonkey/dynamic_html/

Webmonkey consistently has great tutorials on the latest browser technologies and these DHTML tutorials are no exception.

Jeff Rule's Dynamic HTML Demos

http://www.ruleweb.com/dhtml/

Another great DHTML site. There are plenty of examples that work in both Internet Explorer and Navigator as well as some that are browser-specific.

Inside DHTML

`http://www.insidedhtml.com/`

Inside DHTML has extensive examples, tutorials and articles worth checking out.

HTML Editors

However, if you prefer to deal with HTML…

Allaire HomeSite

`www.allaire.com/products/homesite/index.cfm`

HomeSite is an award-winning HTML editor. You can download an evaluation copy before deciding to purchase either the packaged version ($99) or the electronic version ($89).

Bare Bones Software BBEdit

`http://web.barebones.com/products/bbedit/bbedit.html`

This leading HTML editor for the Macintosh costs $119. You can also download a demo before ordering.

Web Editors

Would you rather have a Web-based editor than an HTML editor? Here are some of the best.

Microsoft FrontPage

http://www.microsoft.com/products/prodref/571_ov.htm

Not surprisingly, Microsoft's excellent FrontPage Web editor is incredibly popular with approximately 1.5 million people using some version of the product. The price is $149.

Adobe PageMill

www.adobe.com/prodindex/pagemill/main.html

You can download a trial version of this popular Web editor. PageMill ordered online costs $79 and does not include any templates or third-party products.

FileMaker Home Page

www.filemaker.com/products/homepage3.html

FileMaker Home Page, formerly Claris Home Page, is another popular, useful Web editor. Cost is approximately $90. The trial version runs for 30 days.

FrontPage Web Sites

More than half a million people use FrontPage 98 and another million or so use some other version of the product. Not surprisingly, there are plenty of places for you to turn for FrontPage tips. Here are a few.

FrontPage Forum and Help Page

http://microsoftsoft.miningco.com/msubFrontPage.htm

Josh Andrews offers links to news stories, plug-ins, and reviews related to FrontPage on his Focus on Microsoft Software pages. There are also bulletin boards, chats and newsletters.

FrontPage Tip of the Week

`www.zdtips.com/mfp/zdt-f.htm`

Go here and sign up to receive a FrontPage tip of the week via email from Ziff-Davis. The tips are useful, brief and direct, not long-winded monologues.

MD's FrontPage Tip of the Week

`http://websunlimited.com/mdtips.htm`

MD is a Microsoft-designated MVP (Most Valuable Professional) for FrontPage. He contributes regularly to several FrontPage news groups and is skilled in FrontPage as well as CGI programming. The tips, such as "How to create beveled button hyperlinks" or "How to keep your pages from being stored in the browser's cache," remain on the site for several weeks.

Builder.com's High-Performance FrontPage 98

`www.builder.com/Authoring/FrontPage98/index.html`

CNet's Builder.com offers a multitude of easy-to-follow FrontPage tips and advice.

General and Promotional Help

The following sites can help you tune up your page and attract traffic.

Web Site Garage

`www.websitegarage.com`

The Web Site Garage includes maintenance, promotion and analysis, consulting, and news. The Tune Up area enables you to run critical performance diagnostics on your site; the Browser Snapshot ensures browser compatibility in 18 different browsers, platforms and screen sizes; GIF Lube helps you speed up your site by optimizing your images. There are charges attached to the services.

Submit It!

`www.submit-it.com`

Submit It! offers a number of services to help drive traffic to your site. Many of the services have a price tag attached. Submit It! Free enables you to submit your Web page automatically to seven different search engines—Lycos, Excite, HotBot, AltaVista, InfoSeek, NetFind and WebCrawler.

Register-It

`www.register-it.com/`

Register-It offers free registration with eight search engines, including Excite, Infoseek, and WebCrawler. It also offers a paid service to as many as 400 engines, Web site maintenance and analysis, and Web site communication.

Web Site Post Office

`http://websitepostoffice.com/`

The Web Site Post Office is a place to turn if you are considering adding a mailing list to your site. The free version enables you to send and manage newsletters without adding any software.

Doctor HTML

`www2.imagiware.com/RxHTML/`

Doctor HTML retrieves HTML pages and reports problems, helping you improve your pages.

Web Graphic Tutorials

Scanning Images FAQ

`www.i-us.com/associate/scanfaq.htm`

The Scanning FAQ presented by i/us breaks the scanning of artwork and photographs into four primary categories and also covers advanced issues such as resolution, copyright and JPEG vs. PhotoCD.

i/us

`www.i-us.com`

This extensive graphics community covers 3D, animation, royalty-free images, fonts and type, freelancing, PhotoCD, plug-ins, shareware, Web design, and more.

Optimizing Web Graphics

`www.webreference.com/dev/graphics/`

Poorly optimized graphics are certain to drive away visitors. These tips can keep them coming back for more.

Image Map Tutorials

`www.cris.com/~automata/tutorial.shtml`

This site has numerous links to tutorials and other information related to the authoring and serving of image maps.

Lynda Weinman's Links

`www.lynda.com/dwg/links.html`

Lynda Weinman's favorite links related to Web design, graphics, and authoring tools.

GIF89a Animation on the WWW

`http://member.aol.com/royalef/gifanim.htm`

Nearly endless information on creating GIF89a animations.

Graphics Editors

Graphics make the Web world more interesting, and these editors can do the same for your graphics.

Paint Shop Pro

`www.jasc.com/psp.html`

Paint Shop Pro is an excellent, inexpensive image creation and editing program for Windows will help you create a visually exciting page. The product costs $99.

Adobe ImageReady

www.adobe.com/prodindex/imageready/price.html

ImageReady is a robust and rather expensive ($219) graphics editor for Windows or Macintosh.

Macromedia Fireworks

www.macromedia.com/software/fireworks/

Fireworks, a graphics editor for Macintosh or Windows, costs $299 for the packaged edition or $269 for the electronic version.

Animated GIF Creation Tools

All of the above programs let you create animated GIFs, but these products, which focus specifically on the process, are less expensive alternatives specifically for GIF creation.

Ulead Gif Animator

www.webutilities.com/

This is an award-winning product for Windows. There is a 15-day trial version; registration cost is $39.95.

GifBuilder

http://iawww.epfl.ch/Staff/Yves.Piguet/clip2gif-home/GifBuilder.html

GifBuilder is a freeware/shareware animation builder for the Macintosh.

GIF CONSTRUCTION SET

www.mindworkshop.com/alchemy/gifcon.html

This popular Web page animator is available as shareware. The Professional registered version is $20.

ANIMATED JAVA TOOLS

Adding Java animation is a relatively inexpensive way to add a fun twist to your site. Here are a couple of top tools.

MICROSOFT LIQUID MOTION

www.microsoft.com/products/prodref/726_ov.htm

Microsoft's Liquid Motion enables you to create and publish animation for your Web site for approximately $150.

INTERLEAF JAMBA

www.jamba.com

Jamba, a visual authoring tool for creating Java applets, costs $199. PC Magazine gave it an Editors' Choice Award in the spring of 1998.

FREE CLIP LIBRARIES

There are a number of free clip libraries that can provide images, backgrounds, textures, GIFs and more for use. Tripod offers you access to one already. For more links, check AndyArt's links page at www.andyart.com/links.htm and these other popular sites.

Cool Archive

www.coolarchive.com

The Cool Archive includes an extensive selection of free fonts, icons, animations, buttons, bullets, backgrounds, sounds and more.

GIF Artist

www.gifartist.com

Includes more than 7,500 3D animated GIFs.

Animation Zone

www.animationzone.com

Animation Zone started as an animated GIF gallery and has added background and clip art.

Astonishing Backgrounds

http://backgrounds.hypermart.net

Tons of textures for background use. Some of them are actually quite astonishing.

Jelane's Free Web Graphics

www.erinet.com/jelane/families/

Just what the name says—free graphics in categories such as themes, thumbnails, and controls.

Sound and Music Production

The Web is alive with the sound of music!

The Audio Guys

www.audioguys.com

The Audio Guys offer information for anyone interested in improving their command of sound recording and reproduction. Includes links to audio tools on the Web.

MidiWeb

www.midiweb.com

MidiWeb offers extensive information on MIDI (Musical Instruments Digital Interface).

MP3.com

www.mp3.com

MP3's are the fastest growing form of music, in CD quality, on the Web. MP3.com offers free music and downloadable software.

Sound Editors

Some sites just sit there, nice and quiet. That's fine, but if you want to offer audio, check out the following.

GoldWave

www.goldwave.com

GoldWave is a digital audio editor for Windows. There is a shareware version worth trying, and the product costs $40 to register.

Syntrillium Cool Edit

www.syntrillium.com/cooledit/index.html

Cool Edit is another Windows digital audio editor. Try the shareware version. Syntrillium offers a $50 Basic Registration and a $25 Lite Registration, which lacks some of the features of the Basic Registration.

Macromedia SoundEdit 16 Plus Deck II

www.macromedia.com/software/sound

SoundEdit 16 is now being packaged with Deck II to offer a software-only recording studio for the Macintosh. The registered product is $499.

Sonic Foundry Sound Forge XP

www.sfoundry.com

Sound Forge XP is a streamlined version of Sonic Foundry's professional editor for Windows. The packaged version is $59.95; the downloadable version costs $10 less.

Flash

Flash is the standard for interactive vector graphics and animation on the Web.

Macromedia Flash Developers Center

www.macromedia.com/support/flash/dev_index.html

Macromedia's Flash Developers Center offers articles, documentation, discussion groups and resources.

SMIL References

To make authoring of multimedia presentations on the Web easier, W3C has designed the Synchronized Multimedia Integration Language (SMIL). The SMIL language is an easy-to-learn, HTML-like language that enables you to use a text editor to write multimedia presentations with streaming audio and video that you can deliver through your Tripod site.

SMIL

www.w3.org/AudioVideo/

The SMIL index at the World Wide Web Consortium, which approved the SMIL 1.0 standard, includes a Web Techniques tutorial, players, authoring tools, background, and more.

JustSmil

www.justsmil.com

Just Smil is an independent site and the leading third-party Web site on SMIL. It includes news, information, guides, tools, a link to the W3C mailing list, and a gallery of source file examples.

Overall G2 Content and Programming Guide

`www.real/com/devzone/library/creating/index.html`

Covers not just the code issues, but also content creation, tips, and tricks for SMIL using Real Networks G2 player.

RealPix

`http://service.real.com/help/library/guides/realpix/htmfiles/tagtable.htm#1005261`

Organized in a chart, this page covers the RealPix tags and how they work with RealMedia's G2 system using SMIL.

RealText

`http://service.real.com/help/library/guides/realtext/htmfiles/texttabl.htm#997671`

Designed in the same fashion as RealPix, this covers the RealText tags and how they work in the G2 system using SMIL.

INDEX

C

D

G

H

J - K

L

M

N - O

P

Q - R

S

U - V

W - Z